W9-AYQ-234

L.A. FREEWAY

DAVID BRODSLY

L.A. FREEWAY

AN APPRECIATIVE ESSAY

UNIVERSITY OF CALIFORNIA PRESS

Berkeley   *Los Angeles*   *London*

UNIVERSITY OF CALIFORNIA PRESS
BERKELEY AND LOS ANGELES, CALIFORNIA
UNIVERSITY OF CALIFORNIA PRESS, LTD.
LONDON, ENGLAND
COPYRIGHT © 1981
BY THE REGENTS OF THE UNIVERSITY OF CALIFORNIA
PRINTED IN THE UNITED STATES OF AMERICA

Library of Congress Cataloging in Publication Data

Brodsly, David.
L.A. freeway, an appreciative essay.

Bibliography—
Includes index.
1 Express highways—California—Los Angeles metropolitan area—History.
2. Los Angeles metropolitan area—Social conditions. 3. Urban transportation—California—Los Angeles metropolitan area—History. I. Title.
HE356.5.L7B76   388.4'11'0979493   80-29620
ISBN 0-520-04068-6

For my parents,
William and Edith Brodsly,
and for Greg Erlandson

CONTENTS

ACKNOWLEDGMENTS

Although the most important acknowledgments in this book appear at the end, in the bibliography, one particular source requires special mention here. Robert Fogelson, in *The Fragmented Metropolis: Los Angeles, 1850-1930,* offers the most detailed study ever published of Los Angeles' most critical period. It was an invaluable aid to my understanding of this city. Although published in 1967, the book is sadly out of print. Sadder still, it is almost nonexistent in local libraries. The invisibility of this book speaks very poorly for Los Angeles' sense of self-awareness.

This essay began at the University of California, Santa Cruz, and I wish to thank Stevenson College, and particularly the Modern Society and Social Thought Program, for supporting interdisciplinary study and encouraging serious undergraduate research.

A number of people have read parts or all of the manuscript, lending their support, suggestions, or criticisms. The criticism of Greg Erlandson, Carey McWilliams, Mary Milne, John Caughey, Rosalie Avery, Robert Kinsman, and Richard Gibb have all improved the final product. I am especially grateful to Jim Borchert and Larry Veysey, for the generosity of their repeated readings and continuing encouragement.

Staff at the California Department of Transportation's District VII office in Los Angeles were very patient in explaining the details of maintaining a freeway system. I owe special thanks to Robert Goodell for sharing his extensive knowledge of the system, and for leading me through the bureaucratic maze.

I received diverse assistance in acquiring the graphic materials for this book. Especially generous help was provided by Alan Jutzi of the Huntington Library, Mason Dooley of the City of Los Angeles Planning Department, and most especially, Bob Rose, chief of CALTRANS' photography section in Sacramento, who gave me access to his extensive archives. Thanks are also due to Henrik Kam, for providing photographs and photographic guidance, to Amalie Brown, who prepared a number of the maps and charts, and to Nancy Applegate for additional maps and cartographic advice.

Chris Micaud is responsible for the four striking photographs that open the four main chapters.

Without the support of the people at the University of California Press, this book, of course, would be impossible. I am particularly indebted to Grace Stimson, for her careful and detailed editing of the manuscript. It is impossible properly to thank Jack Miles, who sponsored this book at the press. Without his encouragement and advice, from the time this was simply a graduation requirement through the present, this essay would be only a dusty thesis on my parents' bookshelf.

Finally, only with the continued support of my friends do I complete anything, and my deepest appreciation goes to all who have endured me the last few years; too many names deserving of acknowledgment come to mind. I will indite only Peyton, Belmont and Associates, all those associated with the Colegio House, and Shelly Vaughen, Mary Milne, Jim Steele, Marangus Erlandson, Megan Gallagher, Greg Erlandson, and my family, all of whom are directly responsible for this book, and all of whom I thank, once again.

O Thou steeled Cognizance whose leap commits
The agile precincts of the lark's return;
Within whose lariat sweep encinctured sing
In single chrysalis the many twain,—
Of stars Thou art the stitch and stallion glow
And like an organ, Thou, with sound of doom—
Sight, sound and flesh Thou leadest from time's realm
As love strikes clear direction for the helm.

Swift peal of secular light, intrinsic Myth
Whose fell unshadow is death's utter wound,—
O River-throated—iridescently upborne
Through the bright drench and fabric of our veins;
With white escarpments swinging into light,
Sustained in tears the cities are endowed
And justified conclamant with ripe fields
Revolving through their harvests in sweet torment.
—HART CRANE, "Atlantis"[1]

Contrary to what one might expect of an essay on freeways, this one is neither a diatribe nor a paean. Sometimes I hate freeways and sometimes I actually love them, but that is not the point. The point here is simply to spend some time thinking about a subject that most of us take for granted. It is an "appreciative" essay in the formal sense of the word. To appreciate freeways is not necessarily to like them but, more important, to consider them rightly. In essence, it is merely the act of seeing, in this instance of seeing the everyday with something more than everyday eyes.

My hope was to understand the freeways, not to judge them. Even now, I do not know quite how I feel about them, not having reconciled myself to living in a world where the automobile is a vital appendage. But, if I were called on to cast my judgment on the L.A. freeways, it would be simply this: they make sense.

What follows is really a series of short exercises in freeway appreciation, an exploration of a context for thinking about Los Angeles' freeways. I look at present-day Los Angeles to see what kinds of general statements one can make about the freeway metropolis, to sketch what it means to live in relation to the center lane. I discuss the system as a product of history, not only of the history of transportation, but also of the history of a place and of the people who shaped that place. There is also, in the epilogue, a brief musing on what the future might bring. And an appendix glances backward once again, to consider the road not taken—rail rapid transit.

The freeway is literally a concrete testament to who we are, and it continues to structure the way we live. Both the dominant role the freeways play in transportation and their sheer permanence have made them the backbone of southern California. They rank with the mountains and the rivers in influencing the organization of a changing city, and uncontestably they are the single most important feature of the man-made landscape. Driving the freeway is absolutely central to the experience of living in Los Angeles, and any anthropologist studying our city would head for the nearest onramp, for nowhere else would he or she observe such large-scale public activity. Time spent on the freeway is for many of us a significant chunk of our lives. The way we think about place, both the city at large and our home turf, is intimately tied to cars and freeways. Perhaps the most basic feature of freeways, and the one most overlooked by the preoccupied commuter, is that they are impressive structures, the most awesome works of design in the daily lives of most of us. They can even be beautiful.

Although tourists and schoolchildren look to Olvera Street for a visible sign of Los Angeles' illusive history, the freeway stands as a living monument to our past. It is a final product of succeeding generations of transportation systems which have been superimposed on the southern California landscape: the early Indian and Mexican colonial trails, the steam railroads, the electric railways, and the automotive highways.

Through a hundred-year-long process of transportation development an urban metropolis was etched out of the desert, an act of creation which is revealed by a historical view from the road.

The original Spanish settlement, founded in 1781 as El Pueblo de la Reina de los Angeles, was a village located about fifteen miles due east of the Pacific Ocean and another fifteen south of the San Gabriel Mountains on a coastal plain now called the Los Angeles Basin. The basin is ringed by the high, often snowcapped mountains of the coastal range, its flatness interrupted by a few smaller ranges including the Santa Monica Mountains and La Puente Hills.

The early and continuing pattern of transportation in the basin comprises five lines of movement radiating from the Los Angeles pueblo (present downtown Los Angeles) toward other early Spanish settlements: a line running northwest toward San Fernando, another west toward Santa Monica, a third south toward San Pedro, a fourth southeast toward Santa Ana, and a fifth east toward San Bernardino. This pattern is implicit in the physical geography of the region, dictated in large measure by points of access to the outside world through mountain passes and natural harbors. The introduction of railroads set these routes as the primary matrices for all subsequent development, and their courses remain more or less faithfully articulated by the freeways. A quick genealogy shows that the route northwest along the Los Angeles River into the San Fernando Valley became a Southern Pacific line and later the Golden State freeway; the route west to Santa Monica became the Los Angeles and Independence Railroad and later the Santa Monica freeway; the route south to San Pedro became the Los Angeles and

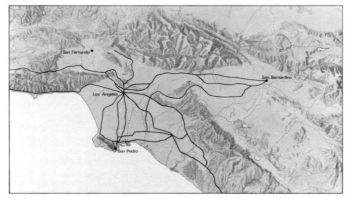

Footpaths and Roadways, pre-1860

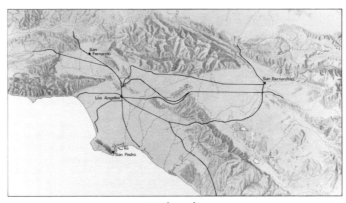

Railroads

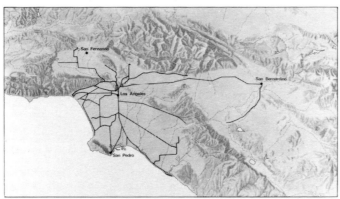

Pacific Electric Railway

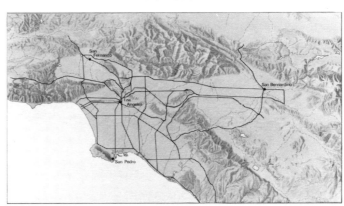

Automotive Highways

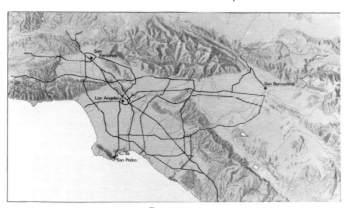

Freeways

Transportation Overlays

These maps show highlights of the major systems of transportation which have served the Los Angeles area. Architectural historian Reyner Banham has labeled the region a "transportation palimpsest," a huge earthen tablet revised by subsequent generations. Evident in the maps is a marked degree of continuity, as succeeding forms of transportation elaborate an increasingly dispersed urban structure.

San Pedro Railroad and later the Harbor freeway; and the route southeast to Santa Ana became another Southern Pacific line and later the Santa Ana freeway. Three railroads headed east through the San Gabriel Valley, as do three freeways today. The Pasadena freeway and the Foothill freeway east of Pasadena descend from the Santa Fe, the Pomona freeway descends from the Union Pacific, and the San Bernardino freeway is partial heir of the Southern Pacific. Both the Foothill and the San Bernardino freeways now have railroad tracks built within sections of their center dividers.

The legacy of Los Angeles' once extensive electric railways, though not so obvious, can also be found in the freeway system. The freeways were designed to serve the same territory covered by the trolleys. They could not have done otherwise, as it was through the electric streetcars, especially the interurbans, that a metropolitan Los Angeles first suggested itself. The most striking testament vanished when the Pacific Electric disappeared. We no longer have the red cars sharing the rights-of-way of the Hollywood freeway over Cahuenga Pass or the early segments of the San Bernardino to remind us of this continuity. Some railway lines actually met their fate as a direct result of freeway construction. Several Pacific Electric rights-of-way were usurped by their land-hungry stepchildren, the freeways striking the final blow to a system long suffering from public neglect.

The relationship of the freeways to their highway predecessors is the most obvious and the easiest to understand. The freeways were built to relieve the most popular surface highways of through traffic. The names associated with the freeways in the early mas-

ter plans of the 1930s and 1940s make this intended superimposition particularly clear: Sepulveda Parkway, Colorado Parkway, Ramona Parkway, Atlantic Parkway, Olympic Parkway, Crenshaw Parkway, and so on. The parallel was even more pronounced in the plan for a freeway and expressway system adopted by the state legislature in 1959, which was to replace practically every major state highway with a freeway. What was actually built, however, more closely resembles the earlier rail patterns than a comprehensive highway grid. The radial routes usually received higher priority and were constructed first, and several major bypass routes were subsequently deleted owing to funding shortages and routing controversies.

The Los Angeles freeway is a silent monument not only to the history of the region's spatial organization, but to the history of its values as well. Rather than representing a radical departure from tradition, the freeway was the logical next step in making the Los Angeles dream a reality. Los Angeles' appeal lay in its being the first major city that was not quite a city, that is, not a crowded industrial metropolis. It was a garden city of backyards and quiet streets, a sprawling small town magnified a thousandfold and set among palms and orange trees and under a sunny sky. When the city began drowning in the sheer popularity of this vision, the freeway was offered as a lifeline. The L.A. freeway makes manifest in concrete the city's determination to keep its dream alive.

The L.A. freeway embodies a tension long present in American culture: the pastoral versus the technological. It is a drama that historian Leo Marx called, in an excellent book of the same title, the "Machine in the Garden." American arts and letters have, since Jefferson expounded his agrarian ideals, been struggling with acceptance of the urban industrial age. Only a few have suggested reconciliation through acceptance, replacing the bucolic imagery with some technological counterpart. Henry Adams, in his autobiography, made an uneasy truce with the technological age through the image of the dynamo. He saw the electric generator as a modern equivalent of the medieval Virgin, as a new goddess of power and fecundity. As the Virgin had inspired the building of Chartres, so the force of the dynamo would infuse the works of technological man. The American poet Hart Crane, in his most famous collection, *The Bridge,* supplied the missing element in Adams's equation. For Crane, the Brooklyn Bridge was like a cathedral of the machine age. In steel, concrete, and cable he could see, as Adams had at Chartres, the evocation of an entire epoch.

Both Adams's essay, ''The Virgin and the Dynamo,'' and Crane's American epic function better as literature than as modern secular theology. The electric generator is simply too far removed from our experience to have any symbolic force, and the Brooklyn Bridge seems today more a monument to our past. As I survey the world I live in for a better metaphor to evoke the contours of the machine-age soul, I find none more appropriate than the freeway. For here the abstract image of the dynamo becomes an active metaphor in the automobile. It is the machine most fully integrated into our lives, the dynamo with a face; it has become an extension of our bodies, both as appendage and as an expression of personality, a technological icon. And the freeway is the automotive basilica.

Later in this essay I quote Joan Didion, who calls the freeway experience ''the only secular communion Los Angeles has.'' The more I think about the parallel, the more I realize how correct she is. Every time we merge with traffic we join our community in a wordless creed: belief in individual freedom, in a technological liberation from place and circumstance, in a democracy of personal mobility. When we are stuck in rush-hour traffic the freeway's greatest frustration is that it belies its promise.

The L.A. freeway is the cathedral of its time and place. It is a monumental structure designed to serve the needs of our daily lives, at the same time representing what we stand for in this world. It is surely the structure the archeologists of some future age will study in seeking to understand who we were. This essay suggests that we ourselves can turn to it for the same reason.

6

It is interesting, if not useful, to consider where one would go in Los Angeles to have an effective revolution of the Latin American sort. Presumably, that place would be in the heart of the city. If one took over some public square, some urban open space in Los Angeles, who would know? A march on City Hall would be inconclusive. The heart of the city would have to be sought elsewhere. . . . The only hope would seem to be to take over the freeways.

— CHARLES M. MOORE, dean of the
Yale School of Architecture[1]

Sprawl and Order

In 1966 United States Senator Claiborne Pell, in a book ominously entitled *Megalopolis Unbound,* warned American cities to "ponder the plight of Los Angeles since that city became the freeway capital of the nation."[2] Senator Pell was a major force in the federal government's discovery of an urban mass transportation problem, and he expressed an implicit assumption held by many critics of contemporary Los Angeles. The City of the Angels has become the chief symbol of a common urban—or suburban, or metro-politan, or megalopolitan—malaise, and the freeway system for which Los Angeles is infamous is often thought to lie at the heart of that disorder. Saddled with the blame for a sprawling, faceless metropolis, the erosion of neighborhoods and communities, and a generally destructive and dehumanized quality of life, the freeway has come in many minds to shoulder the burden of Los Angeles' modern history.

That such an indictment is misplaced becomes evi-dent when one glances backward from the contempo-rary situation. With a little sense of the area's history

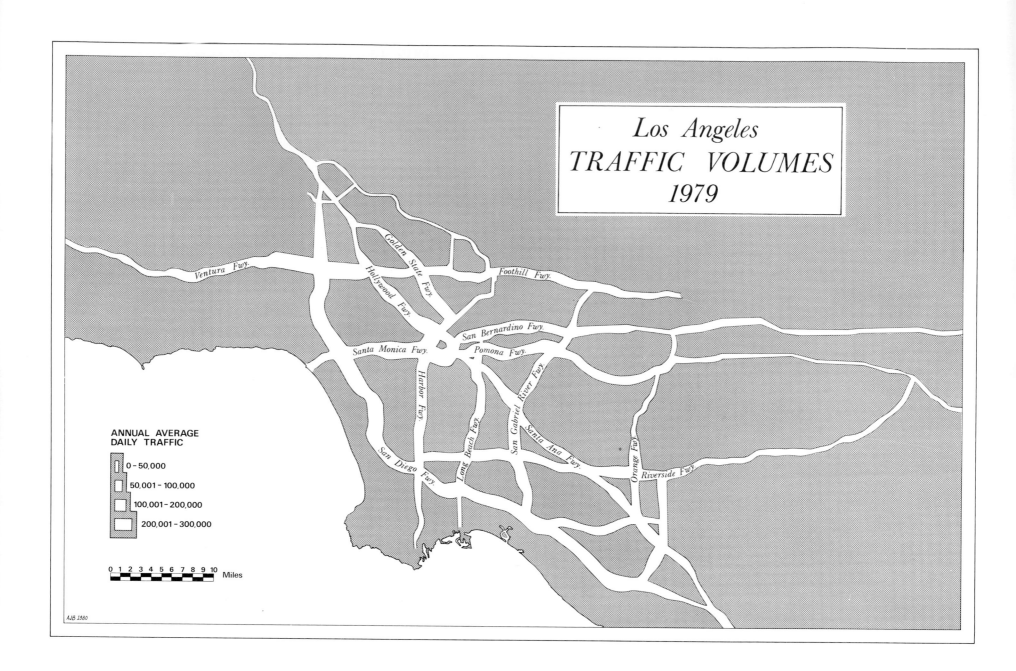

Los Angeles
TRAFFIC VOLUMES
1979

Ventura Fwy.

Golden State Fwy.

Hollywood Fwy.

Foothill Fwy.

San Bernardino Fwy.

Santa Monica Fwy.

Pomona Fwy.

Harbor Fwy.

Long Beach Fwy.

San Gabriel River Fwy.

Santa Ana Fwy.

San Diego Fwy.

Orange Fwy.

Riverside Fwy.

ANNUAL AVERAGE
DAILY TRAFFIC

0 - 50,000

50,001 - 100,000

100,001 - 200,000

200,001 - 300,000

0 1 2 3 4 5 6 7 8 9 10   Miles

AJB 1980

8

one can begin to penetrate the mysteries of southern California. What one discovers is that the freeways were really more a product than a cause of the prevalent urban form. They were consciously conceived and executed to serve a long-established pattern of decentralized, low-density development. Nevertheless, the freeways are important—their very notoriety suggests significance—although it is still too early to say exactly how important. Most of the freeways were completed only in the 1960s and 1970s, and their wide-ranging effects are not going to be felt immediately in a society blessed with automotive flexibility. Yet they have quickly asserted their dominance as urban paths. Many freeways have been crowded practically from their opening day, draining surface streets of much of their regular traffic, as well as continually encouraging new trips.[3] Even though they account for only 4 percent of the total surface area of streets and highways, they carry more than 40 percent of all metropolitan traffic.[4] On an average weekday, the freeways in the Los Angeles metropolitan region are used for more than 5.8 million trips and accommodate an incredible 75.2 million miles of travel.[5] An organizer of human activity on so unprecendented a scale is bound to have an impact on the structures of a society.

That the increased subdivision of undeveloped land for residential use is a corollary to the construction of freeways is perhaps the only important point on which critics and defenders of the system agree. As the more centrally located land becomes more densely populated, suburbanization has been pushed farther out into the hinterland, the freeways making these areas more easily accessible to commercial and industrial

Automotive Suburbs

A major product of the automotive revolution in transportation
was the suburban explosion in housing, of which Los Angeles
provides the classic example. The availability of privately owned
cars divorced real estate development from public transit, and
land that was inaccessible by trolley could easily be cut up with
roadways and sold in more spacious lots. The top left photo
shows Westwood Village in 1929, an early center in the development of Los Angeles' fashionable west side. The mass production of the automobile was eventually followed by the mass production of housing. The first large-scale development of this kind
was Lakewood, shown at bottom left in 1951. Lakewood, located
north of Long Beach, was a pioneer of the planned community.
The city contained the largest subdivision of its time—with more
than 17,500 homes built in two years—and was built around the
first regional shopping mall in the West. The planned community
has come of age with residential minicities such as Westlake,
shown on the right during the mid-1970s. Westlake is buffered
from the urbanized San Fernando Valley by 15 miles of sparsely
developed land. The Ventura freeway (center of photo) ties the
community to the Los Angeles metropolis, while a lavish master
plan protects it from encroaching urban sprawl. (Westwood
photo courtesy of UCLA, Department of Geography/Spence Collection; Lakewood photo courtesy of City of Lakewood; Westlake
photo courtesy of the Prudential Insurance Company.)

centers. New developments spring up to help fulfill the southern Californian's quest for the pastoral. The freeway's relation to suburbanization is similar to that of the interurban electric railways, whose original routes shaped the subsequent metropolitanization of undeveloped lands. The completion of the Ventura and Hollywood freeways accelerated the already extensive development of the San Fernando Valley, making it one of the more heavily settled areas of southern California, with more than a million inhabitants. (If the Valley was incorporated separately it would be the second-largest city in the state.) Freeway construction has also been associated with the rapid expansion of the area's three other major population growth centers: the San Gabriel Valley, the South Bay area including Inglewood, Torrance, and Palos Verdes, and Orange County.[6] The latter, with 130 miles of freeway, not only was rapidly developed, but through completion of the Santa Ana and San Diego freeways it was effectively united with Los Angeles County to form a single megalopolis.

The newest and most sophisticated permutation of the bedroom community a la small town is the string of residential minicities along the freeway radials. Typical of these modern villages are the trend-setting developments of Irvine and Westlake at the southern and northern peripheries, respectively, of the southern California metropolis. Similar settlements adorn the eastern freeways toward Pomona, Riverside, and San Bernardino and the Ventura freeway, and flourish in other areas where open land has been made available to the urban commuter. Here rurality proves to be a supreme middle-class value, as many workers willingly assume daily drives lasting one or two hours in order to live in rugged and picturesque settings of mountain-sheltered valley locations, free from smog and blighted landscapes. Enjoying parklands and greenbelts, with recreation facilities and playgrounds, usually a golf course and always a tennis court, perhaps a man-made recreational lake, and served by well-designed shopping centers, restaurants, and cocktail lounges (but not bars), these new planned communities may offer a model for posturban America.[7]

It is the sheer relentlessness of this auto-oriented landscape which so beguiles the uninitiated and leads observers such as Daniel Boorstin to complain that "whatever the other virtues of Los Angeles, it had surely become one of the least 'legible' of the great settlements of the world." The freeway has certainly done its share in facilitating the continuing sprawl of a medium-density urban landscape, but it is merely the latest in a long series of technological and social improvements to do so. Mass-produced automobiles, mass-produced housing, and a growing population able to afford them were the key ingredients in Los Angeles' present development. None of these elements remains uniquely southern Californian; and so Boorstin must amend his statement, adding that Los Angeles "offered the visual future of American cities in caricature."[8]

The problem Boorstin alludes to—the problem of sprawl—is really the automotive problem, an issue that has been attracting the attention of concerned social critics since the vehicle ceased being a plaything of the rich in the decade 1910-1920. The automobile gave mobility to all who could come up with the purchase price and undermined any geographical order bred of constraint. As one Los Angeles planner complained in 1965, "as long as unbridled fluidity exists, there can be no permanent pattern."[9] The fact that city and regional planning commissions sprang up throughout the country at the beginning of the automotive era was no coincidence.[10] "Los Angeles County's problems of growth which forced the creation of the commission may not have been caused by the advent of the auto," wrote the authors of *Master Plan of Highways* in 1941, "but the latter was in any case one of the most powerful factors, and certainly accounted for the prevailing form of those problems and their early incidence in this region."[11]

Regional and city planning, limited in its regulatory powers to zoning and highway construction, was institutionalized in large measure as an effort to combat the potential chaos of the privatization of transportation. A system of major highways, designed to provide some control over the use of land and to ensure an ordered urban environment, culminated in the freeway system. The freeway itself did not revolutionize transportation in Los Angeles; it was an extension of the automobile, the radically new form of transportation which did revolutionize urban development.

The freeway system was in fact a conservative force, promising the metropolis the clear and coherent structure it had lacked since the decline of the urban railways. As the end result of the automotive revolution, the freeway system has tended to stabilize a particular order of social change. It has given structure to the Los Angeles area by creating a stable gradient of accessibility. The freeways serve as the arbitrator of urban development, as any specific place is made more or less desirable by its accessibility to the metropolis through the freeway system. Areas that are readily served by the system are suddenly "freeway close," and they become appropriate locations for economic activities whose major criterion is accessibility. Accordingly, the freeways have fostered a rash of new construction in several key economic sectors. Large and sometimes dramatic buildings compete to catch the motorist's eye and leave a lasting impression. These new monuments to the corporate economy, which have granted renewed visual clarity to the Los Angeles environs, suggest the freeway's power to reorganize and solidify the economic geography of the region.

The Heart of the City

The most dramatic effect of the development of the freeway system has been the rebuilding of downtown Los Angeles. In 1950 a sociologist tied the decline of the central business district and the appearance of competing districts throughout the southland to the relative inaccessibility of downtown by automobile.[12] The construction of radial freeway routes connecting the central hub to major suburban nuclei has to some extent reversed this trend. As early as 1961 one Division of Highways official, writing about the "renaissance" of downtown Los Angeles, attributed the construction of new civic and corporate buildings to the easier availability of the central city.[13] But the most impressive outburst of new construction was yet to come. With the lifting of the 150-foot height limitation on buildings in Los Angeles, the relatively low-density area immediately west of downtown would be radi-

Downtown's New Main Street

Crowding into the west side of the downtown freeway loop along the Harbor freeway (shown in 1953 and 1979), the new monuments to the corporate economy dominate the downtown cityscape, both as a major center of activity and as a visual focus. The sites just east of the Harbor freeway were recommended not only by their easy access to the freeway system, but also by the availability of relatively inexpensive downtown property. Such high-rise construction required zoning changes to permit buildings more than 150 feet tall, robbing City Hall of its distinction as the tallest building in Los Angeles. (Left photo courtesy of CAL-TRANS; right photo by Mason Dooley.)

cally transformed, a process that will continue well into the 1980s and beyond.

The Harbor freeway, which ties into every major arterial feeding the downtown area, has become what a prominent Los Angeles architect called the new "Main Street" of Los Angeles.[14] Along its eastern flank has appeared a large number of skyscrapers housing the corporate headquarters of banks and petroleum companies, the futuristic Bonaventure Hotel, several shopping plazas, tall office buildings, and multilevel parking structures. New construction continues, and soon Bullock's department store—which in 1929 became the first store of its kind to open a branch outside the downtown district—will relocate its parent establishment near the freeway. This new wave of building has done more to redefine the look of the central city than anything since the completion of City Hall in 1928. The difference is apparent as one approaches downtown on the Harbor freeway. The skyscrapers combine with the increasing frequency of overpasses to create the visual excitement one expects to feel when entering a major metropolitan center.

By completing the transfer of the city's commercial core several blocks to the west, further separating it from the civic center, the Harbor freeway has defined a new financial district. It has also effected a 90-degree shift of the district's historic north-south axis. Moving from their older locations on Spring Street, which parallels the freeway, major banking facilities are now establishing themselves on Fifth and Sixth streets, which feed directly into the freeway. As a corollary result, retail stores have increasingly concentrated on Seventh Street, adjacent to the new financial section and anchored by the new Broadway

The Freeway and Tomorrowland

The location of Disneyland was recommended by the Stanford Research Institute, which conducted a yearlong study to aid in the planning of the park. A primary advantage of the Anaheim site was its easy accessibility to the "traffic-carrying potentialities" of the Santa Ana freeway. The park is shown in 1956, a year after its opening. Harbor Boulevard is in the foreground, with the freeway running diagonally in the midground. (Courtesy of CAL-TRANS.)

The Freeway and Industry

Several major industrial districts can be seen in this aerial photograph of the Central Los Angeles area. The two prominent swaths of white are the concrete channels of the Los Angeles and San Gabriel rivers.) The central manufacturing district, stretching from Vernon eastward through Commerce and Montebello, runs roughly parallel to the Los Angeles River and the Santa Ana freeway, which bisects its western extension. The Santa Fe Springs and Norwalk industrial area lies just east of the San Gabriel River freeway. At the bottom of the photo is the Carson–Wilmington–Long Beach industrial area, served by four freeways: the Harbor, the San Diego, the Long Beach, and the Artesia. (Courtesy of U.S. Geological Survey and NASA/EROS Data Center. Photo #576 0023 984613, Frame 4615.)

Plaza. Older stores on and near Broadway, which parallels Spring Street, have been almost completely abandoned to Mexican Americans, most of whom live just east of the central city, making Broadway by far the liveliest pedestrian street in all downtown Los Angeles.[15]

The rejuvenation of the central city has not dramatically reversed the major pattern of Los Angeles' organization. Although the downtown area remains the largest business district, employing about 240,000 people, it accounts for only 3 percent of all retail sales for the metropolitan area. (Inclusion of the adjacent Wilshire district in the definition of downtown would substantially boost that figure.)[16] And despite the much-touted Bunker Hill tower apartments located near the new financial district, only a minor resurgence of downtown residence has as yet occurred. (Although several new condominium and apartment projects may indicate that a major movement toward downtown living is in the works.)

The Los Angeles metropolitan area has always been multifocused, and the freeway system was designed to serve other urban centers as well. The high-speed transportation it makes possible is transforming suburban communities such as Long Beach, whose central business district reflects the impact of the freeway running to that city.[17] Though the freeway was routed to the western harbor district rather than directly to the city, it has had an impact on the traffic pattern in downtown Long Beach, attracting through traffic from the eastern residential areas. The overall effect has been to improve the central district's economic position, as indicated by accelerated increases in land values. It is particularly noteworthy that the Long

Beach freeway has wrought changes in landscape similar to those in downtown Los Angeles. The focus of business activity has shifted from the north-south streets fed by surface highways to east-west streets, especially those with direct access to the freeway. Furthermore, whereas retail floor space (though not selling activity) continues to drop slowly, service, office, and financial enterprises have shown marked growth. Long Beach has also experienced a surge of new construction, creating a new downtown skyline. Other traditional satellite communities, such as Pasadena, Hollywood, Glendale, Santa Monica, and Santa Ana, have in some degree experienced a similar rejuvenation, as have newer urban centers like Van Nuys, Westwood, and the area around Los Angeles International Airport, all conveniently served by freeways.

A freeway can have a similar impact all along the corridor it articulates and supports. Given a positive economic climate for the general area, property near a freeway increases in value more rapidly than property farther away, and higher values encourage more intensive use of land. The effect of easier accessibility is seen in the shopping center, suburbia's equivalent to the urban service and retail district. In the competition for retail trade, freeways define points of maximum accessibility to suburban residents; new shopping centers are usually built on sites approachable by freeways.[18] Huge enclosed malls now give automotive commuters a pedestrian environment in which to shop.

Ironically, freeway construction can indirectly increase the accessibility of bypassed areas by removing the barrier of heavy through traffic. In general, only businesses serving a strictly local clientele are likely to reap this benefit; I have become more aware of shoestring shopping strips which, abandoned by many former customers, must now struggle for survival in the face of new and improved competition. The notable exceptions are the chic establishments clustered around Wilshire Boulevard in Beverly Hills, for whose customers convenience and the economics of mass sales are usually lesser considerations. The appeal of such shops is often the inaccessibility that lends prestige.

The entertainment business has been no less aware than commercial enterprises of the advantages of being close to and visible from a freeway. Early in the construction program, Disneyland, after an extensive independent study,[19] decided on a site just off the Santa Ana freeway. Freeway accessibility has likewise played a role in locating other big-money entertainment facilities, including the Dodger and Anaheim stadiums, the Ontario Speedway, Magic Mountain, the Los Angeles and Anaheim Convention Centers, and numerous golf and miniature golf courses.

Industrial location has been particularly responsive to freeway routing. Proximity to a freeway is almost a necessity in an economy where goods are usually transported by truck. Virtually every major industrial district in Los Angeles County is close to a freeway, except for the old Alameda Street district stretching south along the railroad lines. This fact alone is misleading, as freeways were originally designed to serve industry and were purposely routed along existing rail corridors through land previously zoned for industrial use.[20] But the freeway has shifted the advantage to newer industrial sites, where large undeveloped lots provided an ideal opportunity for expansion. Every

Urban Corridors

Apartment buildings, shown at left, crowd the streets on either side of the San Diego freeway, shown just south of the interchange with the Santa Monica freeway in 1971. Some of the earlier high rises along Wilshire Boulevard in Westwood are visible in the background. In residential areas, the commercial potential of freeway-closeness translates into multiunit structures, and the freeways become the focus of concentrated corridors of high-density residence and commerce spreading through suburbia. (Photo by Mason Dooley.)

Overleaf: Cementing a Fragmented Metropolis

The freeway provides the warp of a dispersed urban fabric, integrating on at least one level the sprawl of Los Angeles. A prime example is the San Diego freeway, which acts as a bridge over the barrier of the Santa Monica Mountains. Whereas 40,000 cars used the old Sepulveda Boulevard, nearly 200,000 use the freeway connecting the west sides of the central basin and the San Fernando Valley. The first photo shows the summit cut under construction in 1960, with the new Mulholland Drive bridge and the old Sepulveda hairpin curve in the foreground. Construction of this "Brooklyn Bridge" for Los Angeles constituted perhaps the single most impressive piece of engineering in the L.A. freeway system: more than 18 million cubic yards of earth were moved in widening and straightening the tortuous Sepulveda Pass. The second photo shows the completed freeway heading north into the valley, with a realigned Sepulveda Boulevard running parallel. The Mulholland bridge spans freeway and boulevard in the left center of the photo. (Left photo courtesy of CALTRANS; right photo by Mason Dooley.)

19

20

freeway of any length has attracted new industries, with the San Diego, Long Beach, Pomona, San Bernardino, Golden State, and Santa Ana freeways being particular favorites.[21] The Santa Ana freeway has not only extended the central manufacturing district, but has shifted its alignment to the southeast.[22] It is significant that the City of Commerce, incorporated in 1960, is located on the Santa Ana freeway in this new district, whereas the City of Industry (1957) is merely a long stretch of frontage land along the Pomona freeway.

Besides acting as a force behind peripheral growth and new residential subdivision, the freeways have affected the form of residential development as well. Specifically, by clearly defining stable urban corridors, they encourage denser settlement patterns. The rise in property values often leads to the conversion of single-dwelling sites into income property. For example, proximity to both the Santa Monica and San Diego freeways has stimulated the construction of middle-class and upper-middle-class apartments and condominiums in Westwood.[23] A study of the Ventura freeway through Glendale revealed similar changes in land uses.[24] Reyner Banham found the same process at work in much of the Los Angeles area:

Whenever a freeway crosses one of the more desirable residential areas of the plains—say, the San Diego south to a point just beyond International Airport—it seems to produce a shift in land values that almost always leads to the construction of dingbats. This useful term—"the basic Los Angeles Dingbat"—denotes the current minimal form of multi-family residential unit.[25]

In Los Angeles, a fairly consistent high-density residential band (with as many as 15,000 persons per square mile, comparable to Chicago or San Francisco) parallels Wilshire Boulevard from Hollywood to Santa Monica; it is bounded by the Santa Monica freeway to the south and the Harbor and Hollywood freeways to the east.[26] Such changes in the traditional Los Angeles demography are by no means a result of the freeway system; they have been brought about rather by rising land and construction costs and by population shifts. Nevertheless, the freeways have certainly influenced the spatial organization of these alterations.

It would be naive to exaggerate the freeway as a factor in restructuring urban geography. Other forces are always at work; accessibility is not an all-important ingredient. While the homes of corporate executives on Palos Verdes Peninsula are some 20 minutes away from the nearest onramp, the extended ghetto of south central Los Angeles is bisected by the Harbor freeway. Easy access to the freeway has done little to revitalize the latter area economically. Economic choices are always informed by a variety of perceived amenities, as congested Wilshire Boulevard continues to attest. The Los Angeles County town where I grew up, for instance, was served by two enclosed shopping malls, one in the predominantly black city of Carson, the other in the predominantly white city of Torrance. Although Carson lay within sight of a freeway offramp and Torrance required all surface travel, the latter was far more popular because it was in a more "familiar" neighborhood.

After surveying the empirical literature on the subject of highway impact, Anthony Downs of the Real Estate Research Corporation summarized the effects of a freeway on adjacent land: (1) A new traffic artery has no positive impact on the value of adjacent land unless other economic factors favoring urban growth are present in the area; (2) the greater the dynamic strength of economic forces in the area served by a new artery, the greater its potential positive impact upon land values; and (3) the highest potential values for land adjacent to a major artery exist where the highest intensity is supported by the local economy.[27]

In other words, the freeway does not act independently in transforming land uses. Division of Highways studies have shown that Los Angeles freeways have little impact on stable communities, especially when routed along neighborhood boundaries.[28] If, however, an area is undergoing changes, the introduction of a freeway will reinforce those changes, geographically organizing existing economic trends in terms of intensity of land use. The same holds true in the suburban "hinterland," when agricultural property is converted to single-family housing tracts; in the more central suburbs, where older single-family homes are replaced by multiple units; and in urban cores, where the most intense uses, whether commercial, industrial, or high-rise residential, prevail. The freeways, though not working single-handedly, are helping to reshape the geography of Los Angeles by delineating corridors of more intensive land use in the push to be accessible to the automotive metropolis.

A Sense of Place

The Los Angeles freeway system has also changed the way people think about the urban landscape and therefore about the metropolitan area. Earlier modes of transportation created a multicentered way of life served by widespread patterns of movement, but development of the freeway system is the critical stage in the formalization of that process. Greater Los Angeles is not a series of suburbs in close proximity to one another; it is, rather, their integration into a fluid system of exchanges, of which the freeway system is the most important nexus. In 1960 *Life* magazine argued that "more important than the Dodgers or civic buildings in giving Los Angeles its new personality are the ribbons of freeway which are gradually tying the city's scattered pieces together."[29] This "new personality" emerges because the freeway makes manifest the true nature of the metropolis. In an area of sprawling suburbanization and hundreds of randomly attached communities, the freeway serves to evoke a sense of clarity and sharpness, to delineate and integrate urban space. It has created a new sense of place.

The freeway system provides an integrating design for an expanse of humanity too large to consider at a glance. Testimony to this fact abounds. Any contemporary map of Los Angeles shows the freeways in wide red bands, while municipal boundaries fade into the background. The Western Economic Research Company, which publishes in map form the latest census data for major California cities, provides a transparent overlay for the Los Angeles series which fits all the specialized sheets; it is a map of county boundaries, major place-names, and freeways. The freeway system is even redefining the general sense of what is "downtown." More and more frequently it is mapped as simply the area within the downtown freeway loop, a delineation not completely in consonance with the geography of business, government, and historical sites.

Anybody who has lived in southern California knows the psychological truth portrayed by the freeway's prominence in maps of the area. The real estate section in any Sunday issue of the *Los Angeles Times* presents dozens of advertisements for new homes, most of them containing a map showing the nearest freeway. The system is crucial to a driver seeking to cross the city without risking becoming hopelessly lost. Instructions to a crosstown traveler almost always begin with directions as to how to reach the nearest freeway. (The simplest directions do not necessarily point to the quickest route, but usually to the route with the least use of surface streets.) To be lost in Los Angeles is to be unable to find a freeway onramp or not to know which way to turn after exiting.

Perhaps the freeways have yet to define a sense of urban space as distinct as that associated with previous modes of transport, as in "the other side of the tracks," but they do evoke a sense of social areas. The Harbor freeway is black; the Foothill freeway is very white and middle class; and to at least one resident, "living east of the San Diego Freeway is a kind of death."[30] In many of the flat stretches of the coastal basin, the freeways, each personalized by a given name, are the only distinctive feature of the physical landscape to which one can attach such associations.

Nevertheless, although the freeways may provide Los Angeles with a metropolitan imagery of one sort, they are in another sense almost invisible. Kevin Lynch, in his classic study of urban images, found that freeways were perceived as being somehow dissociated from the surrounding landscape.[31] Downtown workers, when mapping their everyday environment, often overlooked the freeways' existence altogether.

They might, for example, trace an imaginary path which would necessitate walking across the Hollywood freeway. These urban motorways, often depressed below street level and visually obscured by landscaping, were not felt to be "in" the rest of the city. Major surface streets, such as Figueroa, Sunset, and Olympic, were regarded by downtown employees as stronger boundaries of the central business district than the theoretically more prominent freeways.

The dissociation of freeways from their surroundings is especially conspicuous during transitions to or from surface streets. As a result, according to Lynch, decisions to exit are made under pressure, and coming off an exit results in a moment of "severe disorientation."[32] A later study by a graduate student at the University of California, Los Angeles, further illustrates how the freeway does not quite "fit" into the everyday urban environment.[33] Subjects exhibited little ability to locate a freeway onramp from numerous contextual clues, such as traffic patterns or the presence of high-rise buildings; they usually waited for explicit freeway signs or sight of the highway itself.

This contradiction in the role of the freeway as urban image in Los Angeles—overwhelmingly important on one hand and almost invisible on the other—points to a paradox in the metropolitan environment. The schism in urban imagery stems from an underlying duality based on competing senses of orientation—one localized, the other metropolitan. The former sense of place exists as places have always existed. Oriented on the human scale, it is articulated by familiar and specific artifacts with which one has a personal association. It is the place of one's residence,

Invisible Freeways

Almost like a subway tunneling through the city, a depressed freeway disappears from view. The effect is a lessened visual and aural impact on surface-level activities, but at a cost. Thousands of motorists are denied a view, and the freeway remains poorly integrated in one's sense of the local landscape. (Photo by Henrik Kam.)

of one's work, of one's play. It is the location in which people live, in the sense of staying in a place and cultivating it.[34] The localized dwelling place implies the familiar environment connoted by the word ''neighborhood.''

The metropolitan orientation is a more abstract sense of place. One's relationship to the metropolitan environment could never be so intimate as it is, for instance, to the street on which one lives. The scale alone defies such a relationship. Metropolitan life suggests the disintegration in space and time of an individual's various dwelling places. Often living in ''communities without propinquity,''[35] the individual metropolitan must somehow confront the task of reintegrating his or her environment. The metropolis, therefore, provides the context for dwelling. One does not dwell in the metropolis; one passes through it between dwelling places.

The freeway emerges as a particularly apt orientation toward the Los Angeles metropolis, because it defines the nature of the passage. Movement through metropolitan space, particularly in Los Angeles, is experienced in terms of automotive corridors, and the freeway is the automotive corridor par excellence. The freeway system suggests relevant location, as a way that an individual can relate to a plethora of places. An urban environment of distinct points on the highway grid is in part replaced by a set of freeway-defined vector relationships. These vectors are freeway routes, whose magnitudes are measured in minutes and whose directions are disembodied place-names. For example, to get to my present home in Westchester from downtown L.A., I travel the Santa Monica freeway for 20 minutes following the signs for

Santa Monica (the place-name associated with the westward direction) and then travel the San Diego freeway for 10 minutes following the signs for Long Beach (south) without ever catching a glimpse of either community. Sometimes a freeway never even passes through the community whose name marks the direction of travel on the interchange sign. But by relating significant places to these freeway vectors, they are fixed according to a standard that is rooted in daily experience and are thereby reintegrated into a meaningful context.

The freeway system, however, does not provide one unified conception for all Los Angeles; imagery is always dependent on the individual's personal connection with place. In my experience, for example, of growing up in San Pedro, Los Angeles was a triangle formed by the Harbor, San Diego, and Santa Monica freeways. Similarly, the image held by a child going to a local school will differ from that held by an adult driving forty-five minutes to work and back each day. This fact is confirmed by a cognitive mapping study of Los Angeles.[36] Residents of several areas were asked to draw maps of the city. The differences between maps emanating from a poor minority area such as Boyle Heights and those from middle-class Northridge are striking. The Boyle Heights composite map covers a very small area and contains only local landmarks. The Northridge map covers much of the county and shows distant place-names and, predictably, the main routes of travel, that is, the freeways and a few major surface streets. This contrast in perspective clearly suggests the relationship between mobility and the perception of the urban environment.

The results of the study also suggest, as one would assume, a correlation between social class and mobility. Families in the Los Angeles area earning less than $3,000 a year in 1967 generated on an average only 2.2 trips a day per household; families earning more than $25,000 a year generated 12.1, or five and a half times as many, trips per household. The upper half of the income scale generated on an average 10.2 trips a day, the lower half, 4.8.[37] This single factor of mobility does much to explain the types of neighborhood associated with social class and the heavier dependence of poorer classes on their neighborhood area.[38] It is sadly ironic, therefore, that so much of the damage caused by removal of housing in freeway construction has afflicted the poorer urban neighborhoods, the most dramatic example perhaps being the east Los Angeles Mexican American community, which is intersected by six different freeways. In addition, these same communities are most likely to perceive the freeway as a barrier. Underpasses and overpasses for surface traffic would do little to restrict the mobility of residents predominantly transported by automobile, but the isolated pedestrian bridges arching high above an eight-lane freeway mutely assert its capability to discourage pedestrian movement. A study of a small black community partly displaced by the Santa Monica freeway found that 49 percent of a sample of the remaining residents felt local communications had been disrupted; 80 percent of these people came from families without a car. Of those who felt no disruption, 60 percent owned two or more cars.[39] One cannot help but wonder to what extent highway planners with upper-middle-class life-styles are sensitive to the needs of such a community.

But even for the true metropolitan citizens of Los Angeles, such as those living in Westwood or Northridge, the sense of the local place remains im-

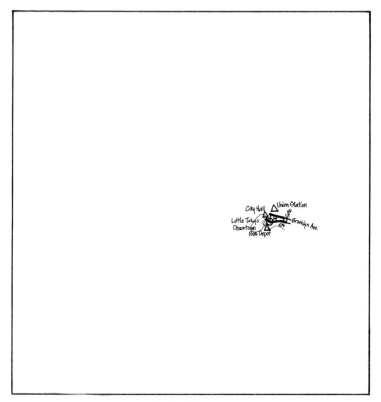

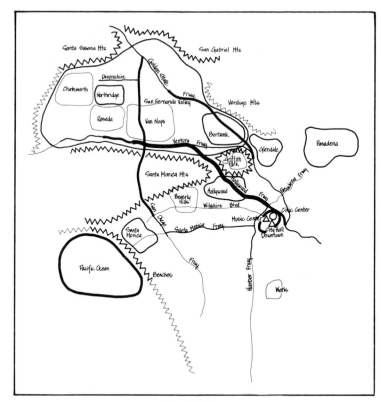

Boyle Heights

Northridge

Images of the City

*These composite maps come from a study in which residents of
different areas in Los Angeles were asked to draw a map of the
city. Obviously, Los Angeles is a very different place to members
of different socioeconomic classes. Boyle Heights has among the
highest percentages of households with no automobile in the
city, and their images reflect this restricted mobility. For the
urban commuters of Northridge, home is the metropolis and the
freeways are a significant feature of the landscape. (Source: Los
Angeles Department of City Planning,* The Visual Environment of
Los Angeles, *1971.)*

portant. Despite the fact that so-called communities are no longer strictly identified with particular neighborhoods, the sense of place is by no means irrelevant to the Angeleno. A number of studies have shown that residents retain a strong sense of neighborhood identity. Nelson and Clark characterize these findings as follows:

> Residents of the Los Angeles area separate the supposedly amorphous city into distinct neighborhoods. Moreover, they indicate considerable identification with and knowledge of the locational aspects of their home neighborhoods. It is likely, however, that they lack complete information about more distant neighborhoods. Their judgments reflect an inability to know all the communities in a very large metropolitan area.[40]

To a child growing up in southern California, home is Compton, or Canoga Park, or Temple City, and so on. In my own case, it was only on leaving the area that I discovered that I really lived in Los Angeles.

The freeways will undoubtedly play a larger role in influencing one's sense of the local neighborhood. Again drawing from my own experience, I have thought of the boundaries of my home communities in Los Angeles in terms of freeways. As far as I was concerned, San Pedro was separated from Wilmington by the Harbor freeway, and now I think of Westchester and Inglewood as being divided by the San Diego freeway; the Inglewood sign west of the freeway seems out of place. Part of this sense of borders reflects real differences in urban land use marked by freeway structures, and as freeways continue to reorganize urban geography the idea of a freeway-defined locality will be reinforced. The concept of freeway neighborhoods is especially important for children, as

East Los Angeles Interchange

The residential areas just east of downtown are home not only to a large Mexican American community, but also to a web of freeways and connector roads. This photograph of the Santa Ana, Pomona, and Golden State freeways illustrates the structure's potential as a barrier in both a positive and a negative sense. The first two freeways divide residential neighborhoods, but the third isolates incompatible land uses, protecting a residential section from the further encroachment of the Los Angeles River industrial area. (Courtesy of CALTRANS.)

freeways are regularly used to determine school attendance areas.

The existence of opposing senses of place complicates any discussion of the Los Angeles metropolitan experience. When the area is considered to be the whole of Los Angeles, few separate localities are appreciated as dwelling places. What one sees is a "vast urban sprawl [in which] the tracts of houses are relieved by freeways and shopping centers."[41] From the local perspective, however, the same tracts are one's neighborhood, one's home. The potential for conflict is well illustrated by freeway-routing controversies. Although from the metropolitan perspective a particular route may seem absolutely necessary to serve "the needs of the travelling public as a whole,"[42] to the individual living in the right-of-way it signals the destruction of the family home.

The conflict was only exacerbated by some questionable early planning practices of the Division of Highways. Until 1965 freeway routing was required by California state law to take the "most direct and practical location," a directive that was not likely to encourage sensitivity to the more subtle local community values. The routing of freeways was an exercise in civil engineering, rather than in regional planning, and was primarily concerned with motorists' priorities and with keeping down construction costs. Although the situation continually improved, thanks in large measure to increasingly organized protests, highway designers were regularly accused of treating "the space between the points joined by a freeway [as] a social wasteland devoid of human significance."[43]

The problem embodies the age-old dilemma of the individual versus a general will; it is in essence a political problem. Yet from a purely metropolitan perspective, any conflict between metropolitan and local priorities is easily decided, and its political nature is obscured. The following scenario presented by Tunnard and Pushkarev illustrates the possibility of conflict between competing senses of place:

The street pattern is historically far more permanent than that of the buildings. Today it happens that a freeway is bent out of its way to miss a supposedly important building, which, three years later, is pulled down anyway as part of private or public redevelopment. The obstacle is gone but the detour will remain for decades, promising to make the freeway obsolete functionally long before it seems obsolete structurally.[44]

Implicit here is an argument for the maintenance of metropolitan priorities, whose logic is presented as unquestionable when considered from the metropolitan perspective. Of course, the definition of metropolitan priorities is itself a political problem, a fact that many freeway supporters prefer to ignore. The rise of formidable opposition to any further commitment to freeway construction has forced the reassessment of that definition.

The power of the freeway system to shape a metropolitan sensibility cannot be understated. The freeways have almost single-handedly expanded the realm of the accessible, and thus they have enlarged what most people recognize as their metropolitan environment. A map of recent changes in the thirty-minute isochron shows one measure of accessibility, suggesting the increase in the amount of space that can be taken in during a relatively short time. (A thirty-minute drive to work is not at all uncommon.)

Right-of-Way Clearance

More than a quarter of a million people have been displaced by freeway construction in Los Angeles, Orange, and Ventura counties. Right-of-way clearance, like any form of urban renewal, places an undue burden on displaced households, ranging from the disruption of established neighborhood relationships to uncompensated monetary costs incurred in relocating. Although California has long been a leader in the development of increasingly just compensation policies, the majority of the relocated households would not receive the full benefit of this liberal trend, since reimbursement was not retroactive. It is ironic, but not at all coincidental, that the most disruptive civic venture should produce the most profoundly permanent impact on Los Angeles' urban geography. The photo shows the site of the San Gabriel River freeway through Norwalk in 1962. (Courtesy of CAL-TRANS.)

As a result of new freeway construction and of highway improvements, the area of land within a thirty-minute drive from the civic center rose from 261 square miles in 1953 to 705 square miles by 1962, an increase of 175 percent.[45]

Such changes in temporal accessibility are in most respects much more important than spatial measures of territorial expansion in affecting the quality of the metropolitan experience. In the metropolis, distance becomes a function of time, and the expanding isochron must reflect an expansion in the individual's sense of place. Some of the resulting changes were noted earlier in my discussion of the relationship of the metropolitan area to the dwelling place. But the situation is more complex. Who knows what changes occur with a growing irreverence for distance and an increasing impatience with time? Most places then become merely points to pass through, and interaction with such a place is just an obstacle on the way toward a destination. Perhaps our destinations, the localities where we dwell, also lose their distinctiveness. The individual mobility epitomized by the freeway frees us from the constraints of the locality. Yet in doing so it may also destroy the integrity of the locality. People concern themselves less with places and more with functions, and place becomes simply the location of an institution providing a functional fulfillment. Redondo has a nice beach, Venice a good movie theater, and Long Beach a good Mexican restaurant, but all lose their identity as coherent environments. Concurrently there is a decreased appreciation of and commitment to locality. Immobility breeds diversity, which the expanding range of the accessible undermines; places lose their charm and interest, and we become less sensitive to their attractions.

Urban sociologists, with some sadness, have regularly noted changes of this sort. A survey of a central Los Angeles neighborhood in 1929 reported "decreasing social dependence upon the locality and an increasing lack of concern about it."[46] There are good reasons for feeling nostalgic about the losses imposed by the transition to a highly urban society. Yet we must not get too idealistic about a mythical golden age of community lest we lose sight of the realistic expectations of a modern society and of its primary values, for these values continue to inform the choices that govern our lives.

The growth of the new metropolis represented by Los Angeles has been spurred by distinct advantages. Perhaps never before has a city's form been so much the product of individual choice rather than of the constraints of geography and economy. It is easy to dismiss these choices, to expose them as "contradictory" and "antisocial," to sneer at an anemic and misdirected suburban life. But in doing so we forget their history. Los Angeles has grown as a response to what was perceived as a less satisfactory way of life, and in many ways it has succeeded. It is a living polemic against both the large industrial metropolis and the provincial small town.

There are many defenders of the urban form pioneered in southern California. Among them is Sam Bass Warner, Jr., who is far from an automatic supporter of the status quo in urban development:

The land-use and transportation structure of Los Angeles gives glimpses of a more humane environment than we have yet enjoyed. The special factor of the city's social geography is its

33

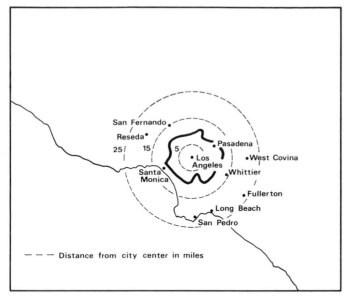

1953

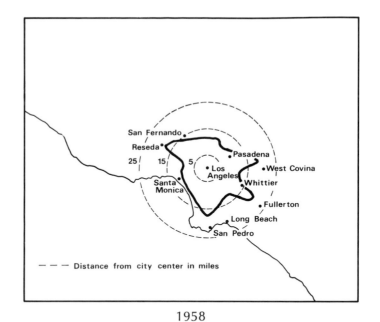

1958

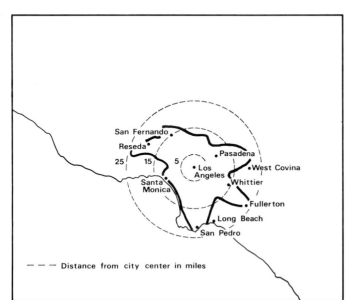

1962

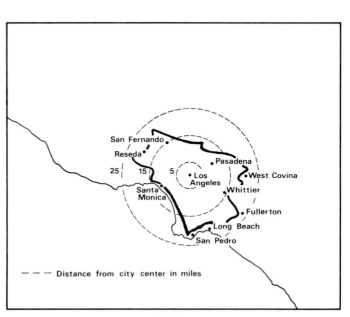

1971

low density of settlement, the ease and scope of movement of the overwhelming proportion of its citizens, and its comparative lack of domination by a single downtown area. It has thus escaped the rigid core, sector, and ring structure of business and residential occupation that tyrannized the industrial metropolis and from which older cities are only now beginning to extricate themselves.[47]

For almost a century southern California has been attracting millions of new inhabitants from across the continent. Although Los Angeles County has recently shown population losses of almost 1 percent a year, its neighboring areas in Orange, Riverside, and Ventura counties, which are part of the Greater Los Angeles area, continue to draw people in large numbers. Their populations increased through in-migration alone by 17 percent, 15 percent, and 12 percent, respectively, in the six years from 1972 to 1978.[48]

Mass popularization of the automobile has democratized transportation for most of the area's residents. The vast majority of households (85 percent) have access to at least one vehicle. "Such a distribution of automobiles and freeways," writes Warner, "gives the Los Angeles employee the widest choice of job opportunities ever possible in an American city."[49] Such freedom (like all "freedoms") is not universal, and the poor, the young, and the old remain handicapped in a world that seems designed to run on four wheels. The lack of adequate mass transit was in fact noted as contributing to the frustrations inciting the Watts riots of 1965. But as Robert Fogelson has written, "the South Central Ghetto is indeed isolated, but not for reasons as simple and reassuring as dreadful bus service."[50] And public transit has been slowly improving in the past fifteen years; the buses of a unified transit district now carry 1.3 million patron-fares a day, and

Changes in the Thirty-Minute Isochrone

The single most important factor in the increases in accessibility shown here was progress in freeway construction. The dramatic increase from 1953 to 1962 of land area within a thirty-minute drive of downtown reflects the priority placed on the radial routes of the freeway system; note that each point of the irregularly shaped stars corresponds to a freeway. During 1962-1971, construction shifted to the periphery, thus having little effect on the accessibility of the central region. In a few instances congestion has worked to undo these gains, as is evident, for example, in the contracted 1971 isochrone at the Ventura and Santa Ana freeways. (Source: Howard J. Nelson and William A. V. Clark, The Los Angeles Metropolitan Experience *[Cambridge, Mass., Ballinger Publishing Co., 1976].)*

they are supplemented by several good (and not so good) municipal lines.

It is all too easy to dismiss the city whose life-force "lurks in a very strange place: under the hood of the automobile."[51] Yet for those who have the technological equipment it all seems to work fairly well. In Los Angeles, most people think little of driving for every purpose: to see a friend, to buy cigarettes or an ice-cream cone, to watch the sunset. Your world is centered on the automobile, which gives you an unprecedented and addicting degree of freedom. The freeway becomes as much a part of your life as the street you live on—perhaps you even know the former more intimately. You accustom yourself to enjoy as much or as little of any particular amenity that you choose to pursue on the road: "The freeway allows you to create your own life. Your community is formed not by geography or ethnicity but by common interests, and it is not unusual to drive 45 minutes for a casual dinner with friends."[52]

There are distinct social costs for such freedoms. One can drive anywhere in Los Angeles, but there are usually few places worth walking to. The two most immediate concerns, air pollution and energy resources, are too complex to be discussed here in any detail. (The latter is briefly treated in the epilogue.) But, ultimately, it makes little difference if many of us cannot completely reconcile ourselves to a fully automotive society. The automobile seems to reflect an overwhelmingly popular consensus rarely matched by social movements, and it flourishes because it continues to serve that general will.

Modern Streets

The juxtaposition of shopping mall and freeway offers an interesting study in urban environments. Both are specialized street scenes where a single function has been isolated and reorganized on a grand scale. The freeway supersedes the street as a conduit of traffic. Abutting property serves merely as a buffer to ensure the exclusive requirements of rapid movement. The enclosed mall is the most recent evolutionary phase of the commercial street. Here cars are parked on the periphery, with the main entrances of the stores facing onto a pedestrian gallery. Most malls are intended to recreate the sense of space—and occasionally even the building facades—of a preautomotive marketing plaza. It is ironic that, especially in Los Angeles, one has to drive to find a place to stroll or just to loiter. (Photo by Mason Dooley.)

Private Lives and Zen Freeway

The southern California megalopolis is a society integrated by rubber tires. Of all trips made on an average weekday, about 96 percent are made by automobile or by truck; the figure is 99 percent for the weekend.[53] The automobile is not just another way to get around; it is *the* way to get around. As such, it has transcended the level of mere transportation and has become a dominant cultural phenomenon in the area. And the freeway is the central manifestation of this cultural experience, both for the large volume of travel it carries and for its unique position in the automotive environment. It is hardly an exaggeration to call the freeway experience, as Joan Didion does, "the only secular communion Los Angeles has."[54] The well-publicized hoax of the couple who lived in a trailer home on the freeway[55] contains so much pyschological truth that it is immediately convincing. The mythical pair surely ranks among the pantheon of Angelenos. Although not all students of the subject would concur,[56] I agree with Reyner Banham when he suggests that "the freeway system in its totality is now a single comprehensible place, a coherent state of mind, a complete way of life, the fourth ecology [with the beaches, the foothills, and the basin plains] of the Angeleno."[57]

Our language alone tells the story. Never would one "take a freeway to work" or "take the freeway system to work"; one simply takes "the freeway." An extensive system serving more than 1,000 square miles exists singularly in the local psyche.

What the university is to the scholar, what the church is to the faithful, the freeway is to the Los Angeles motorist. It is not the only place where the activity of driving occurs, but it is a sanctuary for such activity, designed specifically to serve its needs. The freeway represents an unprecedented evolution in the form of the street. It is a monofunctional street from which all other forms of street life have been banned except unidirectional movement. Nothing else of what has traditionally been considered street life—residence and play, loitering and walking—remains. Of the buying, selling, and displaying of goods, all that survives is the billboard, already prohibited from much of the system and surviving tenuously on the rest in the face of often conflicting city, county, and state regulation aimed at controlling it. The illuminated business sign can only lure you toward the off-ramp, back into the realm of "gas, food and lodging."

The freeways were constructed with a single purpose: to supply unrestricted auto-mobility. They are good for only one type of activity—driving—a fact testified to by the anxiety caused by a freeway breakdown. Changing a tire, walking for help, or simply waiting for a passing highway patrolman has been called "one of the most traumatic disruptions in the routine of urban life."[58] It is the uniqueness of this ultimate street, this hyperfunctional environment, which makes it a distinct ecology.

Central to the freeway's functional separation is its visual isolation, both planned (through landscaping, depressed or elevated roadways, and sound walls) and consequential (with the speed of motion itself blurring

A Three-Second Spot

The freeways offer the largest live audience to which a business can pitch its wares. Here three enterprises take advantage of their location at the southeast corner of the San Diego and Harbor freeways interchange by erecting tall signs designed to survive the blur of 55-mph vision. An even more sophisticated approach lies across the way: the Datsun building is a prime example of freeway-side corporate-image architecture. It is simple yet imposing, built largely of eye-catching reflective glass. The few billboards that adorn the freeway must abide by a myriad of municipal, county, and state ordinances; most of them are located in industrial areas. (Photo by Mason Dooley.)

details). As a result of the de-emphasis on peripheral involvement with the urban landscape, the dissociation of the freeway from the urban context described by Lynch is not surprising. As an environment, the freeway does not exist "within" the surrounding landscape. It is in this sense like a tunnel, boring through the city without physical or psychological obstacles, a Los Angeles subway system.

This isolation sets the freeway apart from its immediate environment. While opening up the city by making distant points more accessible, it simultaneously creates a situation that discourages the individual's involvement with much of the city. As a hyperfunctional metropolitan street, the freeway reinforces the sense of the metropolis as consisting merely of points to be passed by on the way to one's destination. Commuting is not touring: it is not taking in the charms or experiencing the drama of the everyday world of others. Indeed, the automobile has long since driven most of what is charming and dramatic off our streets, and the subtleties that remain are obscured by the blur of motion.

Rarely thinking of anything beyond the embankment, one can pass through the most depressed parts of the city without ever being directly confronted with poverty. In discussing the Watts riots, Thomas Pynchon observed that

The panoramic sense of black impoverishment is hard to miss from atop the Harbor Freeway, which so many whites must drive at least twice every working day. Somehow, it occurs to very few of them to leave at the Imperial Highway exit for a change, go east instead of west only a few blocks, and take a look at Watts. A quick look. The simplest kind of beginning. But Watts is country which lies, psychologically, uncounted miles further than most whites seem at present willing to travel.[59]

Freeway Through the Ghetto

To keep right-of-way expenses under control, freeways were often routed through inexpensive property, with the result that a disproportionate number of those affected by relocation or disruption were poor, minority, or elderly—those least able to absorb uncompensated expenses, and those least served by the projects. Most commuters are probably unaware of the irony, for the freeway offers a continued shelter from engagement with ghetto areas. As a result, few of the whites who travel the Harbor freeway, shown here, have probably ever set foot in Watts, which lies just east of the freeway and is the home of one of Los Angeles' most significant, but least visited, monuments, the Towers of Simon Rodia. (Photo by Mason Dooley.)

Similarly, the east L.A. interchange, site of probably the worst peak-hour congestion as it feeds suburban commuters into the central business district, lies just at the edge of a huge Mexican American community; again, few of the daily visitors to east Los Angeles would ever leave the freeway for that foreign milieu. The isolation of the freeway environment from its immediate urban context suggests social consequences that go beyond problems in cognitive mapping and direction finding.

The freeway serves as a bridge over the barriers of both social and natural geography. The Harbor freeway is perceived by whites as their "safe passage" through the south central black community. For east–west travel there are only the Santa Monica and the Artesia freeways at the elongated ghetto's perimeters, and a white traveler will go out of his or her way rather than drive at surface level. And of course, the freeway spans physical barriers as well. The San Diego freeway through the Sepulveda Pass, connecting west Los Angeles with the San Fernando Valley, is functionally similar to the Brooklyn Bridge, connecting Manhattan with the once less accessible Brooklyn suburbs.

The disengagement of the freeway environment from its immediate context serves its purpose: it makes it easier for the driver to reach his destination. Because peripheral distractions are muted and all but unidirectional movement is eliminated, he is freed from all considerations irrelevant to the task of efficient transportation. As a result, driving a freeway usually creates less tension than driving a major surface street, at least according to one series of studies. In fact, the re-searcher who conducted the studies concluded that the main reason people switch to freeways is precisely because they suffer fewer tensions and find more driving comfort; they do not necessarily do so to save time. Ironically the shift is often self-defeating, for drivers were found to take advantage of the ease of freeway travel and accelerate until they reached a particular threshold of driving tension.[60]

Anyone who has seen Los Angeles at five o'clock in the afternoon knows that most drivers prefer to use the freeways. People tend to take a freeway whenever it is at all feasible, often driving a less direct route to do so. "A surface street," quips Joan Didion, "is anything around Los Angeles that is not a freeway—'going surface' from one part of town to another is generally regarded as eccentric."[61] On the surface, one has an overabundance of visual input. Cars are coming from every direction, crossing intersections and pulling out of parking spaces. Traffic signals, cyclists, and unobservant pedestrians all seemingly conspire to plague the motorist. The obstacles are not simply psychological; they also slow you down. Despite above-capacity usage, the freeways are still usually faster than their corresponding surface highways, though not by so much as some proponents have claimed. Furthermore, freeways have fewer accidents per vehicle-mile than surface streets (though Los Angeles has the highest motor vehicle fatality rate per capita of any major metropolis in the nation).[62]

Certainly few cruise the freeway all day like Joan Didion's heroine Maria, who "drove it as a riverman runs a river, every day more attuned to its currents, its deceptions."[63] But the experience of driving a freeway has a special quality, a sort of "detached involvement" with the environment, which is indeed common to many. The involvement is very real, and many writers stress the complexity of making rapid decisions and high-speed maneuvers. Yet the average Angeleno, whose first driving test is a major rite of passage into full membership in society, manages the freeway with half a mind. With reflexes conditioned even to peak-hour congestion, he is often only partly aware that he is driving. The rest of his mind wanders at will or, to employ the colloquialism, he "spaces out." Perhaps no aspect of the freeway experience is more characteristic than the sudden realization that you have no memory of the past ten minutes of your trip. The point was driven home for me by my first speeding ticket. The highway patrolman told me I was going twelve miles an hour over the speed limit, changing lanes, and passing cars; all I could remember was the song on the radio.

Christopher Rand, writing on Los Angeles for the *New Yorker,* was unquestionably correct in observing that "one sees little activity on the L.A. freeway besides driving," but he was mistaken in saying that "time spent on them can be counted as lost."[64] One sees little activity, it is true, but what one does not see is that driving provides a scheduled opportunity to do nothing. The ritual of driving, for the most part, appropriately occurs right before and right after the working day, thus easing the transitions of a fragmented life. The freeway commute is Los Angeles' distinctively urban form of meditation.

Most freeway drivers probably do not realize that they "battle the freeway" twice daily in order to relax.

Most of them would more readily accept as true the following scenario: "You find yourself congealed in August afternoon smog at 5 o'clock in a shimmering hallucination of hell and molten metal. By the time you reach home, the early stages of what you have come to recognize as carbon monoxide poisoning have made an anger that takes an hour and two drinks to wash out."[65] Indeed, there are such days. But the comments about hellish traffic jams which so commonly fill casual conversation are, as Banham observed, "little more than standard rhetorical tropes, like English complaints about the weather."[66] Such talk is a ritualistic exchange carried out, not to dispense information, but rather to establish a commonality; bucking the rush-hour traffic, like enduring bad weather, is one of the few experiences that are so widely shared, so utterly mundane, that they are a surefire basis for conversation.

It is true that the opportunity for relaxation during rush-hour traffic may seem slight compared with that afforded by sitting on the bus and looking out the window, but it holds up well when compared with riding a crowded New York subway; and it has advantages: one never "misses his car," waits to transfer, or walks more than a short distance. Since time spent in waiting and walking is considered time lost by commuters, it is a source of frustration. As Melvin Webber, a Berkeley transportation researcher, recently noted,

During the past 15 years, at least a dozen major studies have investigated the ways travellers assess costs when deciding how they will make intrametropolitan trips. With remarkably small variation among the cities examined, the studies all conclude that *the time spent inside vehicles is judged to be far less onerous than the time spent walking, waiting, and transferring by a factor of up to three or four times. For commuters waiting on platforms, the factor may be as high as 10 times!* [emphasis in original][67]

It is easy to forget that rush-hour congestion is hardly unique to Los Angeles. Yet a rush hour is, by its very nature, a time of congestion.[68] One need only visit another major city to discover the virtues of our freeway traffic, as Hunter S. Thompson reminds us:

One of the best and most beneficial things about coming East now and then is that it tends to provoke a powerful understanding of the "Westward Movement" in U.S. history. After a few years on the Coast or even Colorado you tend to forget just exactly what it was that put you on the road, going west, in the first place. You live in L.A. a while and before long you start cursing traffic jams on the freeways in the warm Pacific dusk . . . and you tend to forget that in New York City you can't even *park*; forget about driving.[69]

If you can avoid those four rush hours when everybody is on the road, driving the freeway can be a true pleasure, with its numerous lanes, graceful curves, banked interchange ramps that require no braking, and the sense of speed without danger. Driving the freeway can create a rare, and distinctly urban, moment of joy when the car drives well, the freeway is uncrowded, and there is a good song on the radio. The freeway lifts you over the city or through a pass, and the view from the side windows is framed by the greenery of the embankment landscaping. Although I often dislike driving, I love to drive the freeway when the day is good.

While it may appear farfetched to compare a peak-hour commute with a stroll down a country road, the freeway has a certain quality that makes driving it the nearest equivalent to such an experience the average

Angeleno is likely to have during a typical day. For here, rather than in Griffith Park or along the beach, one receives a daily guarantee of privacy. Safe from all direct communication with other individuals, on the freeway one is alone in the world. You can smoke, manipulate the radio dial at will, sing off key, belch, fart, or pick your nose. A car on a freeway is more private than one's home.

It is the freedom to be alone, coupled with the corollary freedom to be independent, which feeds the freeway addict's habit and thwarts the best-laid schemes of many a transit planner. Since roughly 87 percent of all vehicles using the freeway to travel to work and back contain only the driver, the occupancy rate for freeway commuters is 1.2 persons per vehicle.[70] With freeway construction at a standstill, Caltrans is now seeking to raise that figure by 0.1 and is spending hundreds of thousands of dollars locally to that end. Only a limited number of freeway commuters are at all responsive to programs to raise vehicle occupancy. One study of the Hollywood freeway found two out of three users to be "hard-core" solitary drivers.[71]

The importance to the individual of driving alone is difficult to assess. A few newspaper articles have included statements from psychologists, artists, and other "experts" on the human psyche, testifying to the value of the daily commute in providing an island of peace, a period in which to fantasize, a time when one can be uninhibited.[72] John Lilly has gone so far as to describe driving on the freeway as having "all the characteristics of the most esoteric and far-out discipline that you could find in the Far East. You have to be in an expanded state of awareness in regard to the external world or you'll have a head-on collision. At the same time, you can deal with the problems within your own head."[73] Perhaps this duality explains why est guru Werner Erhard experienced his visionary breakthrough while driving on the freeway.[74] Friends claim that they do some of their best thinking on freeways, even while struggling with stop-and-go traffic, a paradox which Thomas Pynchon also noticed:

Amid the exhaust, sweat, glare and ill-humor of a summer evening on an American freeway, Oedipa Maas pondered her Trystero problem. All the silence of San Narciso—the calm surface of the motel pool, the contemplative contours of residential streets like rakings in the sand of a Japanese garden—had not allowed her to think as leisurely as this freeway madness.[75]

Time spent on a freeway is not always productive. Nevertheless, the freeway does induce a state of mind which, as Banham suggests, has become an integral part of the Los Angeles metropolitan experience.

On the freeway, the private automobile defines a private space set within what is ostensibly the most public of places. Freeways do not, in any meaningful sense, constitute a public space. That is not to say that they do not embody a public order. There is a remarkable degree of coordination and self-regulation in being part of the flow of traffic, and Los Angeles drivers are renowned for their courtesy. One observer describes a "kind of Brotherhood among freeway drivers,"[76] as illustrated at entrance ramps by the way commuters take turns in allowing oncoming traffic to merge. Yet the freeway as a social environment supports none of the social relationships, none of the personal interactions, which characterize the truly public place. Relationships between drivers are completely anonymous, and almost never does one come in contact with another particular driver more than once. The exceptions described in a few journalistic pieces—chatting across the lane during traffic standstills or attempted teenage romantic encounters—are notable only for their striking novelty. In general, the freeway remains perhaps Los Angeles' most exclusive sanctuary of the faceless mass.

The automobile itself is well suited to support a variety of public cultures, and Los Angeles is rich with such activity. Car culture flourishes, however, on streets other than freeways. Cruising occurs in every corner of the metropolis, from Mexican American cholos low-riding down Whittier Boulevard to the heterogeneous traffic jam on Van Nuys Boulevard on a Wednesday night or middle-class suburban teenagers flocking to Sunset Boulevard or Westwood to take in the sights. Would-be race drivers in souped-up dragsters speed along Mulholland Drive every night, and Los Angeles, home of the celebrated car customizers of the 1960s, remains the publishing center for the major automobile magazines.[77] One can see more exotic cars in a week on the streets of Beverly Hills than in several years' back issues of *Road and Track*. Perhaps nowhere else has the auto mystique become so characteristic a quality of an urban environment. As Benjamin Stein observes in the journal of his first year in Los Angeles, whose title is copied appropriately from the license plate of his Mercedes 450SL: "In L.A., a car is everything. It is how a person relates to the world, and it is how he sees himself in the world."[78]

This identification of public face and private automobile is imprinted from the day one turns sixteen. To be a teenager in L.A. without access to a car is to risk being a nonentity, as James Q. Wilson recalls:

A car was the absolutely essential piece of social overhead capital. With it, you could get a job, meet a girl, hang around with the boys, go to a drive-in, see football games away from home, take in the beach parties at Laguna or Corona del Mar, or go to the Palladium ballroom in Hollywood. To have a car meant being somebody; to have to borrow a car meant knowing somebody; to have no car at all, owned or borrowed, was to be left out—way out.[79]

The discussion of the intricacies of car culture is, however, mainly a discussion of life on surface streets. That is where you can be seen; that is where you can see the action. If one cruises the freeway, it is to be alone or, more commonly, to go somewhere.

The car on the freeway is to transportation what the suburban bedroom community is to residence: a private, self-contained environment. One's home is one's castle, and so is one's car. As in the suburban home you are free from the intrusion of the stranger or the door-to-door salesman (for the former you call the police; for the latter you buy a "No Peddlers" sign); in the car there are no strange faces and no one threatens to disturb you. Protected by the detached single-family home and the detached private automobile, the Angeleno can maintain his daily life remarkably free of intrusion. Thus Los Angeles is able to maintain its facade of a garden patch of urban villages, a metropolitan small town, without ever compromising the anonymity that is a hallmark of city life.

This private-public dichotomy has been somewhat confused by the mass media. Whereas the private home has been violated by television, its extension on the road has become closely connected with radio.

One cannot help but suspect that the car radio supports the industry, and that so many stations are able to flourish in Los Angeles because so much time is spent in automobiles. You begin to realize the intimacy between radio and car whenever you haven't driven for a while; you discover that you don't know the latest popular songs. Those who prefer complete control of their environment install tape players. It is likely that Los Angeles has more car tape players per capita than any other area in the nation.

The union of freeway and car radio is most truly consummated, however, by the "sigalert." At least five local radio stations regularly broadcast freeway conditions, making it far easier to find a traffic report than a good song at rush hour. The sigalert has joined the weather report in dispensing crucial environmental information, though its content rarely affects one's day. Except for the occasional catastrophe of a jack-knifed trailer blocking all four lanes, advice to consider alternative routes is usually ignored. As a teenager I never understood why my parents would religiously listen to sigalerts at breakfast, yet such attentiveness served a purpose. The traffic report is news addressed to the everyday world of the everyday commuter, thereby publicly validating the driving experience as significant.

The electronic media have made another inroad on the privacy of the freeway. Perhaps the recent popularity of the citizen band radio in Los Angeles suggests an attempt to bridge the distances set by steel and by speed. But the CB is only a mockery of real communication, as meaningful as a passing smile from a never-to-be seen-again face. A passage from an L.A.-based novel aptly describes the phenomenon: "The CB radio was on, and he listened to the strange, distorted, distant voices talking to one another in their strange private language. He never seemed to hear the same voices twice, just as he never seemed to see the same faces twice in the streets on which he drove. There were so many people, he thought. Too confusing."[80]

In his book on southern California, Richard Lillard sees the freeways as the "most notable public spaces open to significant and admirable movement. They are the Gasoline Age parallel to the boulevards for parades, fiestas, and military movement, to the spaces for fairs, open markets, and religious ceremonies in all old worlds."[81] But the picture is not quite accurate. The freeways are indeed as essential a focus for the functioning of our society as those earlier places were for theirs (as the epigraph that opens this chapter suggests), and they do provide an important shared experience, a cultural phenomenon of the highest order. Nevertheless, the freeway represents the complete subversion of the traditional sanctuary of the public realm—the street. For up to a tenth of every day, the average Angeleno sits in a steel-enclosed private world. More than any other ecology in Los Angeles, more than any single comprehensible place, the freeway is a private space.

The Architectonic Landscape

The freeway lends yet another dimension to the Los Angeles experience which is often unappreciated by the average driver. The freeway structure has made a significant, and often enriching, contribution to the landscape. A project on so enormous a scale is par-

ticularly well suited to the Los Angeles environs, where the terrain is expansive and the urban texture is open. Hence the freeway is easily accommodated; Los Angeles has few of the cramped freeway structures that mar densely settled cities like San Francisco or Boston. As a result, the freeway rarely obscures the scenery by creating a visual barricade. More commonly, by rising above the sea of one- and two-story buildings, freeways open up new vistas of the cityscape. The most striking examples are the interchanges at the sunset hour. The motorist who is temporarily stranded at rush hour on a connector road— say the Santa Monica to the San Diego, or the Hollywood to the Harbor—can enjoy some of the finest views of Los Angeles.

In Los Angeles, at least, the freeway is organic, as organic as any product of a boomtown built in a desert can be. As literary critic Tom Reck has observed, "The city is artificial in a quite literal sense. All its features, whether flora, fauna, or freeway, have had to be imported because it is built on a desert where nothing grows naturally."[82] It seems only natural that panoramas of freeway interchanges should rank with long stretches of white beach and Mediterranean orange trees set against snow-capped mountains as among the classic postcard views of Los Angeles.

The tabula rasa where American culture etched its dreams provided an apt setting for this tremendous act of civic will, which sculpts the earth's surface anew for human settlement. The freeways create a new geography and a new sense of place. Gracing the desert terrain with giant concrete rivers which nature alone could not produce, they provide a rare geographical relief to the sprawling flatness of the central basin. No

San Francisco Freeway

Los Angeles' low-density settlement made it a relatively hospitable environ for freeway development. Freeway construction in more densely settled cities proved less successful. This example from San Francisco shows why. The freeway alone may offer a perversely interesting study in curved lines, but it is so poorly integrated with the surrounding urban landscape that it is a blight. An additional score against freeways in high-density areas is that they took an even higher toll in dislocated residences and businesses during right-of-way clearances than they did in other areas. This photo of the Central freeway was taken in 1959, the year the Board of Supervisors halted all further freeway construction within San Francisco city limits. (Courtesy of CALTRANS.)

one has argued this contribution of the Los Angeles freeways more persuasively than Reyner Banham:

The plains began to impose their style on the freeways—instead of having to follow the landscape, they began to create the landscape. For miles across the flatlands the freeways are conspicuously the biggest human artifact, the only major disturbance of the land-surface, involving vastly more earth-moving than the railways did. In areas like Palms, or Bell Gardens, or over between Willowbrook and Hawthorne, the banks and cuttings of the freeways are often the only topographical features of note in the townscape, and the planting on their slopes can make a contribution to the local environment that outweighs the disturbances caused by their construction—a view of a bank of artfully varied tree-plantings can easily be a lot more rewarding than a prospect of endless flat backyards.[83]

Despite all the pastoral rhetoric that embellishes freeway criticism, the freeways do provide the city with an extensive greenbelt. In one of the most generous public commitments to landscaping, the Department of Transportation is currently spending $5 million a year simply for new plantings in District VII and another $9 million to keep existing greenery on the freeways alive. The plantings are often exquisite. More than 100 varieties adorn embankments, with carefully planned arrangements of trees, shrubs, and ground covers. Acacia, eucalyptus, oak, pine, palm, pepper tree, jacaranda, Chinese pistachio, oleander, lantana, myrtle, sumac, ivy, ice plant, and juniper are included in the wide range of California natives and imports from other "Mediterranean" climates of the world (notably Australia and New Zealand) which are used. A succession of blossoms at the side of the road marks the changing seasons. In a city with less and less undeveloped space, driving a landscaped freeway becomes one of the best (or at least most regular) es-

capes from the world of stucco into an urban preserve of open space and greenery.

Not only does the freeway shelter nature but, when viewed from a distance, it takes on a naturalistic quality of its own. Sitting in the revolving bar atop downtown's Bonaventure Hotel, one views the freeway as one might watch the waves crashing at a beach, the traffic moving with an almost natural rhythm of ebb and flow. Perhaps the ultimate testimony to the pleasure of watching the freeway flow is the McDonald's restaurant in east Los Angeles whose picture windows overlook the San Bernardino freeway. Countless office buildings and apartments enjoy similar views.

The freeway as a general form lends itself well to a consideration of its aesthetic potential. Freeways are imposing, consciously designed structures, and the best of them can be strikingly beautiful. Outstanding examples are the interchanges. The Santa Monica and San Diego interchange, the one most often cited, is a spectacular piece of architecture, with its long, graceful connector ramps that are as much a pleasure to drive as to look at. But the area abounds with notable examples. The old downtown "stack" (four-level interchange), with its simple lines, is particularly elegant, and some of the newest interchanges, such as those constructed in the north part of the San Fernando Valley or the giant Kellogg Hill interchange in Pomona, are powerfully dramatic. In fact, nearly every major interchange constructed since the early 1960s is of genuine aesthetic interest, providing an interaction of straight and curved shapes which delineate space much as a work of modern sculpture does. Perhaps it is no coincidence that Alexander Calder's

Environmental Sculpture

The integrity of so many of the interchanges as artistic forms helps raise the Los Angeles freeways above the level of mere automotive thoroughfares. Yet, like so many other "externalities" in freeway construction, aesthetic considerations were hampered by a narrow interpretation of the constitutional limit on highway fund uses. The additional rights-of-way required for the more graceful structures and for extensive plantings came only with additional expenses. (As late as 1975 the local district was denied funding for landscaping in order to save money.) The traditional highway lobby was the most vocal opponent of such expenditures, complaining that money was being wasted on the "frosting" when more "cake"—that is, more freeways—was the most important priority. Fortunately, the state scenic highways program and the national beautification movement both worked to militate against such narrow interests. The monumental Kellogg Hill interchange of the San Bernardino and Orange freeways, set in a landscape of native vegetation, is a good example of a freeway as functional sculpture. (Photo courtesy of CALTRANS.)

sculpture for the Security Pacific skyscraper—just off the Harbor freeway—consists of a few sweeping arches, defining its setting like a reassembled interchange. The work is a fitting reminder to the Angeleno that a few simple curves can provide aesthetic structures of monumental proportions.

What makes the freeway, and most notably the freeway interchange, so special is that it is, in Lawrence Halprin's words, "a new form of urban sculpture for motion."[84] Each exit ramp offers a different visual as well as kinesthetic sensation. The interchange is like a mobile in a situation where the observer is the moving object. It is the experience of an effortlessly choreographed dance, with each car both performing and observing the total movement and the freeway architecture providing the carefully integrated setting. Even the clean, gentle sweep of the broad ribbon of freeway before you as you drive can be, if properly viewed, extremely beautiful. Or, to return to Halprin,

The great overhead concrete structures with their haunches tied to the ground and the vast flowing cantilevers rippling above the local streets stand like enormous sculptures marching through the architectonic caverns. These vast beautiful works of engineering speak to us in the language of a new scale, a new attitude in which high-speed motion and the qualities of change are not mere abstract conceptions but a vital part of our everyday experiences. Though man is dwarfed by the size of the immense structures, he regains his relationship to them by participating in their use. Freeways involve each of us visually through the strength and urgency of their structure and also through qualities of motion which they make possible.[85]

The first time I considered such views they struck me as just short of absurd. But perhaps their apparent novelty speaks more for the narrowness of our prevailing conceptions of aesthetics than for the formal qualities of the freeway itself. We make pilgrimages to museums of art while remaining blind to whatever substance and beauty can be found in the everyday world. Certainly freeway builders have often failed to live up to the creative challenge of their task. But then, they too are a product of a society that so often seems to suffer from aesthetic anemia.

The Freeway as Symbol: What I Say and What I Mean

In this essay I am trying to pay heed to Anselm Strauss's directive for urban research, to "study an area which is enmeshed in public debate only after taking steps to minimize ideological entrapment."[86] Although I make no claim to have transcended my personal involvement, a questioning attitude toward prejudices—both my own and those I have encountered in others—has been implicit in my process. When studying what others have written, one discovers that the notion of the freeway evokes a number of associations in the minds of most people, and that these associations influence their treatment of the subject. The freeway has taken on symbolic proportions. Its symbolic qualities are often dismissed by those concerned with the "realities" of transportation as at best overstated or, more often, as fantastic. Yet we do not live in a "real world"; we live in a world of cultural constructs, a world of metaphors and fictions. As Emerson suggested, "we are symbols, and inhabit symbols." Accordingly, the freeway exists as more than a mere traffic artery; it is a cultural artifact around which a whole complex of meanings can cluster. If we

Filmex, 1979

This advertisement for the 1979 Los Angeles International Film Exposition combined two of the principal leitmotivs of the city — the movies and the freeways — and set them in a landscape of palm trees and the Hollywood Hills to form a unified restatement of classic Los Angeles images. (Courtesy of Filmex.)

forget this simple fact we render unintelligible much of what has been said about freeways, as well as about any social issue. To understand fully the freeway's place in the Los Angeles experience requires that we consider its position as a central element of the native imagery.

The freeway system supplies Los Angeles with one of its principal metaphors. Employed to represent the totality of metropolitan Los Angeles, it is the city's great synecdoche, one of the few parts capable of standing for the whole. Freeway imagery — a graceful interchange or a bumper-to-bumper rush hour — is one of the area's principal leitmotivs. Its uses are manifold. Postcards flourish with shots of the downtown stack or a freeway set against a panoramic vista. A *National Geographic* article on the city is subtitled "Babylon on the Freeway."[87] As a movie or a television program opens, a shot of a freeway places the setting as precisely as any caption.

The leitmotiv is reinforced as the seemingly constant reliance on the freeway system impresses itself upon the memory of the millions who visit Los Angeles every year. Nervously clinging to the freeway for orientation, much as a visitor to Paris might rarely venture beyond walking range of the metro, the tourist or the passer-through returns home with an image of all of sprawling southern California melting into a freeway.

More often than not, the freeway as a symbol carries negative connotations. As a *New York Times* bureau chief has suggested, " 'Freeway' has become an emotional word in recent years, like 'hippie' or 'mugger.' "[88] Freeways may be associated with all the ills of a modern, and particularly automotive, me-

tropolis: air and noise pollution, congestion, the destruction of neighborhoods, the specter of a concrete blanket over the landscape. When country singer Jerry Jeff Walker sings of getting off the L.A. freeway, he longs to leave every perceived evil of city life behind.

By extension, the metaphor also serves for less tangible modern evils. As a product of some of the most powerful political organizations in both state and nation (particularly the California Division of Highways, the Federal Highway Administration, and various automotive and highway lobbies), the freeway can symbolize the evils of an omnipresent and insensitive bureaucracy. The testimony of a homeowner association representative seems typical, characterizing the Division of Highways as "a colossus, a state agency which can ruthlessly roll over and through communities."[89] Forced removals for right-of-way clearance and lightning changes in the physical landscape of local communities reveal the powerlessness of the individual. Dissenters feel like helpless victims to a conquering force of government and special interests. A frustrated resident of South Pasadena could only complain to the editor of the *Los Angeles Times* about the "mutilation" threatened by "the forced rape of this beautiful city by the freeway gang."[90]

The use of the freeway as a symbol of bureaucracy is closely associated with its use as a symbol of an equally maleficent technology. The freeway serves as the latest incarnation of the machine in the pastoral garden.[91] Richard Lillard's warning is representative of the genre: "As 1970 draws near, and the Age of Superhighways is at hand, many Californians see as a new menace the white serpentine tentacles of concrete that wind around communities and smother the

Roadside Editorial

A mural by Sandy Bleifer, executed below the Havenhurst over-pass of the Ventura freeway, comments on the activity regularly taking place above. (Photo by Henrik Kam.)

54

environment. Eden has become the world's biggest concrete asphalt desert."[92] Under the guise of the freeway, bureaucracy and technology combine to produce a modern Promethean metaphor. The concrete artifact becomes a focus for anger and frustration directed at pervasive yet intangible forces. A stanza from a folk song illustrates these sentiments:

There's a cement octopus that sits in Sacramento, I think,
Gets red tape to eat, gasoline taxes to drink,
And it grows by day, and it grows by night,
And it rolls over everything in sight.
Oh stand by me and protect that tree
From the freeway misery.[93]

The predominance of serpentine imagery, augmented by related images such as octopus tentacles or aberrations of the natural world, suggests the freeway's power to represent the modern equivalent of primordial evil.

Just what such metaphorical references have to say about urban highways is less clear. The freeway can assume qualities in the abstract which are not necessarily associated with actual freeways in daily life. For example, studies have shown that people living near freeways like them more than people who live farther away.[94] Similarly, as late as 1973 almost 50 percent of residents polled in southern California favored continued construction of freeways, while 38 percent desired only limited cutbacks.[95] Since then public opinion has rapidly changed, and a poll taken only three years later found 80 percent of its respondents agreeing to some extent that transit improvements were more important than new freeways.[96] But of one thing

After the Fall

Like a severed umbilical cord, the ruin of a freeway stands on the mainland shore across from a future Isle of California, as portrayed in this West Los Angeles mural. There is something very fitting about the often-forecast major earthquake. One suspects that if southern California were not already slated for an apocalypse, the rest of the nation would have invented one. (Photo by Henrik Kam.)

we can be certain: 80 percent of those polled would not have preferred that existing freeways had not been built in the first place.

It is important, particularly in matters of public policy, not to confuse the different levels of the freeway's associations in people's minds. The freeway as part of a complex of social phenomena is often isolated, not for purposes of accuracy, but for purity of expression. When employed for rhetorical purposes such artistic liberties often obscure fundamental issues. Nevertheless, the symbolic uses to which the freeway is popularly put reflect real and legitimate concerns. The freeway's range as a negative symbol speaks poorly for the quality of life perceived by many in the automotive metropolis.

As a literary device, imagery of this sort is both common and effective. Perhaps the outstanding instance of reliance on the freeway for literary setting and metaphor is Joan Didion's *Play It As It Lays*. Published in 1970, this novel made the first major statement that the Los Angeles freeway's importance transcended its role as a main automotive arterial. Suggesting a phenomenon of cultish proportions, the protagonist drives the freeway as a daily ritual. Maria, her life crumbling before her, is a tragic heroine; when her husband leaves her she turns to the freeways for sustenance. The routine fills the void in an otherwise empty existence, and she prepares for her sojourn "every morning with a greater sense of purpose than she had felt in some time."[97] On the freeway, absorbed in the driving, she discovers a sense of place and meaning:

Again and again she returned to an intricate stretch just south of the interchange where successful passage from the Hollywood onto the Harbor required a diagonal move across four lanes of traffic. On the afternoon she finally did it without once braking or once losing the beat on the radio she was exhilarated, and that night slept dreamlessly.[98]

The freeway is in fact her drug, her addiction, her escape from a dread that threatens to consume her:

She had only the faintest ugly memory of what had brought BZ and Helen together, and to erase it from her mind she fixed her imagination on a needle drizzling sodium pentathol into her arm and began counting backward from one hundred. When that failed she imagined herself driving, conceived audacious lane changes, strategic shifts of gear, the Hollywood to the San Bernardino and straight on out, past Barstow, past Baker, driving straight on into the hard white empty core of the world. She slept and did not dream.[99]

There is never anybody else of significance on the freeway; it is a private domain. For Didion's heroine, the freeway is indeed a special place, a place without attachments, without commitment, without interpersonal encounters, a place free of the angst that troubles daily existence in the world.

The freeway as a private world is viewed quite differently in a sex-and-violence intrigue appropriately entitled *Freeway,* in which the system is the principal setting for a tale about an automotive sniper. Here the freeway stands as a symbol of extreme alienation in the modern metropolis. The element of individual isolation is exaggerated. The freeway is most often portrayed at night when, a lonely and fearful place, it seems the Los Angeles equivalent of the dark alley. This setting is the background for the novelist's portrayal of daily life. Peopled with characters who are vulnerable and alone, the novel depicts an over-

Twentieth-Century American Landscape Painting

A manic interchange is loosed upon an industrial landscape in one of Wayne Thiebaud's metropolitan visions. The neat rows of palm trees are lost in a scene succinctly titled "Urban Freeways." (Courtesy of the artist.)

whelming sense of personal frustration. A scene in a highway patrol station is typical: "There had been a five-car freeway pileup during the day, and everybody was yelling at everybody else about that, about stupid drivers, and about the fucking freeway."[100] Virtually no sense of joy, beauty, friendship, love, or hope is to be found in the world described. The denouement discloses that the freeway sniper was not even one of the novel's lonely characters, but rather an anonymous young man who lived alone in downtown Los Angeles and had "no determinable history."[101] But the reader has seen enough to understand. Given the sense of the freeway metropolis portrayed, the only surprise is that everybody has not broken down. A young black highway patrolman performs the role of a Greek chorus: "'People are crazy here,' he said. 'I'm getting outta L.A.'"[102]

Thomas Pynchon, in his Los Angeles-based novel *The Crying of Lot 49*, makes the most versatile use of the freeway's potential for metaphor. Employed as a minor symbol, the freeway for Pynchon suggests no intrinsic meaning. It may be employed simply to convey both the ugliness of sprawl and noise or the beauty of clear, meditative thinking. Working from the natural metaphor of the arterial nourishing the metropolis, Pynchon twists the image of the vital city: "What the road really was, she fancied, was this hypodermic needle, inserted somewhere ahead into the vein of a freeway, a vein nourishing the mainliner L.A., keeping it happy, coherent, protected from pain, or whatever passes, with a city, for pain."[103] Pynchon's image reflects Didion's notion of the freeway as a drug; Los Angeles is like Maria, struggling to achieve a victory in merely surviving. The passage closes with an unsentimental recognition of the individual's ultimate place in the urban drama: ". . . but were Oedipa some single melted crystal of urban horse, L.A., really, would be no less turned on for her absence."

Later in the novel Pynchon again addresses what has become a metaphorical cliché, contrasting the concrete freeway with the pastoral earth. While contemplating a bottle of dandelion wine whose ingredients were collected from a graveyard since removed for a right-of-way clearance, the heroine sadly imagines: ". . . as if their home cemetery in some way still did exist, in a land where you could somehow walk, and did not need the East San Narciso Freeway, and bones still could rest in peace, nourishing ghosts of dandelions, no one to plow them up. As if the dead really do persist. . . ."[104] But while accepting the power and importance of such pastoral imagery, Pynchon recognizes what is essential a longing for the mythical. He never denies the freeway a rightful place in the new landscape. In fact, he suggests that the freeway has crept into the local psyche. As one would go home to die, his characters return to the freeway to consider suicide. Oedipa rides the freeway at night without lights for a while, "to see what would happen. But angels were watching."[105] The freeway has even found its place in the unconscious, in "a boozy, black-and-white dream of jumping off The Stack into rush-hour traffic."[106]

Finally, there is a short piece by Los Angeles poet Lawrence Spingarn called "Freeway Problems."[107] Here the freeway is portrayed as oppressive, as, in fact, a nest of anxiety. The imagery and rhythm conspire to agitate the reader, to recreate the sensory overload of a freeway experience at its worst. The second half of the poem concludes:

> There is no free time on the freeway:
> Only a quick look in the rear mirror
> To identify the black-jacketed pursuer
> Roaring with his muffler out, gaining
> On your best intentions, screaming
> Curses through his windshield. Mister,
> These days we all need safety belts.
>
> And it is miles, more octane miles
> To the rocker and the rug on your knees,
> The cat purring by the Franklin stove,
> The victrola playing "Hearts and Flowers."
> Have you heard your master's voice again
> Or measured the cell for length and width?
> Here's where the road ends and dark begins.

In contrast with the speed and noise of the urban imagery, the poet offers the image of the home. Approaching clichés, he emphasizes the traditional comforts and security. Of course, the poem does not end with so pat a contrast; rather, it ends with darkness. The fast paced, superenergized urban environment associated with the freeway distracts from the confrontation of the darkness—but that is not the freeway problem. As if addressing naive critics of the modern age, Spingarn redirects the reader toward that which transcends both the frantic city and the tranquil home, toward our mortality, toward the ultimate. Thus the true contrast to the freeway is no longer the pastoral, but rather death. The poet discovers in Los Angeles an updated image of the Road of Life, infusing the metaphor of the freeway with an appropriate richness that evades simple characterization.

The American poet Hart Crane argued that literature should be able to absorb the products of the machine age "as naturally and casually as trees, cattle, galleons, castles, and all other human associations of the past." Yet in spite of a few noble beginnings, Los Angeles has yet to produce its own Hart Crane and the freeway has yet to find its poet. When such a poet emerges, the freeway will be seen as something more than a series of construction projects engineered by the Department of Public Works or a particular mode of transportation. The freeway will be more fully revealed as an expression of the total complex of signification that is our culture and will "appear in its true subsidiary order in human life."[108]

60

It was only as the great current of traffic swept them into L.A. that Jim began to relax a little. He began to feel secure in his spot, in his lane, and the spectacle of the river of cars was astonishing, almost majestic. After years on the tributaries he had finally reached the Father of Waters, where traffic was concerned. From every entrance cars poured into the freeway. Jim was in a strange, tired, trancelike state and for a few miles he enjoyed the flood of cars. It was as if the whole country was emptying itself into the freeways of Los Angeles—cars from all over America, leaving garages, creeping down country roads, moving out of little towns, swarming out to suburbs, millions of them flowing toward the river he was in, leaving the long regions of the country empty again, not even Indians to disturb it, not even buffaloes. Everyone had come to California, or if not, they were on their way.
— LARRY MCMURTRY, *Moving On*.[1]

The Railroads

Despite a regional penchant for mispronounced Spanish place-names and "Spanish-style" architecture, the beginning of Los Angeles' history as a city should be marked by the introduction of a rail link to the English-speaking East, one hundred years after the official founding of El Pueblo in 1781. The arrival of the transcontinental railroad was the first step in the transformation of a relatively isolated stretch of rangeland and a small agricultural town into what would become one of the world's most important metropolises. With the completion of the Southern Pacific line from San Francisco in 1876 and the area's linkage with industrialized America, Los Angeles emerged as the urban center for the southern California region. Its favored position was not inevitable, coming only after a heated competition with San Diego for the rail connection. It seems that Los Angeles' chief advantage, ensuring its regional leadership, was that it had a poor harbor as compared with its rival and therefore offered little competition to San Francisco, where the railroad developers' hearts, and

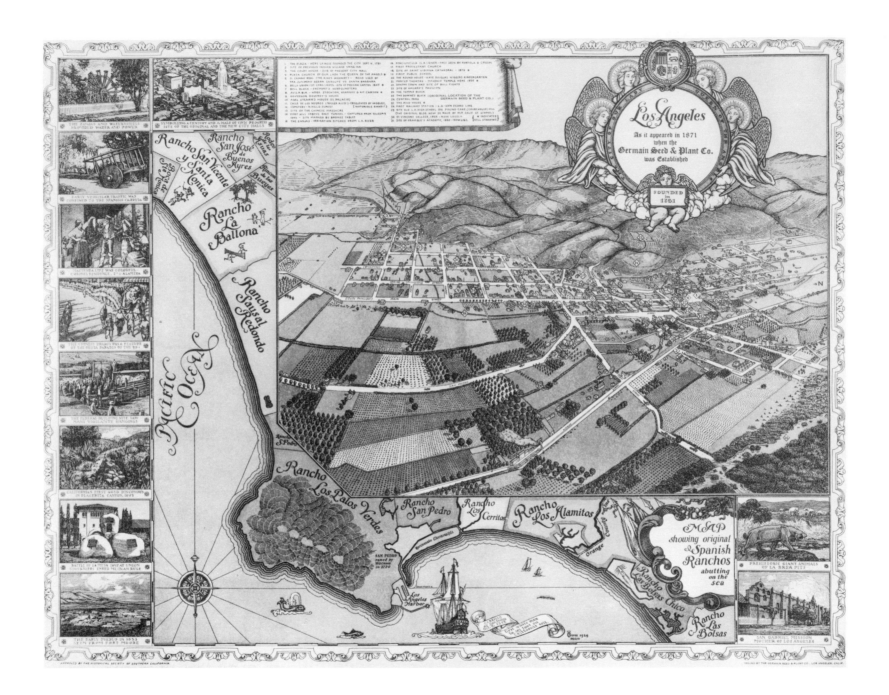

Los Angeles, 1871

With the annexation of California in 1848, Los Angeles began an accelerated transformation to an American town. Taxation and the end of Indian slave labor brought the self-sufficient ranchos into the market economy, a situation reinforced by the lucrative business to be had in supplying cattle to the gold rush-swelled towns to the north. When the cattle market collapsed the ranchos were sold to American ranchers. Subsequent droughts further injured the rancho economy, and these large tracts of land were broken up to be sold to American farmers and land speculators. Pictured here is a Los Angeles of some 6,000 inhabitants on the eve of the first great population boom. The railroad in the lower part of the map is the Los Angeles and San Pedro, which connected Los Angeles to its crude harbor via Alameda Street. (Courtesy UCLA Special Collections.)

capital, were chiefly located.[2] The city's dominance was reinforced by the completion of two direct rail links with the East: the Southern Pacific in 1881 and the Santa Fe four years later.

The two railroads spurred and facilitated the great boom of the eighties, the first major influx of new inhabitants into the area. It is impossible to know exactly how many people passed through southern California during this period. In the peak year of 1887 (during which, as a result of a rate war between the two rail lines, a ticket from Kansas City briefly dropped to a remarkable $1 a head) the Southern Pacific carried 120,000 people into the city, with the Santa Fe running three and four daily passenger trains as well.[3] The region saw many temporary visitors; during just the second half of 1887 the Los Angeles post office handled mail for about 200,000 transients.[4] Although population was drastically reduced in the wake of the inevitable bust that came the following year, the great boom left a swollen population of permanent residents. From 1870 to 1890 the population of the provincial outpost of Los Angeles proper had jumped from 6,000 to more than 50,000, while in the same period about 85,000 new residents were added to the 15,000 previously living in the county as a whole. In addition, 30,000 more people could be found in newly created Orange County.[5]

This early flurry of settlement established a crucial cultural dimension of the southern California area. Los Angeles' curious attraction for those seeking some sort of promised land, what James Vance calls "the geography of the ideal," is a legacy of this period.[6] Several factors served to create this mystique early on. The sunny Mediterranean climate was seen as tailor-made for invalids, in keeping with the increasingly popular practice of medical climatology, whereas others, influenced by nineteenth-century romanticism and the American agrarian tradition, came seeking an "agricultural arcadia." The success of the early agricultural colonies only strengthened the promise of the bountiful garden, whose land was attributed a fertility of mythic proportions. Land was plentiful, thanks ironically to a drought that had served to break up the remaining ranchos and to destroy the cattle industry, and real estate speculators eagerly joined rail companies in conducting an unprecedented advertising campaign for the region. Los Angeles, remote enough from the eastern seaboard and the Midwest to be regarded as naturally exotic, catered almost perfectly to a popular appetite for paradise. Historian Glenn Dumke cities a particularly choice example of regional proselytization:

Certainly many advantages offer to the invalid. The climate permits him to be almost constantly out-of-doors. The sky is blue, the sun unclouded, nearly every day in the year, and he can go into his orchard and concern himself about his Navel or Brazilian oranges, his paper-rind St. Michaels, and his Tahiti seedlings, with little let or hindrance.[7]

These early residents, the true founding fathers of the Los Angeles metropolis, did not comprise a cross section of the American people. On the contrary, they were disproportionately well-to-do. Southern California was attracting the social cream of the East and the Midwest, retiring farmers, businessmen, and professionals. Dumke, noting that "the outstanding quality of the newcomers was their prosperity," quotes a San Francisco paper: "The quality of the newcomers is not less noteworthy than their numbers. They are almost invariably persons of American birth, good education, and some means. . . . This is the best American stock; the bone and sinew of the nation; the flower of the American people."[8]

The "astonishing procession of the gifted, the successful, and the desirable,"[9] as another contemporary described the newcomers, came armed with aspirations, and they had the financial resources to see their hopes at least partly realized. The climate, the landscape, and the rudiments of a "native" culture (with the romantic mission legend) framed a tabula rasa for America's wealthy and provided the beginnings of a mystique of possibility, which would infuse Los Angeles' popular image throughout its subsequent development.

This early period also defined a fundamental structure for the region's social geography. The first railroads were the major axes for the emerging settlement, though they in turn reflected the region's natural geography; in general, they followed routes that had previously been used as Indian, Mexican colonial, or American stage trails.[10] In 1869 the first local line, the Los Angeles and San Pedro Railroad, connected the Wilmington wharves with the inland town. Three years later it was offered by the city to the Southern Pacific as part of the package used in enticing the transcontinental rail link to Los Angeles. In 1875 a second local line, the Los Angeles and Independence, was constructed by Nevada Senator John Jones to connect his Santa Monica property with downtown. Two years later this narrow-gauge railroad also joined the Southern Pacific holdings. The Southern Pacific

IN WINTER. L.A. CAL.

Residences, Circa 1880

The Los Angeles of the late nineteenth century was an oasis for wealthy Americans. As one local magazine put it in 1896, "Southern California has become populous with a quarter of a million people of the class who have the brains and the money to live where they deem life worth while" (Land of Sunshine, Dec. 1896). Accordingly, these new pioneers strove to duplicate their well-to-do eastern origins in both their institutions and their architecture. A drawing of these two homes appeared in an article on Los Angeles in Harper's Weekly *(18 Oct. 1890) to illustrate "typical housing." (Courtesy UCLA Special Collections.)*

Second Street Cable Railway, Looking West

As in all American cities, transportation became the key to selling real estate. A number of small railway companies were launched to make private landholdings accessible from the small downtown area. By 1888 more than 44 miles of cable and electric railways were in operation. Most of the companies were short-lived, and after a series of mergers they became part of the Los Angeles Railway system. (Courtesy UCLA Special Collections.)

itself set the third axis, entering the city from the only major northern approach, through the San Fernando Valley along the Los Angeles River. The rail company further entrenched its position by completion of an eastern access, connecting with Yuma and Texas. This line, passing through Pomona and Ontario, ran about five miles south of San Bernardino because that town had refused to contribute land to the railroad company. The Atchison, Topeka and Santa Fe soon mounted a challenge to the Southern Pacific's monopoly, acquiring the latter's Mojave division road and crossing into San Bernardino. During its first year and a half it entered Los Angeles by using the Southern Pacific's eastern road, but by 1887 it had acquired its own right-of-way and subsequently accelerated the rate war. By purchasing the Los Angeles and San Gabriel Railroad constructed a year and a half earlier, the Santa Fe entered via the San Gabriel Valley, passing through Pasadena on its way downtown. The two companies extended local facilities throughout the 1870s and 1880s, often through similar consolidations with small independent lines. The Southern Pacific opened a branch line to Anaheim, while the Santa Fe extended its service southward to San Diego and built a branch road through the western part of the basin to Redondo Beach, through what is now Inglewood. (During the 1890s the San Pedro, Los Angeles and Salt Lake Railroad and the Terminal Railroad were constructed, the former running eastward parallel to and just south of the Southern Pacific, the latter southward along the Los Angeles River to San Pedro. The two lines consolidated, and in 1905 the joint company connected with the Union Pacific to create a third direct transcontinental rail passage.)[11]

The construction of the railroads stimulated what Howard Nelson called Los Angeles' "first genuinely urban land boom" in the 1870s.[12] Several agricultural settlements, including such centers as San Bernardino, Riverside, Pasadena, El Monte, Pomona, and Long Beach, were founded in anticipation of transcontinental linkage and the related prospects for marketing produce. Some towns were established in connection with the process of railroad construction; an example is San Fernando, which served as Southern Pacific's terminus during the building of the Newhall tunnel between 1874 and 1876. But the largest number of settlements directly resulted from the much bigger boom of the eighties. In this period of remarkable growth more than 100 towns, with room for half a million lots (though actually populated by only 2,350 inhabitants), were parceled off, or platted, in Los Angeles County.[13]

The new settlements fleshed out a social geography structured by these first routes. As Nelson reports, "the railroads were not only the motivating factor in the boom, but the location of their lines influenced the alignment and provided the focus of the new subdivisions."[14] Twenty-five settlements, for example, paralleled the Santa Fe road at intervals of a mile and a half. More than half of these boomtowns failed, but more than thirty survived to provide nuclei for subsequent growth in the county. They were Alhambra, Altadena, Arcadia, Avalon, Azusa, Belvedere, Burbank, Claremont, Covina, Eagle Rock, Gardena, Glendale, Glendora, Hawthorne, Hollywood, Inglewood, La Verne, Lynwood, Monrovia, Puente, Redondo Beach, Rivera, San Dimas, Sawtelle, Sierra Madre, South Pasadena, Sunland, Tropico, Tujunga, Verdugo Hills, Vernon, Watts, and Whittier. Additional communities in outlying counties included Buena Park, Chino, Corona, Coronado, Cucamonga, Escondido, Fullerton, Oceanside, and Rialto.

The Trolley Lines

The 1870s saw the construction not only of local railroad lines but also of streetcar lines to provide more frequent local passenger service. The first one was opened in 1874, and within thirteen years there were no fewer than forty-three separate franchises for lines operating in the city of Los Angeles, propelled by horses, mules, cables, and (starting in 1887) electricity.[15] In addition, a number of narrow-gauge steam railroad lines were built, as were the streetcars, by private developers to promote real estate.

The big breakthrough in local interurban transportation, however, came in 1895 with the opening of Sherman and Clark's electric railway from Pasadena to Los Angeles, followed by a line to Santa Monica a year later.[16] In the next fifteen years numerous electric streetcar lines were constructed in Los Angeles and neighboring cities, with electric interurbans built to connect them. The central figure in this activity was Henry Huntington, nephew of Southern Pacific's Collis Huntington, who entered the scene in 1901 with the organization of the Pacific Electric Railway. Through various holding companies Huntington was an important figure in most of the area's electric rail operations before 1910, along with the Southern Pacific–held Los Angeles Pacific (acquired from Sherman and Clark) and the independent Los Angeles and Redondo.[17]

In 1911 the entire electric interurban network was consolidated by the Southern Pacific and operated as the Pacific Electric Railway Company; Henry Huntington retained control of a consolidated inner-city streetcar system, the Los Angeles Railway Company. Operating over 1,110 miles of track and providing about 700 route miles of service by 1925, the Pacific Electric gave the Los Angeles metropolitan area the largest electric interurban railway in the world.[18]

The electric interurbans substantially fleshed out the geographic framework created by the steam railroad lines. With their incorporation into the interurban systems, small rail outposts were transformed into major regional centers. For example, the population of Long Beach was only 200 in 1900, two years before a line was opened to the city. By the end of the decade, population had increased to 1,700, a jump of 610 percent.[19] Watts, a small station on the Southern Pacific line, was transformed by the trolley into what was perhaps the first full-fledged bedroom community in the city. Supporting only minimal commercial activity itself, it became one of the Southland's most important centers in the electric rail system.[20] The interurban also helped to fill in the regional framework by making possible the establishment of new communities. The development of both Venice and Glendale, soon to become major terminuses of interurban lines, was dependent on the laying of electric tracks. Similarly Hollywood, which incorporated with a population of 600 shortly after the Pacific Electric branch was completed in 1903, had grown to 10,000 by the time it was annexed to the city of Los Angeles seven years later.[21] Of the 42 cities incorporated in the area by the mid-thirties, 39 owed their early growth to the electric railway.[22]

Thus the existence of such a transportation system was crucial in stimulating the spread of population throughout the Los Angeles area. The decade of 1900-1910, in which the electric trolley held a virtual monopoly of interurban transport, witnessed the metropolitan area's largest relative increase in population in the twentieth century: 180.4 percent (from 180,920 to 507,300). Although nearly twice as many people moved into the central part of the county as into all the remaining areas combined, the relative rates of growth in the latter were still tremendous, ranging from 201 percent in the San Fernando Valley to 122 percent in the southeast (including Orange County).[23] Even the central city itself was pretty much a "streetcar suburb." Los Angeles never had time to develop a large, dense urban core as earlier industrial cities had. As soon as the railroads marked the traditional plaza area as "downtown" for an emerging city, subdividers were building railways for horse-drawn cars, cable cars, and electric streetcars to make it easier to sell lots. Thus central Los Angeles retained the feel of a giant village of single-family homes.

Concurrent with the widespread distribution of population came the expanding of the city boundaries through the incorporation of new territory. The city of Los Angeles almost quadrupled in size during the period from 1876, when the first rail lines reached the city, until 1914, growing from 28 to 108 square miles. A new policy formulated that year, making annexation or consolidation a prerequisite to receiving municipal utilities, spurred further annexation. The city's area

nearly quadrupled again between 1915 and 1925, increasing to 415 square miles.[24] In addition, other suburban communities were expanding their boundaries through "empire-building" annexations. Between 1900 and 1920 such independent municipalities as Glendale, Pasadena, and Long Beach were further encouraging regional expansion and decentralization.[25]

Although the trolley lines brought dramatically dispersed residential patterns, their effect on business and industry was not so marked. Electric rail transit made the movement of people cheaper, but the intracity movement of goods was still dependent on inefficient modes of transportation, such as horse and wagon or human labor. These economic factors were constraints to decentralization. The economies of scale possible in rail transport, on the other hand, tended to concentrate economic activity at major shipping and receiving points.[26] The electric railways did effect some decentralization of industry, but in general it remained clustered in the downtown, southeastern, and harbor areas. Likewise, most business and commercial enterprises continued to be centrally located. According to Robert Fogelson, the inadequate market potential of low suburban densities, the monopolization of radial transit routes, and the limited availability of freight service and public utilities all encouraged the continued concentration of economic activity within the downtown Los Angeles area.[27]

The relationship of the interurban system to the spreading of an increasingly urban populace over the region was far from casual. Electric rail transportation

preceded population and spurred it, as ambitious entrepreneurs sought immediate real estate profits as well as the more distant gains that they hoped would come from transporting people.[28] The most notable example was Henry Huntington, whose original Pacific Electric Railway Company, Los Angeles Interurban Company, and San Gabriel Valley Water Company joined his Huntington Land and Improvement Company in the promoting and selling of real estate. Huntington's plan of attack was first to select the choicest land for development and to decide on a route to serve the area. The construction of a line through Monrovia, for example, followed his purchase of substantial parcels there, as well as in South Pasadena and San Marino.[29] Not only were the peripheries of existing settlements built up, but no fewer than thirteen new towns resulted from his personal promotions, all but one located on his interurban lines.[30] Smaller rail companies encouraged subsidies of cash or land for the extension of interurban lines to a community or a new subdivision, as when Sherman and Clark were given a 225-acre parcel for the development of the Santa Monica line.[31] From the outset, the electric railways were a significant element in the strategy employed by private enterprise to expand and develop the region.

Interlude: Los Angeles As the Port of Iowa

As if in some laissez-faire fairy tale, private capital and public consumption seemed to harmonize perfectly during the early period of expansion in the Los Angeles area, with a tremendous influx of newcomers

71

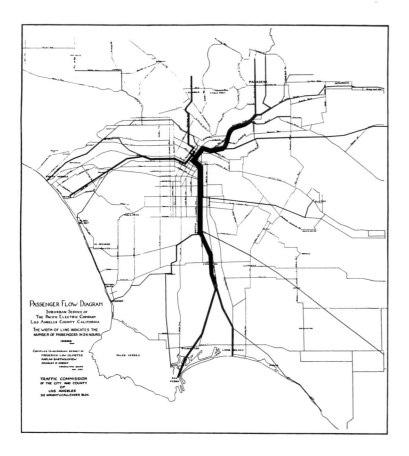

*Interurban Passenger Flow on the
Pacific Electric Railway*

This map of electric railway transportation suggests the downtown area's domination as an employment and shopping center in the Los Angeles of 1924. It also shows that the most heavily populated residential areas were the central and northeastern flatlands, which were particularly attractive to villagers and farmers who settled in Los Angeles. (Source: Los Angeles Traffic Commission, Major Traffic Street Plan.)

eager to fulfill many a subdivider's dreams. Successive waves of in-migrants swelled the area's population and settled into the new residential developments. The city of Los Angeles grew from 50,000 inhabitants in 1890 to half a million thirty years later and the county's population jumped from 100,000 to 935,000 in the same period, giving the area the highest rate of growth for any major metropolitan center in the nation in those three decades.[32]

An important factor in this rapid growth was the early availability of transit service, which made accessible a tremendous amount of undeveloped land tied together in an urban network and led to the creation of new residential communities. Of course, partly responsible for the development was the magnetic force of Los Angeles, a force that would continue to draw people long after the trolley had yielded to the automobile. The region's emergence as the first great sprawling metropolis cannot be explained simply on the basis of its extensive interurban and streetcar network. Every American city of any importance had built similar, if more modest, systems, but none effected so dramatic a dispersal of population as was characteristic of southern California. The reason for the difference is found elsewhere.

Los Angeles became the central city of a growing southern California metropolis at a time when the United States as a whole was undergoing a dramatic transformation. During the second half of the nineteenth century, following on the heels of accelerated industrialization and improvements in agriculture and transportation, America became an urban nation. From 1860 to 1910 American cities recorded a sevenfold increase in population. Although the largest

Small Town America

If the palms were replaced by poplars, this scene could easily have been a community in Iowa or Ohio, but it shows Holt Avenue in Pomona in the early 1900s. Southern California was in many respects a colony of the American Midwest, and its origins were reflected both in its social institutions and in its man-made landscape. The old patterns of the homogenous Protestant community were especially maintained in the early suburban communities, such as Pomona, Santa Monica, Long Beach, and Pasadena, which often existed as isolated villages. This photo was taken by the Pacific Electric Company for publicity purposes. (Courtesy Henry E. Huntington Library.)

share came from foreign immigrants, nearly one-third of the total increase in urban population came from rural America.[33] Rising urban productivity was offering American farmers an alternative to the hardships, uncertainty, and loneliness of an agrarian existence. The routine of farm labor, growing more tedious with increasing specialization, compared poorly with the inevitable exaggeration of "the other life," the freedom and potential of the city.[34]

In no part of the country was the process more evident than in the Midwest, America's rural heartland. All the major cities there—Chicago, Minneapolis, St. Paul, Detroit, Milwaukee, Columbus, Cleveland, St. Louis, Kansas City, Omaha, Lincoln, Des Moines— experienced tremendous growth. Local hamlets and small towns were growing as well, often serving as way stations for people bent on moving to the city. Besides, there was a large movement westward, into Kansas, Nebraska, the Dakotas, Colorado, and of course California. This American "wandering of the nations," as Arthur Schlesinger, Sr., has called it in his classic history of the period, left much of the Midwest devastated. Rural sections of Missouri, Iowa, Illinois, Indiana, Michigan, and Ohio were the most extreme examples.[35]

The Midwest's loss was, to a significant extent, Los Angeles' gain. In the first great boom of the 1880s most of the area's new residents came from northeastern states, but midwesterners were soon flocking to the region in large numbers. Census figures show that from one-fourth to one-third of the total population living in Los Angeles during the period 1890-1930 had been born in midwestern states.[36] The area's

nickname, "the port of Iowa," was no misnomer. According to McWilliams, hundreds of thousands of immigrants to southern California came from Iowa alone, though a majority of these were perhaps born in the neighboring states of Illinois, Ohio, and Missouri.[37] Iowa, like the Midwest in general, had itself been a boom territory. First opened to homesteaders in 1830, all its free lands were completely gone sixty years later. By 1930, however, more than 2,000 Iowa towns had been abandoned.[38] Los Angeles had become the focus of the final phase of Protestant Americans' historic trek west, the latest journey of a restless Mayflower.

The character of the new communities created by the in-migration reflected the origins of the newcomers. Los Angeles developed much as a midwestern town transplanted onto the southern California landscape, embodying what Fogelson has characterized as a native American vision of the good life:

The native Americans came to Los Angeles with a conception of the good community which was embodied in single-family houses, located on large lots, surrounded by landscaped lawns, and isolated from business activities. . . . Their vision was epitomized by the residential suburb—spacious, affluent, clean, decent, permanent, predictable, and homogeneous—and violated by the great city—congested, impoverished, filthy, immoral, transient, uncertain, and heterogeneous.[39]

"In the process of settlement," wrote McWilliams, "they reverted to former practices and built not a city, but a series of connecting villages."[40] The typical home throughout much of this period (more specifically, from 1907 to 1927), was the "California bungalow," an easily constructed utilitarian house with hor-

California Bungalows

The California bungalow is considered the first architectural style native to the West Coast. As this street scene shows, it is more an eclectic combination of styles than a single coherent form. The original bungalows were probably converted barns intended to provide temporary shelter until the "real" home was built. Roughly executed by journeymen carpenters, the common bungalow was an appropriate structure for meeting the pressing housing demands of the boom town. It was sometimes, however, produced by such noted architects as Greene and Greene, who did much to popularize the style. The peak period for bungalow building was 1907-1927, to be followed by the stuccoed "Spanish" style. Note the high-pitched roofs, an imported feature that in its native climes is designed to shed snow. The street in the photo is Harvard Boulevard between 29th and 30th streets. (Courtesy Los Angeles County Museum of Natural History.)

izontal weatherboarding and columned porches, which structurally had more in common with a rural barn than with an urban Victorian or a town house.[41]

It became almost a cliché to observe that life in Los Angeles resembled Main Street, USA. "Within its vast contours," wrote one visitor, "it is basically the same existence that is led, half-actually, half-imaginatively, in Shelby, Indiana."[42] As Raymond Chandler reflected nostalgically in 1949, "Los Angeles was just a big dry sunny place with ugly homes and no style, but good-hearted and peaceful."[43] Indeed, Los Angeles was becoming a full-blown American suburban ideal.

The suburban life-style, the combination of small-town or country-style residential communities with an urban economy, was by no means unique to Los Angeles: in the 1820s Brooklyn grew into a wealthy bedroom community for New York; by 1870 Chicago was surrounded by almost a hundred suburban communities tied together by steam railroads; by 1900 nearly half the families of metropolitan Boston were living in a suburban environment, thanks to a good streetcar system. Housing patterns were changing throughout urban America, as the freestanding house, set back from the street, emerged as the new standard.[44] But suburbs in the East, defined in relation to an older sector of a city, offered an escape from a dense urban core. Residential patterns in Los Angeles, on the other hand, were commonly all suburban. It was a city of single- and two-family detached homes, a category that, as late as 1930, comprised 93 percent of all dwellings. In comparison, Chicago had 52 percent and Boston 49.5 percent detached housing. Whereas 32 percent and 27 percent, respectively, of families in

LOS ANGELES

THE SOUTHWESTERN METROPOLIS
—
THE TOURISTS' PARADISE
—
THE HOMESEEKERS' REFUGE
—
THE EXPOSITION CITY OF THE COAST
—
1903

The PROGRESSIVE CITY of the Twentieth Century ● ●

Write to the
Chamber of Commerce
For Full Information

Early southern California was blessed with few natural resources and supported little industry. What it offered was land and sunshine, and speculators worked hard to capitalize on those "commodities." Their fortunes, and indeed the economy of the entire southland, were based on population growth, like a pyramid scheme that assumed a continually swelling base. The first great boom in the 1800s was a railroad company promotion, but soon the city got into the business of selling itself. By 1900 the Chamber of Commerce, three years after its inception, had distributed some 2 million pieces of literature; Los Angeles was the best-advertised city in the world. An interior caption from this example reads: "Cost of Living Same as Middle West." Obviously, the promoters knew their market. (Courtesy Henry E. Huntington Library.)

those cities owned their own homes, in 1930 the Los Angeles figure was 40 percent.[45]

The emerging southern California metropolis may have seemed "typically midwestern" or "typically suburban," but an entire metropolis of such proportions was not typical. For one thing, Los Angeles did not receive its share of the foreign-born immigrants who had so much impact on the development of the large, well-established cities in the East. During the fifty years from 1890 to 1940, only 20 percent of the residents of Los Angeles County were either foreign-born or nonwhite, a figure less than half that for New York or Chicago. "Unlike the typical American metropolis," observes Fogelson, "Los Angeles did not have at any time in its history a vast group of European immigrants."[46] And the contribution of the existing nonnative and nonwhite communities, mostly Mexicans, Mexican Americans, and blacks, was obscured by the tide of white, native-born Americans.[47]

Even then the impact of the majority population in creating a regional character was only partly owing to the impressive numbers of native-born Americans, who themselves underwent a further economic filtration. Southern California still had a fledgling economy (supported more by the process of growth than by any particular industry), and in-migrants seeking material betterment often went elsewhere. Those who chose Los Angeles did so for what two sociologists in 1941 called "hedonistic" reasons, attracted more by climate and legend than by superior job opportunities.[48] They had enough financial security to be able to risk the uncertain economy of Los Angeles. The composite of the "typical" new arrival, as portrayed by Fogelson,

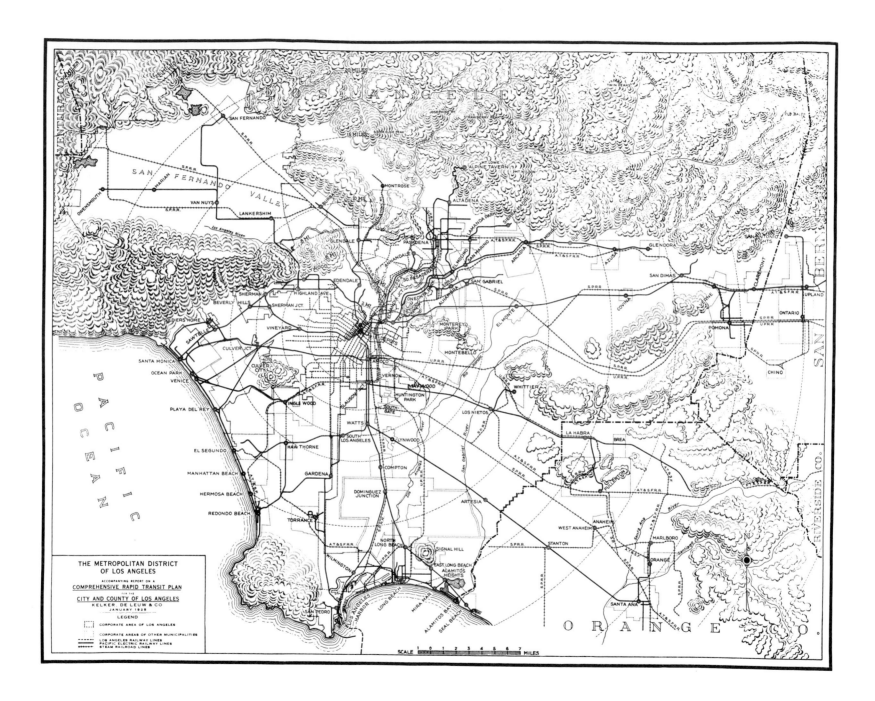

THE METROPOLITAN DISTRICT
OF LOS ANGELES
ACCOMPANYING REPORT ON A
COMPREHENSIVE RAPID TRANSIT PLAN
FOR THE
CITY AND COUNTY OF LOS ANGELES
KELKER, DE LEUW & CO
JANUARY 1925

LEGEND
.... CORPORATE AREA OF LOS ANGELES
----------- CORPORATE AREAS OF OTHER MUNICIPALITIES
━━━━━ LOS ANGELES RAILWAY LINES
+++++++ PACIFIC ELECTRIC RAILWAY LINES
+++++++ STEAM RAILROAD LINES

SCALE   1 0 1 2 3 4 5 6 7   MILES

78

was a midwestern farmer who had sold his property at a time of general economic prosperity and had come west in rejection of agricultural life, if by no means in pursuit of urban life.[49] Carey McWilliams characterized the immigrants as "predominately middle-class, middle-aged people seeking to retire."[50]

Of course, to describe the average is not to suggest absolute homogeneity. Many newcomers did not fit such stereotypes and, with the expansion of local industry in the 1920s, lower-middle-class families began to make a major contribution to the area's newly arrived population.[51] But the fact that so many had adequate resources as well as adequate skills and therefore were able to choose the residential environment they wanted had a vital impact on the region's development.

Los Angeles was continuing to provide a "geography of the Ideal." The alluring image of the southland, emerging with the well-to-do seekers of the 1880s, was developing almost spontaneously. It was as if the openness of the Los Angeles landscape was a kind of Rorschach test for the times. And business interests, particularly real estate, soon recognized the area's new appeal as a mecca for midwesterners. Ambitious advertising was targeted on the Midwest, proffering a good climate, a beautiful landscape, and a suburban life-style. "Instead of promising prospective immigrants material prosperity, Southern California's promoters," according to Fogelson, "offered them an easier, more varied, less complicated, and well-rounded life."[52]

Like other attributes, the value placed on noneconomic amenities was not uniquely southern Californian. As Fogelson makes clear, they reflected a

Railway and Railroad Systems, 1925

Los Angeles was exceptionally well served by rail. Three railroad companies—the Southern Pacific, the Atchison, Topeka, and Santa Fe, and the Union Pacific—brought new arrivals to the area and provided the infrastructure for the southern California economy. The Pacific Electric, whose "Big Red Cars" operated on more than 1,100 miles of standard-gauge track, carried passengers to all corners of the Los Angeles area and offered its own freight services as well. The Los Angeles Railway Company served the central area with 370 miles of narrow-gauge tracks. (Source: Kelker, De Leuw, and Co., Comprehensive Rapid Transit Plan for the City and County of Los Angeles.*)*

growing redefinition of the good life which had eastern and midwestern roots. The late nineteenth century saw the rise of a new American attitude toward success. In contrast with the Protestant ethic of material success, so strongly a part of midwestern culture in particular,[53] there was a growing concern with "the balanced life," emphasizing the importance of leisure, family life, and the enjoyment of nature.[54] This new ideology, which historian Richard Weiss describes under the rubric of "New Thought," was expressed in its most extreme form in a wide variety of cultish religions and secularized movements. Los Angeles' strong identification with "New Thought" values is perhaps most easily illustrated by its early notoriety as the cult capital of the nation.[55] These same values, however, had broad-based appeal and were infusing mainstream American culture. Los Angeles was simply the sanctuary for their realization. Thanks to massive organized promotional campaigns and to the proselytizing fervor of new converts writing home, Los Angeles took shape in the popular mind as a new Eden for easy living.

This "philosophical restlessness" was a reflection of a general restlessness that was growing in American life. Industrialization, despite the material improvement it brought to many, was a profoundly disruptive force. Increased agricultural productivity combined with expanding economic activities in the cities to facilitate movement from rural to urban areas. The growth of an urban middle class, along with improved technologies in transportation, encouraged migration from the urban core to the suburban periphery. "Rampaging industrialism," in soiling the pastoral dream of the small town, spurred population shifts from old communities to new communities.[56] Los An-

geles became identified with all these movements, providing a contrast with farm life, with urban industrial life, and with small-town life. Its phenomenal growth stemmed from the moral confusion of industrialization, creating what was in effect America's first postindustrial metropolis.

Southern California was the first locality where geography, technology, and a sufficient population of well-to-do consumers combined to provide a suburban ideal of the good life on a mass scale. In that development the interurban transit system played a fundamental role, particularly because Los Angeles was well suited to electric rail transportation. Its characteristically flat geography and its mild climate eased the strain on expensive equipment, and a lack of natural fuels such as coal or wood led it to an early dependence on electricity.[57] The region provided an unparalleled opportunity for imaginative entrepreneurs to expand their fortunes by mixing real estate and transportation, establishing transit lines that alone would not be immediately profitable. The expansive system of electric rail transport made it possible for a growing population to participate in a particular vision of the good life, to combine urban patterns of consumption and production with a rural and small-town sense of space and community. As a result, southern California became a dispersed metropolitan region structured around electric railway lines.

The Street Plan

After the advent of the automobile, Los Angeles did not long remain an electric railway–bound city. One author has undoubtedly stated the opinion of many in

Redondo Beach

Glendale

Converts to the Automobile

The world's largest interurban railway operation, as well as a fine urban streetcar system, did nothing to slow the acceptance of the automobile in Los Angeles. On the contrary, it helped to set the stage. The trolley lines provided the technological component for the early pattern of dispersed communities, almost custom-made for the automobile. Other key elements in the region's development during the trolley era, from the gentle climate to the particular type of immigrants who chose to settle in Los Angeles, were equally compatible with the car's popularity. These photos show two early suburbs served by the Pacific Electric, Redondo Beach and Glendale, in 1923 and 1924, respectively. (Courtesy Henry E. Huntington Library.)

arguing that "it is difficult to over-emphasize the fact that Los Angeles is truly a product of the automobile age."[58] Nevertheless, though Los Angeles certainly came of age with its becoming the first great automotive city, it never abandoned its legacy. The spread of a man-made landscape over the region continued to reflect a spatial structure established by rail transport and confirmed by the region's response to the electric trolley.

Many of the factors that worked so well in building a streetcar metropolis served to undermine it as well. The widespread single-use land configurations preferred by the area's pioneering well-to-do and accommodated by the streetcars and interurbans set up habit patterns of long-distance travel. The growth of the metropolis, spurred by the same interests responsible for the electric rail lines, soon outpaced the trolley's capacity to serve the downtown area—the focus of the system—and its business and commercial interests. As early as 1910 the Los Angeles Examiner reported that "there are times in the rush hours when every foot of trackage in the business district is covered with trolley cars."[59] Not only were electric rail companies responsible for the building up of outlying communities but, in compliance with city ordinances, they had constructed and maintained many of the streets and highways needed to make automobile transport practical. Roughly 10 percent of streetcar net revenues went to this purpose.[60] Even the seemingly trivial circumstance of standard residential lots large enough to conveniently store vehicles has been cited as a factor contributing to the automobile's popularity.[61] The climate alone was another crucial element. Unlike eastern cities, whose inclement winters im-

mobilized their residents for months, Los Angeles could use open and unheated autos the year round. In addition, cars as recreation vehicles afforded a new opportunity to enjoy the pastoral qualities of the region through a pleasure drive. Finally, the characteristic middle-class Angeleno family was likely to be able to afford a car and to value the independence it made possible.

The region's "love affair" with the car commenced immediately; as early as 1915, when Los Angeles County had only 750,000 inhabitants, its 55,217 private cars made it the nation's leading county in automobile ownership. Three years later, vehicle registrations in the county had jumped to 110,000 and, by 1924, had risen above 441,000.[62] Auto registration continued to skyrocket with the boom of the 1920s which, fueled by the development of transcontinental highways, has been characterized as "the first migration of the automobile age."[63]

More than 1.25 million new arrivals entered the Los Angeles area during the decade of the twenties. The vast majority of the newcomers continued to be from midwestern states. This far from casual coincidence of the population boom of the twenties with "the widespread adoption of the mass-produced, low-priced automobile as the primary mode of urban transportation" profoundly affected the subsequent development of cities in southern California.[64]

The chief effect of the automobile was in further removing spatial constraints to the region's development. The streetcar had permitted decentralization only along well-defined corridors. City maps drawn between 1902 and 1919 show what one would expect: that few streets existed more than five or six

Tract Opening, 1915

The early leadership of Los Angeles County in automobile ownership among all counties in the nation meant a bonanza for real
estate developers, who were freed from the necessity of subsidiz-
ing the railways, a capital-hungry form of transportation. What is
most striking about this photo of a barbecue celebrating the
opening of a new tract in Montrose is the number of cars that
brought people there. By 1915 more than 55,000 automobiles
were on the road in Los Angeles County. (Courtesy Henry E.
Huntington Library.)

blocks from streetcar lines.[65] The automobile, however, permitted settlement of any area to which a road could be cleared. The result was the real estate boom of the 1920s during which subdividers scrambled to capitalize on the quick profit potential of lands lying on the city's periphery. In some instances development actually shifted away from localities best served by transit lines. According to historian Mark Foster, the South Bay area, where lines were rarely more than two miles apart, saw only modest "filling in." "On the other hand," he adds, "the automobile's triumph exerted a dramatic effect on the remote areas which were not so well served by the trolleys." As the most spectacular example, he cites the extensive development of the southeastern part of the San Fernando Valley as an automotive suburb.[66] Accelerated subdivision of foothill areas for residential communities also illustrates this trend.

Originally the automobile was accommodated, for the most part, at private expense. According to Fogelson, "opening, widening, and paving roads was normally initiated by the property owners and undertaken by the common council." The property benefited by the newly constructed streets was assessed the full cost. Sometimes subdividers would put in thoroughfares that would serve more than local residences, hoping to increase property values. Huntington Drive in San Marino is the most notable example. Other thoroughfares resulted from the obligations of electric railways to pave their rights-of-way. As early as 1909, however, local government began to assume responsibility for road construction, when a $3.5 million bond issue was approved by the County

Board of Supervisors. The next year the state, too, began to allocate funds for highway construction.[67]

These early measures proved less than adequate. The streets of Los Angeles were notoriously ill conceived, giving the city an early handicap. Although nearly 500 miles of improved roads were opened between 1904 and 1914, including several major arteries such as Pico Boulevard and Vermont Avenue, few were more than thirty or fifty feet wide.[68] The next decade saw continued construction and continued expansion of surfaced roadways into the suburbs, but again they were of inadequate width and arrangement. Too often roadways were built for the convenience of and according to the whims of private subdividers. Traffic was regularly impeded by forbidding grades, inconvenient jogs, and inconsistent capacity. City planners complained that

There are surprisingly few streets of generous width in Los Angeles. A width of one hundred feet is exceptional, while greater widths are practically unknown. There are a respectable number of eighty-foot streets, but these are noticeably discontinuous and unrelated. The prevailing standard has been the sixty-foot street, a width totally unsuited for a traffic street of great capacity.[69]

Exceptions like Figueroa feeding from the south and Sunset winding in from the west proved to be self-defeating; overcrowded with traffic, they ran through areas too heavily developed to allow for much improvement. Other major arterials, wide enough through much of their extent, perversely narrowed as they entered downtown.[70]

It was, in fact, in the downtown district that the problem was at its worst. The urban center contained notably less street space than most other American cities. With only 21.5 percent of the area devoted to streets, downtown Los Angeles lagged behind Chicago (29 percent), Pittsburgh (34.5 percent), Cleveland (39.5 percent), and carefully planned Washington (44 percent), to name only a few.[71]

The huge influx of population and the burgeoning auto registration swelled traffic on Los Angeles streets, causing serious downtown congestion and frustrating delays as well as a concern for traffic safety. Foster credits much of the early decentralization by subdividers and businessmen simply to the inaccessibility of the central area.[72] An attempt was made in April 1920 to relieve the situation by banning all daytime parking in the downtown area. The ban, though lasting only nine days after encountering the criticism of businessmen and drivers, did mark the beginning of public regulation of traffic.[73]

The major step in setting up public control of automotive transportation began three years later. The recently organized Traffic Commission of the City and County of Los Angeles employed three renowned city planners, Frederick Law Olmsted, Jr., Harland Bartholomew, and Charles Henry Cheney, to consider the area's traffic problem. Their report, *A Major Traffic Street Plan for Los Angeles,* submitted in 1924, was, with the passing of a bond issue, Los Angeles' first organized attempt to accommodate itself to the automobile.[74]

The document produced by these three planners provided more than a modified street map. The report was an attempt to articulate the vision of a major metropolitan region while its development was still in a period of adolescence and to suggest programmatic steps to ensure smooth realization of that vision. Found in *A Major Traffic Street Plan* are several trends that were to continue throughout the area's development in the wake of the automobile and eventually be incorporated in a freeway system. Though it is difficult to link subsequent development of these trends directly to the Traffic Commission's report, it is important to note the directions in which the organization of traffic movement was headed from the beginning.

The heart of the report was the rationalization of traffic movement, an attempt to create order in a street layout that was perceived as uncoordinated and chaotic. Congestion was blamed on "unscientific" street width and design and on "improper" use of existing street spaces. The plan proposed an organized street system to manage vehicular traffic efficiently. Street arrangement and capacity were coordinated to produce "a balanced scheme for handling a tremendous traffic flow."[75]

Fundamental to the rationalization of vehicular movement was the differentiation of roads according to function. The report, citing the "promiscuous mixture of different types of traffic" as a major cause of disorder and delay, called for the segregation of different types of vehicles as well as a functional discrimination among automobiles themselves. In a section entitled "Streets Must Be Arranged to Suit Their Use," the report suggested that it had become necessary to divide all streets into three basic classes: major thoroughfares, parkways or boulevards, and minor streets. The first group, which would continue to dominate traffic plans, called forth the major suggestion of the planners:

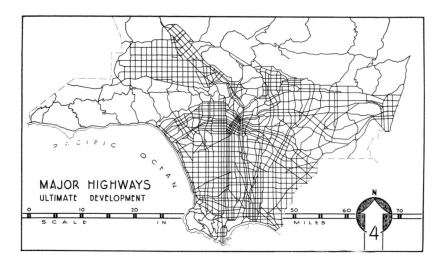

MAJOR HIGHWAYS
ULTIMATE DEVELOPMENT

Street and Highway Planning

Los Angeles was an early leader in the city and regional planning movements. Central to such planning efforts was the accommodation of the private automobile. The city commissioned a street plan for the populated central area (at left), suggesting numerous openings and widenings to increase surface capacity. The county plan (above) provided an extended gridiron of proposed highways through both developed and undeveloped areas. It supplied a major element in the county master plan for the regulation of subdivisions. (Source: Los Angeles Traffic Commission, Major Traffic Street Plan, 1924; Los Angeles Regional Planning Commission, Master Plan Highways, 1941.)

Los Angeles' greatest immediate need in solving its street congestion problem is the development of an orderly and well-balanced system of thoroughfares of such width and arrangement as will facilitate direct and uninterrupted movement from center to center and incidentally facilitate distribution within centers. This is the purpose of the present study.[76]

The thoroughfare system was to include both a radial scheme focusing on the central business district and interdistrict and bypass thoroughfares. The plan was laid out, wherever the terrain permitted, in typical grid fashion, along irregular parallels less than a mile apart. Most of the proposed improvements required the extension of existing roadways, as well their widening so as to accommodate a consistent flow of traffic. The report suggested generous streets of six or preferably eight lanes (allowing two lanes for parking), about 80 feet and 110 feet wide, respectively, between property lines. It is interesting to note the importance placed on pedestrian movement, an issue that was absent from all future highway plans. A thirteen-foot sidewalk was denounced as impractical for a main thoroughfare because of its being "very narrow."[77]

The report functionally distinguished the second class of streets, parkways or boulevards, from thoroughfares in terms of scenic and pleasure values. With their use limited to passenger vehicles, there could be significant overlap of the parkway and thoroughfare systems, though most parkways were to be nothing more than elongated parks for pleasure driving. While the notion of a parkway system received little implementation in the street system of Los Angeles, its vocabulary and imagery continued to haunt city planning for the subsequent two decades.

An underlying theme briefly mentioned, but of the utmost importance, was decentralization. Concentration was cited as a cause of congestion, and zoning was suggested to provide for height and area limits. Addressing critics of Los Angeles' already extensive movement toward decentralization—the most vocal of whom were downtown merchants—the plan redefined the process in terms of specialization and defended it in the language of efficiency and profitability. Ultimately, decentralization as a problem was dismissed from critical consideration as an "inevitable tendency."[78]

The *Major Traffic Street Plan* contained more than simple acceptance of developments already characteristic of the region. Extended-through highways, interdistrict bypasses, boulevards and parkways all were proposed to provide programmatic support for a dispersed and multicentered urban form. Though the report did address itself directly to problems of downtown congestion, the heavy cost of downtown improvements made many of them prohibitive, and most of the proposals concerned construction toward the periphery. A 1927 study showed that less than one-tenth of all work in progress under the plan would directly involve the central district.[79]

The report presented by the three planners shows that as early as 1924 many of the elements that would characterize the freeway system were already under consideration. An integrated system of thoroughfares, composed of radial and bypass arterials, comprises the essentials of the modern system. The report places high priority on removing obstacles to the free flow of traffic and suggests grade-crossing elimination as the ideal whenever auto and rail transportation conflict.

Even more important, apropos a discussion of freeways, is the grade separation of intersecting roadways; it is the lack of obstruction from cross traffic (and not the absence of tolls) which puts the "free" in "freeway." The report contains several discussions of such separations at major intersections.

In fact, the street plan for Los Angeles considers the possibility of a continuous automotive viaduct, in perhaps the first serious local discussion of a freeway:

Probably the most acute situation is that arising from the daily surge of city workers and shoppers whose general destination in the morning hours is towards the central business and retail district and in the evening, outlying residential sections. As this traffic approaches the downtown district it is gradually concentrated from many into a few principal thoroughfares, crossed by transverse movements of street cars, slow moving trucks, and other vehicles. It is to provide for this class of traffic that a complete separation of roadway may become advisable and for this purpose the continuous elevated highway, with approach ramps from side streets, is suggested.[80]

This suggestion appears in an appendix at the end of the report, showing that its visionary character was fully recognized. Even simple grade separations of single intersections are dismissed as largely unworkable owing to excessive cost; they would provide a remedy in only the most extreme circumstances. Given the early date of the report, it is understandable that its authors could not envision a public works program of such a magnitude; even their more modest proposals were often quite bold for the time and would prove difficult to implement.

Olmsted, Bartholomew, and Cheney would hardly have been surprised by the design of the freeways of the city's future. They would even have recognized routes that they had specifically suggested. The proposed river truck speedway eventually came into being, north of downtown, as the Golden State freeway. The importance of this corridor was underlined by the report's suggestion that the parallel San Fernando Road accommodate ten lanes of traffic. The proposal for a speedway heading south along the Los Angeles River was eventually fulfilled by the Long Beach freeway. (The idea was first suggested as early as 1911 in a discussion of the city's transportation problems.)[81] Figueroa Street as a major north-south axis would be replaced by the Harbor freeway, its northern route more precisely recommended by the plan's Arroyo Seco Parkway. The Hollywood freeway was foretold by the suggested diagonal extension of First Street through Hollywood to connect with Cahuenga Pass, thereby providing another major arterial.

Nevertheless, the most important contribution of the 1924 proposal was not its prognostication of a distant future. The plan's immediate impact was in detailed, specific improvements in surface thoroughfares. It became, true to its title, the major street plan for the city. Owing to fiscal constraints, however, actual progress toward implementing the proposals was slow. Only $1 million of construction had been completed by the start of the great depression. But, as Mark Foster observes, "Despite the lack of visible progress during the 1920's, a pattern of opening and widening of streets had been established which had a tremendous impact upon the future."[82]

Traffic congestion continued to be a serious problem, but it was never so serious as it would have been without such a plan. The 1924 city plan and similar actions by the county at least forestalled a major confrontation with the limits of private-auto-on-surface-street transportation for another fifteen years. The existence of numerous through highways of decent width and direct course kept the automobile viable even with the city's huge increases in automotive traffic. And with the supersession of freeways as the primary through arterials, the region was left with the comprehensive grid of distributor and alternative routes which make a freeway metropolis possible.

Perhaps, then, the report's most portentous vision is seen from a statement in the letter of transmittal: "In short, we believe the *Major Traffic Street Plan* here presented provides a broad, practical, well-balanced scheme for handling traffic towards which the city can advantageously grow, and to which it may gradually adjust itself, making improvements piece by piece as they become necessary, each as part of a finished plan."[83] Los Angeles' decision to implement this report, founded on the preceding assumption, may be the city's first self-conscious acceptance of the priority of the motor vehicle and of the efficient accommodation of automotive traffic as the determinative element in the entire region's subsequent development.

Streets into Highways
and the Decline of the Trolley

The growth of the Los Angeles metropolitan area continued through the twenties and thirties. Total population for Los Angeles and Orange counties kept on rising dramatically, from less than a million in 1920 to more than 2.3 million ten years later, an increase of 143 percent. The depression slowed the migration to some extent, but in the 1930s there was still

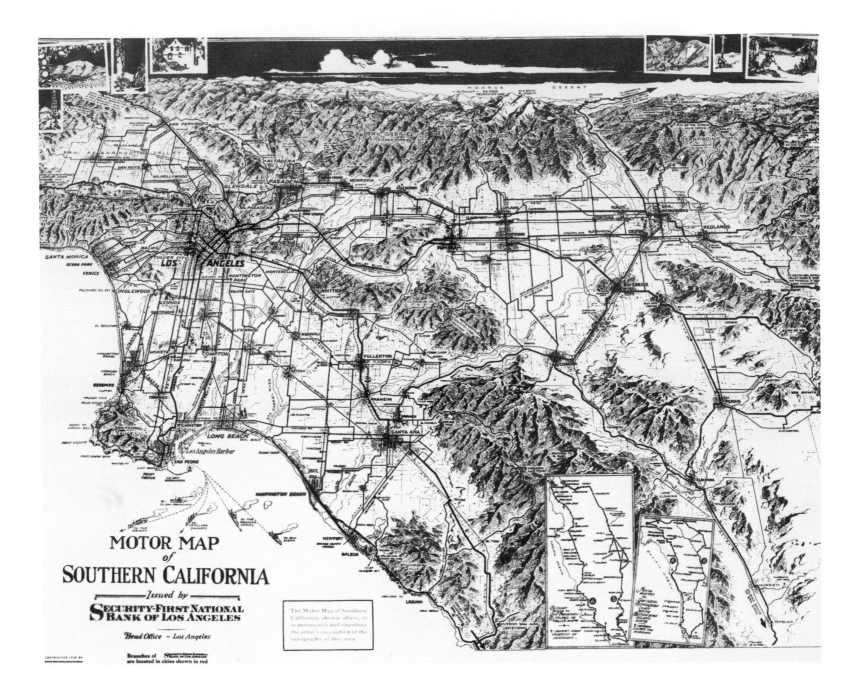

MOTOR MAP
of
SOUTHERN CALIFORNIA

Issued by

SECURITY-FIRST NATIONAL
BANK OF LOS ANGELES

Head Office ~ Los Angeles

The Motor Map of Southern
California, shown above, is
in perspective and visualizes
the artist's conception of the
topography of this area.

Branches of SECURITY-FIRST NATIONAL BANK OF LOS ANGELES
are located in cities shown in red

90

a 25 percent increase in population, adding another half a million people to Los Angeles and Orange counties.

The socioeconomic composition of this in-migration continually widened. Lower-middle-class opportunities were expanding as Los Angeles progressed in its industrial development, most notably in petroleum and rubber production. Yet, as Fogelson points out, in 1930 the labor force was still predominately employed in trade and professional service;[84] the fact that the rate of in-migration was somewhat slowed by the depression suggests that Los Angeles was not viewed as an economic oasis during those hard-pressed times. But it was an oasis of sorts all the same. The area's most important resource remained its image:

All their lives they had slaved at some kind of dull, heavy labor, behind desks and counters, in the fields and at tedious machines of all sorts, saving their pennies and dreaming of the leisure that would be theirs when they had enough. Finally that day came. They could draw a weekly income of ten and fifteen dollars. Where else should they go but California, the land of sunshine and oranges?[85]

The "automobilization" of Los Angeles continued to progress rapidly as well. From the mid-twenties on, motor vehicle registration steadily increased at an average rate of 45,000 a year, and the area maintained a ratio of population to vehicles (2.8) far below its nearest rival (Detroit, at 4.4).[86] The private auto had become the essential transportation element in Los Angeles' growth. New arrivals were increasingly choosing to settle in outlying communities opened up by motor traffic; by 1930 the central area had become the slowest-growing part of the metropolis. From 1920

Motor Map, 1930

By the beginning of the great depression, the highway system in southern California was the dominant feature of the man-made landscape as the automobile became the primary means of transportation. The highway system was more or less superimposed on existing rail systems. The area was still primarily a railway metropolis: few cities were located so as to be independent of rail lines, and most major highways headed toward the downtown district. (Reproduced with permission of Security Pacific National Bank.)

to 1930 it experienced only a 25 percent increase in residential population (still an impressive gain of 146,000, up from 569,000), whereas increases in outlying districts ranged from a low of 100 percent for the San Gabriel Valley to 612 percent for the west side and 525 percent for the San Fernando Valley. The central region, including east Los Angeles, Hollywood, and the midtown Wilshire district, now contained less than one-third of the total population in the metropolitan area; it had been well above one-half at the start of the 1920s. All the peripheral areas continued to outpace central Los Angeles in growth throughout the 1930s, and of course, well beyond.[87]

With the dispersal of residential population came the decentralization of business as well, accompanied by the decline of the central business district. Mark Foster reports that while in 1920 only 16.1 percent of the city's dentists and 21.4 percent of its physicians had offices outside the downtown area, by 1930 the situation had reversed itself, with 55 and 67 percent, respectively, having located in outlying districts. The trend was reflected in the locations of banks, department stores, movie theaters, and real estate offices.as well.[88] Perhaps the most dramatic indicator of the process was the creation of Wilshire's "Miracle Mile" in the late twenties, a fashionable strip development several miles from downtown, which Reyner Banham has called "the first real monument of the Motor Age."[89] In addition, motorized transportation brought about the decentralization of industry. Though in general the route of industrial expansion was not independent of rail transport, the dispersal can be directly associated with the growth of rubber-tired transportation, in that it was independent of both passenger rails and residential development.[90]

Really widespread decentralization of economic activity, however, had to wait for reduction in the costs of short-haul transportation eventually provided by the motor truck. Unfortunately, figures for truck registration are inconsistent owing to continual reclassification of statistical categories. But it is clear that truck registration was steadily increasing, at an average yearly rate of 8.5 percent during the 1920s, thus providing the crucial complement to the auto in the distribution of raw materials, goods, and services.[91]

The same decade saw significant changes in patterns of public transportation. Though total patronage rose, electric railway usage was increasingly based on regular daily commuting by passengers who both lived and worked near rail lines.[92] Fifty percent of weekday traffic was handled during two morning and two afternoon hours, and weekend ridership plummeted to half its previous level. "Hence, the motorcars deprived the railways of their cheap and remunerative casual business without relieving them of their expensive and unprofitable commuter service."[93] As roadway (and therefore streetcar right-of-way) congestion continued to mount with the increase in auto traffic, trolleys rapidly lost favor. Even if an interurban line was able to maintain its schedule, it could not compare with the private car in speed, convenience, and even cost.[94] The situation deteriorated as the rail companies, short of funds, spent little on capital improvements, further damaging the streetcar's popular image.

There was much talk of upgrading the public transportation system to make it more competitive. A comprehensive rapid transit program, commissioned by the city and county, was put forward in 1925, and a year later a referendum was conducted on constructing four miles of elevated railway tracks in the downtown area. The proposal was shelved and the referendum was defeated. (For more on these proposals, see the Appendix.) The closest Los Angeles came to having a rapid transit system was the construction of a tunnel four-fifths of a mile long, known as the Hollywood subway, heading from downtown toward Glendale. Even this modest project strained Pacific Electric's funds.

The great depression struck a further blow, drastically reducing the company's patronage and its operating revenue. After only three years of a depression economy, the rate of return fell from 4.7 to 2.1 percent from the Los Angeles Railway urban system and from 2.3 to −0.2 percent on Pacific Electric's interurban network.[95] By 1934 the latter company's overall patronage had dropped a third from its 1929 figure of 107 million.[96] New auto registration experienced only a slight drop and had regained momentum within five years, whereas the electric interurban continued to decline. (Truck registration was even less affected by the business depression. The only decrease in the number of registered vehicles was in 1932, and within only two years registration had completely regained its momentum of the preceding decade.)[97]

In the 1930s population growth shifted from core to periphery simultaneously with the shrinking of rail system patronage from periphery to core. Pacific Electric was forced to abandon its most unprofitable lines, first cutting suburban routes and replacing them with bus lines. A more modest rapid transit plan was offered by the Central Business District Association in 1935, but there was little official effort to pursue its construction.[98] Pacific Electric, which consistently operated at a loss except during World War II, continued to substitute buses for trolleys as fast as Railroad Commission approval could be obtained. Rail officials argued that the company should not be obligated to keep on operating at a loss merely to ensure the public availability of rights-of-way for future rapid transit development. Such preservation, if desirable, would be a public responsibility.[99]

Public authorities, as before, failed to offer assistance. In 1944 the Los Angeles Railway, which operated the downtown narrow-gauge streetcar lines, sold its holdings to National City Transit Lines. The latter's local subsidiary, Los Angeles Transit Lines, maintained the policy of abandoning antiquated rail facilities for motor buses. The fact that General Motors was a major shareholder in National City (along with Standard Oil of California and Firestone Tires) has engendered the popular "GM Conspiracy" myth of the electric railway's demise. The fate of the Los Angeles Railway lines, however, was no different from that of all other urban streetcar systems in the nation, most of them not owned by National City Lines.

The more extensive interurban system operated by Pacific Electric remained an affiliate of Southern Pacific, as it had been since 1911. Southern Pacific had begun to divest itself of passenger services, for the simple reason that they were unprofitable. In 1953

Pacific Electric Bus

The days of railway construction ended with the beginning of the automobile age. Few new lines were opened after 1910; the last new Pacific Electric route (to Fullerton) began operation in 1917. The rail companies increasingly turned to motor buses, not only to serve new routes but to bail out the least profitable trolley lines as well. The gradual but consistent conversion of rail lines to bus routes allowed private transportation companies to continue without direct public subsidy. The accompanying photo shows a Pacific Electric bus stopping in Beverly Hills during the construction of a new housing development in 1925. (Photo by "Dick" Whittington, courtesy of Henry E. Huntington Library.)

OWN A CAR? IF NOT, WHY NOT?

Passport to Arcadia

This editorial cartoon from the Los Angeles Examiner *of 28 April 1926 illustrates how perfectly the automobile was suited to the ethos of the area. The private car is associated with a pastoral landscape, with the middle-class family home, with the good life a la small town. It is the key to some kind of posturban Arcadia. This cartoon appeared two days before an election in which voters rejected the construction of elevated railways. The fact that the newspaper was spearheading the drive for improved rapid transit only highlights the contradictions that were making rail transit the unviable alternative. (Reprinted with permission of the* Los Angeles Herald Examiner.)

Pacific Electric was sold to Jesse Hough, who organized the Metropolitan Coach Lines. Hough did have connections with General Motors; during the 1940s he had held stock in a number of National City–affiliated transit companies and was even president of a few.[100] Only two routes, however, were shut down during his five-year tenure as owner of the system—the Hollywood and Glendale lines—both of which were halted with the closing of the Hollywood subway.[101]

The account most influential in spreading the notion of a General Motors conspiracy was presented by Bernard Snell to the Senate Judiciary Committee when it was considering the Industrial Reorganization Act in 1973. Snell, who confused the two Los Angeles rail operations, claimed that GM was responsible for the demise of an otherwise viable Pacific Electric and consequently for the destruction of the quality of life in Los Angeles. I find the account offered by George Hilton, in subsequent testimony before the committee, more convincing. Hilton attributes the decline of railway transit in Los Angeles, as in the rest of the nation to such factors as changes in public tastes and incomes, changing technological alternatives, and the varying relative values of fuels and other inputs.[102] The ultimate truth is even more disturbing, as it deprives us of an easy scapegoat and leaves us to shoulder the burden of collective choice. It required no conspiracy to destroy the electric railways; it would, however, have required a conspiracy to save them.

What remained of both rail holdings (three interurban and five streetcar lines) was purchased by the Los Angeles Metropolitan Transportation Agency in 1958. Under the auspices of public operation, the last of the

Pacific Electric routes were discontinued by 1961, and those of the Los Angeles Railway by 1963, at the same time as the MTA was pushing a new comprehensive plan for rail rapid transit.

Unlike the abortive attempts to create a rail rapid transit system, highway planning proceeded smoothly throughout this period. The Regional Planning Commission began to work on its own master plan of highways soon after its founding in 1923. Responding to a County Board of Supervisors resolution that same year urging "the necessity of a comprehensive network of through highways extending over the entire county," the commission started to devise a plan for regional development consistent with the *Major Traffic Street Plan* issued in 1924. The county plan was designed to provide a framework for future development throughout the region as well as to satisfy the Board of Supervisors' suggestion "that all preliminary and final plans for subdivision conform to this proposed comprehensive system of through highways."[103]

The first report, issued in 1929, was *A Comprehensive Report on the Regional Plan of Highways: Section 2-E, San Gabriel Valley*. It was followed two years later by *Section 4, Long Beach – Redondo Area*. Both documents emphasized the relationship between highway development and land use. They made specific recommendations for zoning, including a minimum lot size "consistent with the development most desired in California cities . . . to avoid overcrowding in the ultimate stage of developments," as well as the use of highway layout to encourage a sense of community center and identity.[104] The final report, issued as the *Master Plan of Highways* in 1941, was the heart

of the county master plan, but it merely put into final printed form an unpublished plan that had existed since the mid-twenties. The latter plan had long been used in determining the accommodations for highways in new subdivisions as well as county-sponsored street widenings and openings.[105]

By the time the *Master Plan* came out, a new concept for facilitating automotive transportation—the freeway—had been introduced. Though the *Master Plan of Highways* continued to focus on traditionally defined highways, it argued that a highway system alone was no longer adequate. The volume of automobile traffic had continued to increase in the eighteen years since the plan had first been conceived, and a more innovative system of urban transportation was now required if Los Angeles was successfully to maintain its chosen way of life:

In fact, the inescapable conclusion is that as the population of the Metropolitan Area passes from four to six million, one of the *two eventualities will have to be faced—a drastic reduction in the proportion of automobiles to population, or the relief of the highway system by supplemental freeways*, taken and partially completed long before that time.[106] [emphasis in original]

The *Master Plan* did not contain plans for or explicit discussion of the freeway system. By that time, however, there had developed a small but influential body of literature explicitly devoted to this new concept in urban design.

Highways into Parkways

The ideas that were eventually to be embodied in the Los Angeles freeway system reflected national and international developments in transportation design.[107] Pleasure parkways, first designed by Frederick Law Olmsted, Sr., in the 1850s and 1860s, had been built in Boston and in New York's Central Park. In effect they were merely elongated parks with roads through them and were intended for recreational purposes. Landscaped boulevards called parkways continued to be built in several eastern cities, and with the advent of the automobile the concept of the parkway as a specialized roadway was revived. The most striking realization of the automotive parkway was a 114-mile system in three New York counties, beginning with the Bronx River Parkway. First proposed in 1906 and eventually opened in the early 1920s, it incorporated such design features as limited access, grade separation, and access ramps.

The first nonrecreational, general-purpose divided highway in the United States was opened in Detroit in 1924, although without limited access. Four years later the first cloverleaf was constructed at the intersection of two otherwise traditional highways in New Jersey. The first synthesis of the parkway and the superhighway came with the construction of the new Lake Shore Drive, opened in 1933 to handle traffic in downtown Chicago.

The Germans pioneered a more comprehensive system of motor highways, beginning with a six-mile experimental speedway in 1919, and continuing with the autobahn system in the 1930s. The latter comprised, according to Tunnard and Pushkarev, "the first real freeways in Europe," with strictly limited access, no crossings at grade, and wide median dividers.[108] The Germans also demonstrated a regard for highway aesthetics, a concern compatible with the pastoralism of Nazi ideology.

Although the autobahn was the first system-wide embodiment of freeway form, it was designed exclusively for interurban travel and so bypassed built-up urban areas. The construction of a freeway system to answer the needs of urban transportation was an American innovation whose first realization came in New York City. Championed by Robert Moses, the several projects completed between 1934 and 1940 would "radically transform the face of New York."[109]

As noted earlier, some aspects of the freeway had already been suggested for Los Angeles by the 1924 street plan. These included functional differentiation of roads, isolation of through traffic, and grade separation. A report entitled *Parks, Playgrounds, and Beaches for the Los Angeles Region,* issued in 1930 by a citizens' committee which included two of the 1924 planners, contained plans for a parkway system. Although the proposal did share with later freeway plans the idea of an integrated system, its conceived purpose was markedly different. The parkways described were primarily for recreational purposes, having "almost nothing in common with 'boulevards' as that term is generally used." The compilers recognized that the parkway system would have little effect on most automobile travel within the urban region.[110]

Plans for what could be legitimately called an urban freeway in Los Angeles were imitiated in the 1930s, proposing construction of the Arroyo Seco Parkway.[111] Although the earliest suggestions of highway use for Arroyo Seco were made in 1895, the history of the parkway should probably be dated from the 1924 traffic plan, wherein it was suggested as a pleasure parkway for recreational use. By 1934, after a series of political maneuvers and confrontations, the roadway was being planned to divert surface street traffic and was referred to as a "freeway." The next year an extension through an already developed area of South Pasadena was approved. Construction began in March 1938 and was completed two years later. A one-mile stretch of what was later the Hollywood freeway through Cahuenga Pass was also built in the same period.

Until 1937 official reports had centered on individual freeways. In that year the Automobile Club of Southern California issued its *Traffic Survey,* which contained the first published proposal for a comprehensive freeway system. The recommended system of motorways, based on a thorough study of traffic patterns in the metropolitan area, was perceived as being dictated by already existing traffic movement and population trends within a metropolis where 80 percent of all daily transport was handled by automobiles.[112] No attempt was made substantially to restructure transportation patterns. Rather, the report presented an updated plan to preserve the automotive way of life for the Los Angeles region. The letter of transmittal clearly articulates this perspective:

It is apparent to even the most casual observer that in spite of the large sums of money which have been and are being expended in improvement, the streets and highways of the Los Angeles area are daily becoming more difficult and hazardous to travel. It is also apparent that this growing congestion and accident toll is the direct result of an attempt to serve both abutting property and through traffic upon the same street or highway. Your Committee is convinced that the only permanent solution is to provide facilities for the exclusive use of motor vehicles. . . .

We wish to emphasize that the Los Angeles area has grown up with the automobile. Motor vehicle transportation has shaped its growth to the extent that the business and social life of the area is today vitally dependent upon the motor vehicle for the major part of its transportation. If street and highway congestion continues to increase, the day is not far distant when the automobile will in many parts of the area have lost its usefulness. At this time, the economic loss resulting from readjustment alone will have reached a staggering total.

The destiny of the Los Angeles area has ceased to be a matter of speculation. It is now conceded by all who watched its growth that it will become one of the largest population centers of the world. Future orderly growth is vitally dependent upon the establishment of a system of transportation lines serving all parts of the area.[113]

The report called for a system of freeways whose general scheme embodied the basic elements of all Los Angeles' previous modes of transportation. The plan recommended a generally radial pattern, suggesting the influence of the rail routes. The original steam lines are all represented, including the southward sweep through Inglewood toward Redondo Beach, as well as the five-pointed star connecting at Santa Monica, San Pedro, and San Fernando and leading toward Anaheim and San Bernardino. (In fact, both Southern Pacific and Santa Fe routes are incorporated in the plan.) The interurbans' influence is also reflected in the above-mentioned routes, as well as in the orientation of the downtown grid, the proposed Cahuenga Pass motorway, and, perhaps most strikingly, in the major node proposed for Watts. And as the Automobile Club plan was based on traffic flow and projected population pattern, the influence of the highway system is readily apparent, particularly in the interdistrict routes that would completely bypass the traditional central business district.

Precursors of the Freeway

Many of the basic principles of freeway design descended from earlier transportation systems, most notably the grade separations of intersecting routes common in railroad building. These photos show two local examples of pre-freeway design. The first is a cable car viaduct near San Fernando Road in Lincoln Heights in 1889. The second is an elevated bicycle path in Pasadena in 1910. The path, constructed by a local entrepreneur and supported by tolls, was originally intended to connect Pasadena with downtown Los Angeles, but only a few miles were completed, as the venture proved to be unprofitable. The path was dismantled and the lumber was sold—at a profit. (Courtesy California Historical Society from Title Insurance collection of historical photographs.)

The First L.A. Freeway

The Arroyo Seco Parkway (renamed the Pasadena freeway in 1954) was an early showcase for the freeway concept. The first full freeway in the West – with fully restricted access from abutting property, access ramps, and no intersections at grade level – it was also a model parkway. The freeway was landscaped with 10,000 plants, most of which died quickly because of incompatibility with the roadway environment. Subsequent plantings were more successful. Unfortunately, the design was less amenable to trial and error. Present-day motorists must contend with narrow lanes, dangerously tight curves, and access ramps that often require entering freeway traffic after making a full stop. Later freeways benefited from these initial flaws. (Photo by "Dick" Whittington, Courtesy of the Henry E. Huntington Library.)

Although specific engineering matters were left for later consideration, a few recommendations were made, including cloverleaf intersections, on- and off-ramps, and grade separations through raised or depressed sections. In residential areas, wide (360 feet) rights-of-way were suggested, with a 3:1 ratio of landscaping to roadway. The illustrated effect is of inconspicuous roadways dwarfed by luxuriously ample greenbelts, a somewhat optimistic reflection of the parkway motif. "Motorway buildings" were proposed for urban motorways through the central business district, housing two floors of retail business and several floors of parking. In addition, the report recommended routing through areas of low property value and through the center of existing blocks. No consideration of the possible social effects of such routing was presented.

The leading advocate of a freeway system for Los Angeles was Lloyd Aldrich, who became city engineer in 1933. According to John Rae, "he grasped the essential element of transportation for a modern metropolis: the time required to complete a journey is more important than the distance traveled."[114] After a trip east to study the New York parkway system, Aldrich organized forty city engineers and city managers to study the area's congestion problem and issue a proposal. Denied funding by the Los Angeles City Council, he enlisted the aid of the president of Bullock's, who raised $100,000 in the downtown business community to help create the Citizens' Transportation Survey Committee in 1938. With funding from the Works Progress Administration, this group conducted a series of traffic surveys which, supplemented by the Automobile Club survey of 1937, two Regional Planning Commission reports, and assorted city materials, became the basis for *A Transit Program for the Los Angeles Metropolitan Region*, issued in 1939 by an ad hoc group called the City of Los Angeles Transportation Engineering Board. Headed by Aldrich himself, the board also included K. Charles Bean, chief engineer for the Board of Public Utilities and Transportation, and the Stone and Weber Engineering Corporation, which had been hired by the survey committee to consider the region's mass transit needs. Madigan-Hyland, a firm that had served as consultant engineers for the New York City parkway system and had been hired by the Los Angeles committee to survey local parkway needs, participated as board associates.[115] The *Transit Program* was probably the single most influential study leading to establishment of the Los Angeles freeway system.

Like the Automobile Club report, this plan was conceived in terms of existing transportation patterns. Emphasized throughout is the point that only intensive use would justify any major construction, and the priority recommendations were based on expected rates of usage. The planners consistently argued that the proposed freeway system was a technical rather than a visionary response. That is to say, rather than perceiving the freeway as a radical innovation designed to implement a particular vision of what the city should be, the plan was conceived purely as the engineering necessary to facilitate such choices:

The Board has studiously avoided efforts to control the development of the City and its environs according to any preconceived idea or objective and has continuously contemplated providing in its comprehensive plan for the orderly, efficient, and free flow of people and goods no matter what regional objective and ar-

rangements might be adopted or carried out. It has striven to avoid uni-directional viewpoints and has aimed to provide fluidity rather than to encourage or to discourage decentralizing trends.[116]

The report proposed an "express highway" system containing the same features as the Automobile Club plan, though with a number of specific changes. Discussion was expanded to include more details of engineering, right-of-way, financing, and policy considerations. The study emphasized that more important than the adoption of a comprehensive plan was the immediate construction of priority routes. Perhaps this urgency was a response to the mistakes of earlier rapid transit proposals involving elevated railways, whose progress continually bogged down in discussions of the comprehensive plan. In any event, a recommended construction program was outlined, with the Hollywood freeway receiving top priority.

Two years later the Los Angeles Department of City Planning issued *A Parkway Plan for the City of Los Angeles and the Metropolitan Area* (1941), which essentially was the official recommendation for adoption of the Transportation Engineering Board's proposals. Many of the themes discussed in this report were simply a restatement of parts of the earlier document. The nature of transportation patterns was discussed at length, and a map was included to illustrate the major "hypothetical line of communication." Superimposition of the proposed system showed its relation both to existing population distribution and to public transportation facilities. The report observes that the freeways would serve substantially the same urban centers as the existing mass transportation facilities. This congruency was a test of the system's advantages:

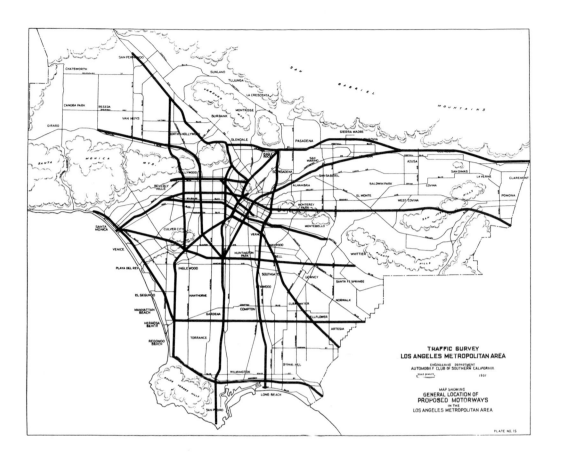

Freeway Plan, 1937

The first comprehensive freeway plan for Los Angeles was prepared by the Automobile Club of Southern California. Despite steady progress in street and highway building, traffic had worsened. The Auto Club concluded that the building of new surface streets and highways was futile, as they robbed property from established commercial districts and made good land unsuitable for residential purposes. Enter the motorways, which were intended to provide adequate facilities for through traffic and preserve southern California as a desirable place to live. (Source: Automobile Club of Southern California, Traffic Survey, 1937.)

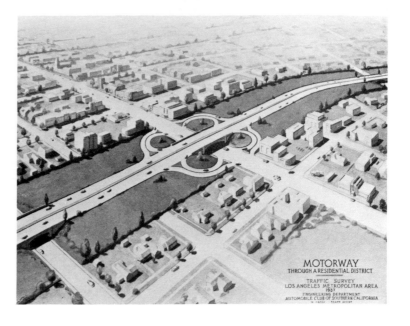

The Freeway Envisioned

These two conceptions of the Automobile Club's proposed motorways illustrate the intended impact of the freeway system on the adjacent landscape. In residential areas they were to be bounded by extremely wide, parklike rights-of-way. The lavish greenbelts would isolate the freeway from surrounding homes. On the other hand, freeways in downtown districts were to be closely integrated into the urban landscape, even passing through special "motorway buildings." Note how little land is required to accommodate the urban freeways in the drawing, an economy made possible by several features absent from future freeways: the draftsman's freeway has only three narrow lanes of travel in each direction, no access or exit ramps, and efficient use of the airspace above and below the roadway. (Source: Automobile Club of Southern California, Traffic Survey, *1937.)*

". . . in many cases the routes parallel each other, and in most cases the parkway takes the most direct route."[117]

The proposed system was praised for connecting a diverse number of points of origin, reflecting residential, industrial, commercial, and recreational uses, by providing for crosstown bypass routes as well as radial routes extending out from the central business district to suburban communities. This pattern was credited with manifesting the economic nature of the metropolis, composed of interdependent suburbs, all of which were "dependent in some measure upon the parent City of Los Angeles."[118]

The 1941 report differs from the 1939 document on which it was based in that it self-consciously champions the freeway as a radical development. It argues that the phenomenal increase in the usage of motor vehicles "has necessitated a radical change in the principles governing the design of highways." A system of roadways devoted exclusively to automobile transportation was recognized as unprecedented and as representing the innovative response necessary for Los Angeles' innovative life-style. The freeway system was heralded as the emerging matrix for the future city, providing "a framework about which the entire structure of the city can be intelligently planned." The freeways would stabilize property value and use, reduce the number of accidents, and counteract the commercialization that blighted standard thoroughfares.[119] As the report's title indicates, the notion of the freeway as "parkway" received continued emphasis.

The county's acceptance of the freeway concept and of the Transportation Board's basic plan came in 1943 with the publication of *Freeways for the Region* by the County Regional Planning Commission. Though based on extensive study again partly financed by the Works Progress Administration, the report was mostly a propaganda device aimed at convincing government officials and the public not only of the necessity but also of the urgency of freeway construction. The arguments remained basically the same as in earlier reports, concentrating on economic gain and safety. Nor is the pastoral imagery of the parkway concept lost. Illustrations show spacious planted borders, whose effect, the report suggests, would be "to produce minor 'green belts'" throughout the region. The report also emphasizes the freeway as representing a democratic ideal. It opens with the flat-out assertion that "all motorists in Los Angeles County, and this means all of us, have felt the need for some superior form of motorway in this region to supplant the existing highways." That the system was virtually dictated by the current situation was dramatically illustrated through the use of flow charts and transparent overlays. An added incentive was the creation of public works projects for a postwar economy. In fact, such planning for the future is portrayed as a wartime patriotic duty, "to prepare for return to a normal volume of automobile usage."[120] There is also a suggestion that Los Angeles had lagged behind in the march of progress, and the report champions the freeway with arguments full of the technological optimism of the 1940s. Freeways on the East Coast and in Germany are cited as tested evidence of the superiority of this modern system of highways.

The report did extend in a few novel directions the discussion of the freeway as more than simply a means of transporting people and goods. There was

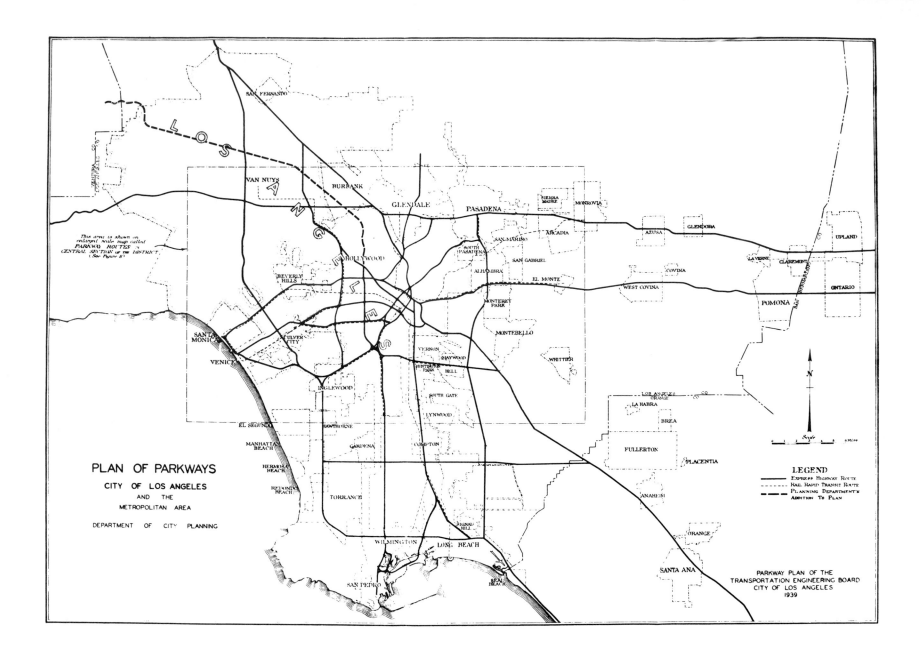

PLAN OF PARKWAYS

CITY OF LOS ANGELES
AND THE
METROPOLITAN AREA

DEPARTMENT OF CITY PLANNING

LEGEND
——— Express Highway Route
········ Rail Rapid Transit Route
━ ━ ━ Planning Department's
Addition To Plan

PARKWAY PLAN OF THE
TRANSPORTATION ENGINEERING BOARD
CITY OF LOS ANGELES
1939

Freeway Plan, 1939

This map shows the proposal developed by the semi-independent Transportation Engineering Board in 1939. The plan was endorsed by the City Planning Commission two years later with only one addition, shown by the broken line. Note that the plan also depicts rail rapid transit routes, many of which share the freeway right-of-way. Rail rapid transit was called the "ultimate solution" for transportation problems in Los Angeles, but the automotive freeways, which were intended for use by express buses as well as cars, were deemed most suitable for the "intermediate stage" of the city's development. (See Appendix.) (Source: Los Angeles Dept. of City Planning, A Parkway Plan for the City of Los Angeles, *1941).*

some recognition that an undertaking as monumental as the construction of a freeway could, by isolating and dividing communities, have a profound impact on the way people conduct their lives. Yet the report for the most part maintains an unabashedly optimistic attitude toward the freeway's potential for creating social changes. For example, freeways are portrayed as protective boundaries rather than as permanent barriers. The report barely discusses the new possibilities for land use a freeway might bring; apparently its authors assumed that such new development would be advantageous.

Although there is even a mention of the necessity to employ designs that do not increase "the destructive aspects of decentralization," the model for future community development in the county document is clearly the dispersed-residence, multicentered urban form for which Los Angeles was already famous. "Satellite communities, well planned within themselves and in relation to a freeway system," could maintain the best of both worlds, to "provide a better way of living and still preserve the social and economic advantages of the urban center." Freeways would be "facilities which are deliberately designed for the decentralized community."[121]

The actual plan for freeway construction differed somewhat from the city proposal. As the report observes, since its primary concerns were for regionally oriented freeways, it had omitted still worthy projects which would serve primarily local needs. Interestingly enough, the two most striking changes —the reduction in the number of downtown belts and the diagonal ex-

Freeways as Parkways

This artist's conception of the 1939 proposal more closely resembles a real freeway, but the roadway is still notably unobtrusive. Part of the negative impact is mitigated by landscaping. By allowing for broad rights-of-way, planners hoped to avoid the objectionable features of "the narrow freeway." "The parkway," a city report optimistically suggested in 1941, "is at once a boon to motorists and advantageous to contiguous and abutting property." This drawing is deceptive, however, for the freeway shown here carries an unrealistically light load. An electric trolley car is using the lane farthest to the right. (Source: Los Angeles Transportation Engineering Board, A Transit Program for the Los Angeles Metropolitan Area, *1939.)*

tension of the Sepulveda Parkway (San Diego freeway)—brought the plan more into line with the present-day system.

Parkways into Freeways

Meanwhile, a cycle of accelerated development had begun in Los Angeles. The end of the thirties marked the beginning of a period of industrial expansion, with the opening of new oil fields and step-ups in auto production. World War II brought further economic growth, most notably in the phenomenal increase in aircraft production. Industrial expansion would continue as Los Angeles became a vital center of the postwar business boom. Between 1950 and 1957, for example, the Los Angeles area accounted for one-sixth of the entire nation's increase in manufacturing employment. The fact that so many of the expanding industries had high land-use requirements became another factor in the spread of an urban landscape.[122]

The tremendous growth of the film industry during the depression years was having its effect as well, and not only as another contribution to the local economy. The region's mystique of possibility, long a commodity for realtors, became an exportable commodity in the motion picture and fused new life into Los Angeles' image. Hollywood represented the fulfillment of fantasy, both on the screen and in the popular imagination. The allure of Hollywood attracted more than the aspiring actor, for it contributed to the romantic image of the region. And like any successful fantasy, Los Angeles' magnetic image was fed by the symbolism of mainstream aspirations. In discussing the period of the 1930s, Gebhard and Von Breton wrote that

the Los Angeles scene, as portrayed in films, weekly radio broadcasts, and the press, seemed to mirror just what most Americans throughout the country felt their world should be like. The Hollywood version of the "average" middle-class American family lived in a quiet, suburban setting, in a spacious Colonial Revival house tastefully furnished in Early American reproductions, with two or more automobiles in the family garage.[123]

Los Angeles continued to play its variations on the American bourgeois ideal of middle-class suburbia.

"The movement of people to Southern California during and since WWII," wrote Howard Nelson, "ranks with the largest migrations in the history of the United States."[124] As the national economy expanded more Americans were joining the middle classes, gaining more choice over how and where they lived. The even more phenomenal growth of the local economy meant that southern California offered tremendous economic incentives for migration. The population of Los Angeles and Orange counties increased by 1.4 million in the 1940s and by 2.3 million in the 1950s, more than doubling the number of residents within two decades.

The newcomers accelerated the long-standing tendency to settle in the periphery of the established metropolitan area, with all subareas except the central one recording dramatic growth—a pattern that was by this time becoming typical throughout the nation. Although the supply of housing was never adequate, liberal Federal Housing Authority and Veterans' Administration lending policies assisted families in purchasing the single-family homes being thrown to-

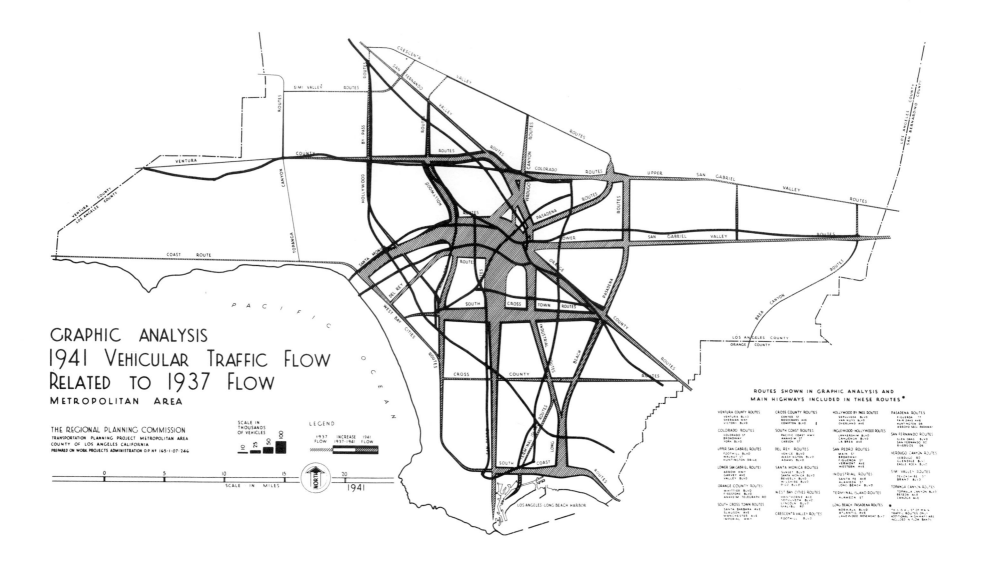

GRAPHIC ANALYSIS
1941 VEHICULAR TRAFFIC FLOW
RELATED TO 1937 FLOW
METROPOLITAN AREA

THE REGIONAL PLANNING COMMISSION
TRANSPORTATION PLANNING PROJECT METROPOLITAN AREA
COUNTY OF LOS ANGELES CALIFORNIA
PREPARED ON WORK PROJECTS ADMINISTRATION O.P. N° 165-1-07-246

SCALE IN
THOUSANDS
OF VEHICLES

LEGEND

1937   INCREASE   1941
FLOW   1937-1941   FLOW

SCALE IN MILES

NORTH
1941

ROUTES SHOWN IN GRAPHIC ANALYSIS AND
MAIN HIGHWAYS INCLUDED IN THESE ROUTES*

VENTURA COUNTY ROUTES   CROSS COUNTY ROUTES   HOLLYWOOD BY PASS ROUTES   PASADENA ROUTES
VENTURA BLVD   CENTER ST   SEPULVEDA BLVD   FIGUEROA ST
SHERMAN WAY   ROSECRANS AVE   VAN NUYS BLVD   FAIR OAKS AVE
VICTORY BLVD   COMPTON BLVD   OVERLAND AVE   HUNTINGTON DR
                                                                                      ARROYO SEC. PARKWAY
COLORADO ROUTES   SOUTH COAST ROUTES   INGLEWOOD-HOLLYWOOD ROUTES
COLORADO ST   PACIFIC COAST HWY   LANKERSHIM BLVD   SAN FERNANDO ROUTES
BROADWAY   ANAHEIM ST   LA BREA AVE   GLEN OAKS BLVD
YORK BLVD   CARSON ST   SAN FERNANDO RD
                                                         SAN PEDRO ROUTES   RIVERSIDE DR
UPPER SAN GABRIEL ROUTES   DEL REY ROUTES   MAIN ST
FOOTHILL BLVD   VENICE BLVD   BROADWAY   VERDUGO CANYON ROUTES
WALNUT ST   WASHINGTON BLVD   FIGUEROA ST   VERDUGO RD
HUNTINGTON DRIVE   ADAMS BLVD   VERMONT AVE   GLENDALE BLVD
                                                         WESTERN AVE   EAGLE ROCK BLVD
LOWER SAN GABRIEL ROUTES   SANTA MONICA ROUTES
ARROW HWY   SUNSET BLVD   INDUSTRIAL ROUTES   SIMI VALLEY ROUTES
GARVEY AVE   SANTA MONICA BLVD   SANTA FE AVE   DEVONSHIRE ST
VALLEY BLVD   BEVERLY BLVD   ALAMEDA ST   BRAND BLVD
                             WILSHIRE BLVD   LONG BEACH BLVD
ORANGE COUNTY ROUTES   PICO BLVD   TOPANGA CANYON ROUTES
WHITTIER BLVD   TERMINAL ISLAND ROUTES   TOPANGA CANYON BLVD
FIRESTONE BLVD   WEST BAY CITIES ROUTES   ALAMEDA ST   RESEDA AVE
ANAHEIM-TELEGRAPH RD   HAWTHORNE AVE   CANOGA AVE
                             SEPULVEDA BLVD
SOUTH CROSS TOWN ROUTES   LINCOLN BLVD   LONG BEACH-PASADENA ROUTES
SANTA BARBARA AVE   MALIBU RD   NORWALK BLVD   *PRINCIPAL STOP N MAN
SLAUSON AVE   ATLANTIC AVE   TRAFFIC ROUTES ONLY
MANCHESTER AVE   CRESCENTA VALLEY ROUTES   LAKEWOOD-ROSEMEAD BLVD   ADDITIONAL HIGHWAYS ARE
IMPERIAL HWY   FOOTHILL BLVD   INCLUDED IN FLOW BANDS

Freeway Plan and Traffic Flow

Freeway planning relied heavily on traffic surveys to suggest the imperative of increased roadway construction. By tying policy to surveys, the engineer acquired the political responsibility of assessing, quantitatively, the public will. The freeways were spawned by an implicit democracy of behavior. This map shows the priority routes of the Los Angeles County plan. (Source: Los Angeles Regional Planning Commission, Freeways for the Region, *1943.)*

gether by housing-tract developers. As increasingly large numbers of blacks and Mexicans arrived to take advantage of improved employment prospects, they began to move into the more centrally located areas of the city—the old suburbs—creating coherent ethnic communities and accelerating new suburban development to meet the demands of "white flight." The tremendous growth in population and the wide dispersion of residential development based on automotive transportation proved a source of continued frustration to city and highway planners as facilities always lagged behind need. It was within this setting that the freeway plans were emerging.

Actually building the freeways was much more difficult than planning them. The big problem was money. A 1939 California law, which officially defined freeways and gave the state authority to deny abutting property owners direct access to them, had also empowered the state to build state highways to freeway standards. But most freeways were still not considered to be the state's business.

A major part of the difficulty was that the first priority freeway recommendations suggested routes through highly urbanized areas, and the state highway program had not yet fully freed itself from its rural bias. It was not until 1933 that urban highways were even included in the state highway system. Before that year, the state maintained only 295 miles of highway in Los Angeles County. Nearly half of those were north of the Los Angeles metropolitan area, and none of them passed through incorporated communities of more than 2,500 population. (A highway ceased to be a state highway as soon as it reached city limits.)[125]

But in 1933, in an effort to bail out depression-strapped cities and counties, the state legislature doubled the mileage in the system to include a large number of county and city roads in various metropolitan areas in California. Los Angeles County received 627 miles of new state highway (making a total of 922 miles) with virtually all the new mileage being slated for the southern part of the county—the Los Angeles metropolitan area. Of the new total, 350 miles traversed incorporated cities, with 202 miles within the city of Los Angeles alone. A number of major highways then in existence were taken over by the Division of Highways, including many whose heavy use would ensure their inclusion as freeways in the local master plans discussed above. Similarly, Orange County received a large share of new state highway mileage. Finally, one-quarter cent of the state gas tax was set aside specifically for highway construction and maintenance within cities, with an additional one-quarter cent added in 1935.[126]

Urban freeways, however, continued to be neglected by the state Division of Highways. They were still regarded as the responsibility of local governments since ostensibly they would meet only local needs.[127] Even had the state chosen to help, it could not have done much as there was not enough money available to divert from the pressing needs of traditional highway construction and maintenance. The earliest attempts at freeway construction were financed by a variety of ad hoc arrangements. The state was able to come up with half of the $5 million needed for the first 6.8 miles of the Arroyo Seco; the other half included money from the Works Progress Administration and the Public Works Administration, city funds, and gas tax revenues from Los Angeles and South Pasadena.[128] Two wartime projects, the extension of the Arroyo Seco downtown and the Aliso Street viaduct (which would carry the Santa Ana and San Bernardino freeways over the Los Angeles River into downtown), received federal financing because they qualified as part of the National Strategic System of Roads, thus ensuring not only federal money but also priority in war-short steel and cement.[129] The Terminal Island freeway, begun at the request of the United States Navy, was built entirely with federal funds. Completed two years after the war ended, the isolated segment was immediately obsolete (and is destined to remain so, since the proposed route 47 freeway connecting it with downtown will never be constructed).[130] By the war's close, only 11 miles of freeway had been opened in Los Angeles, to be followed by a mere 4.3 miles during the next five years.

Keeping highway development apace with population increases had always been a problem in southern California, and the combination of wartime migration, wartime constraints on construction, reduction of gas tax revenues owing to fuel rationing, and roadway damage caused by heavy military vehicles only exacerbated the difficulties. The critical highway shortage was statewide. (Ironically, the slowdown in general construction did allow freeway planners to learn from initial design flaws.)[131] Pressure was applied increasingly on the state by local governments, the public, and by special-interest groups to expand its highway-building activities. The Joint Fact Finding Committee on Highways, Streets and Bridges, headed by state Senator Randolph Collier, was formed to consider a statewide solution to the problem.

The Sprawling Metropolis

World War II set off Los Angeles' biggest population boom, with nearly 4 million people streaming into southern California from 1940 to 1960. During this period of baby booms, television, and drive-ins Los Angeles achieved the status of archetypical American city. This photo, taken in 1953, shows one of the many regional shopping centers built to bring downtown consumer amenities to the suburbs. The Crenshaw center, separated from the civic center by six miles of single-family homes, was within a twenty-minute drive from more than half a million residents at its opening. (Photo by "Dick" Whittington.)

113

Early Freeway

This section of the Ramona Parkway (renamed the San Bernardino freeway in 1954) is shown soon after its opening in 1944. It is part of a 3.5-mile stretch beginning at the Aliso Street Viaduct—a bridge built to freeway specifications over the Los Angeles River—and ending just east of Soto Street in Boyle Heights. The interurban railway car shown to the left of the freeway originally shared the freeway right-of-way as it crossed the river. (Courtesy of CALTRANS.)

As part of the study, local governments were asked to survey their individual traffic needs. Los Angeles responded by appointing an ad hoc committee of various city and planning engineers from the area. Supported by local and state governments, automotive organizations, and local business interests, the Los Angeles Metropolitan Parkway Engineering Committee presented its influential report, *Interregional, Regional, and Metropolitan Parkways,* in 1946. Drawing on city (1941) and county (1943) transportation proposals, the committee's report was a hard-sell presentation of the envisioned freeway system. Its tone is openly propagandistic, with its dramatic flow charts, photographs of congested surface streets, and bold captions such as "In 1945, Automobile Accidents in Los Angeles County Caused 1042 Deaths." The urgent need for freeways was detailed; the lack of sufficient funds was decried. The report closed with recommendations that the state initiate a program of freeway construction.

The plan developed by this committee reconciled the city and county proposals by including both the elaborate downtown configuration recommended by the former and the peripheral routes emphasized by the latter. The report also classified routes according to potential funding sources. In 1944 Congress had appropriated limited funds for a national interregional system of highways, and the committee suggested five freeway routes to be part of that system. Other routes were suggested as state regional highways, and the remaining routes were to be included in a proposed metropolitan system funded by local moneys.

After numerous hearings and studies and several attempts at legislation, a compromise measure was passed by the state legislature in 1947. Known as the Collier-Burns Highway Act, it was designed to bring in new revenues for extensive highway construction by increasing the state gas tax and introducing several new highway-related taxes to be collected by the state, all of which were to be paid into a special highway tax fund. (The law prohibiting gas tax funds from being used for other than highway purposes became part of the state constitution through a voter-approved amendment in 1938.)[132] The Collier-Burns Act brought the state fully into the business of freeway building, providing for full financing of right-of-way acquisition and of planning, construction, and maintenance of urban state highway routes. Although the bill was aimed at the state highway system as a whole, the extent of the tax increases was tied directly to the freeway program. For example, the need for new freeways in the state's metropolitan areas was the primary argument for raising the gas tax 1.5 cents per gallon (up from 3 cents) instead of the 1-cent increase supported by many legislators.[133] With the additional funding California would have "free" roads instead of the toll roads being constructed in eastern states that had more severe fiscal problems. A reshuffling of the state funding ratio gave freeways an additional boost, apportioning to southern California, and especially to Los Angeles County, a larger piece of the pie. The Collier-Burns Act provided both the ideological and financial support necessary for a full-scale construction program.

Passage of the act immediately accelerated freeway construction in the Los Angeles area, and during the following decade most of the major freeways of the system as Angelenos now know it were begun. Total operating mileage was increased four and a half times from 1950 to 1955, as large segments of the Hollywood–Santa Ana and San Bernardino freeways and smaller parts of several other freeways were opened. With the completion of freeway-to-freeway interchanges, the roadways began to function with the intended systemic qualities. The unprecedented four-level downtown interchange, for example, which was fully operating after the Arroyo Seco extension was completed in 1953, integrated freeway travel in four different directions.

Freeway construction received its second major boost when the National System of Interstate and Defense Highways was launched in 1956. The federal response was analogous to that of the state. Highway construction nationally had lagged far behind need, and the federal system was the logical next step in the progression of highway-aid programs which began in 1916. The popular clamor for better roads, along with the more highly organized efforts of highway supporters, called forth a more aggressive response on the federal level. The effect was to pump huge amounts of money into freeway construction everywhere, and Los Angeles, with its rapidly expanding population, was slated to receive a hefty share. A national highway trust fund, much like the one pioneered in California, was set up to reimburse 90 percent of the planning and construction costs of qualifying routes.[134] The San Diego, Golden State, Santa Monica, San Bernardino, Foothill, and San Gabriel River freeways were all built under the program.

Establishment of this important new source of funding was followed by creation of the California Freeway and Expressway System in 1959, again sponsored

Legislating the Freeway

Four Plans for a Los Angeles freeway system were produced between 1937 and 1943, and the California "freeway law" permitting limited-access highways was passed in 1939; yet construction was slowed by a shortage of available funds. The final step in creating a freeway system came in 1947, when the state legislature increased highway-user taxes to finance freeways. The accompanying map is from a 1946 report to the Joint Fact Finding Committee on Highways, Streets, and Bridges formed to study the problem. The report was influential in getting the new tax bill passed. Three complementary systems are shown. The locally funded metropolitan system shown on the map was never created, although several of these routes eventually were incorporated into the state system.

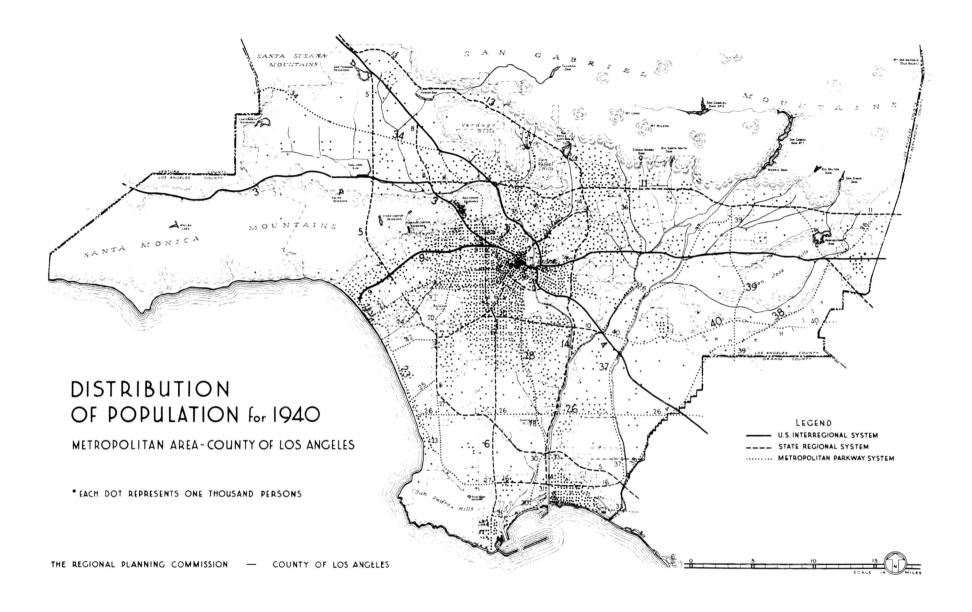

DISTRIBUTION
OF POPULATION for 1940

METROPOLITAN AREA - COUNTY OF LOS ANGELES

*EACH DOT REPRESENTS ONE THOUSAND PERSONS

THE REGIONAL PLANNING COMMISSION — COUNTY OF LOS ANGELES

LEGEND

———— U.S. INTERREGIONAL SYSTEM

– – – – STATE REGIONAL SYSTEM

· · · · · METROPOLITAN PARKWAY SYSTEM

SCALE IN MILES

117

by Senator Collier. The legislation authorized a tight freeway grid for the Los Angeles metropolitan area, which if completed would leave no urbanized area more than four miles from an onramp, and a looser grid penetrating into the less developed periphery. Los Angeles, Orange, and Ventura counties, which composed the state Division of Highways District VII, were slated for an eventual 1,557 miles of freeway, scheduled for completion in the early 1980s.

The system represented formal adoption by the state of the basic plans developed locally in the late 1930s and 1940s. Previously, already established state highway routes were adopted piecemeal as freeways by the California Highway Commission. The commission, a semi-independent appointed body, was empowered to select specific routes for state highways; the legislature, in designating a state highway, usually named merely the points to be connected. The 1959 act classified more than 12,000 miles of highways as state freeways, but the responsibility of setting construction priorities, choosing specific routes, and allocating funds remained in the hands of the Highway Commission. (The California Transportation Commission, created in 1978, assumed the duties of the Highway Commission, as well as those of several other transportation-related boards.)

The legislature's 1959 freeway program was little more than a formal restatement of the tentative projections on which the Division of Highways had already been working. The timetable for construction was, however, made a little more definite by the addition of a proposed completion date.[135]

The state's renewed ideological commitment had been preceded by a 1.5-cent increase in the gas tax in

1956, followed by another 1-cent increase in 1963; the state tax thus rose to 7 cents, with an additional 4 cents being levied by the federal government.[136] This support on both state and federal levels translated into the steady progress of freeway construction throughout California, particularly within District VII.

The age of new freeway construction has, for the most part, ended. The demise of the program resulted from the same circumstances that nearly prevented its full-scale initiation in the first place: inadequate funds. The 7 cents per gallon collected by the state in 1963 was worth only 2 cents in real value by 1979, and highway construction costs have risen at two and a half times the rate of the consumer price index.[137] California simply cannot afford to build much of anything. The squeeze began in the early 1960s, when additional expenses of aesthetic landscaping and environmental protection, plus higher compensation to displaced homeowners and businesses, all aimed at appeasing opposition, began to escalate construction costs. Meanwhile, local opposition to several key routes (most notably the Beverly Hills and Century freeways) became more outspoken, further stimulating a rethinking of transportation goals.[138] All attempts to increase highway user taxes were defeated. The price of an acceptable freeway rose as the value of the dollar fell, and state highway officials were left with the nearly impossible task of reconstructing policy from the ruins.

What remains is a department (the California Department of Transportation, or Caltrans, which superseded the Division of Highways in 1973) whose basic purpose is to keep the existing system running. Offi-

A Freeway Near Every Garage

In 1959 the state legislature approved the California freeway and expressway system which planned for 12,414 miles of freeway. Although the legislative action was little more than a formal approval of then current highway practices, the system did provide a statement of vision. The master plan for the Los Angeles area would have left very few urbanized areas more than four miles from a freeway by 1980. (Courtesy of CALTRANS.)

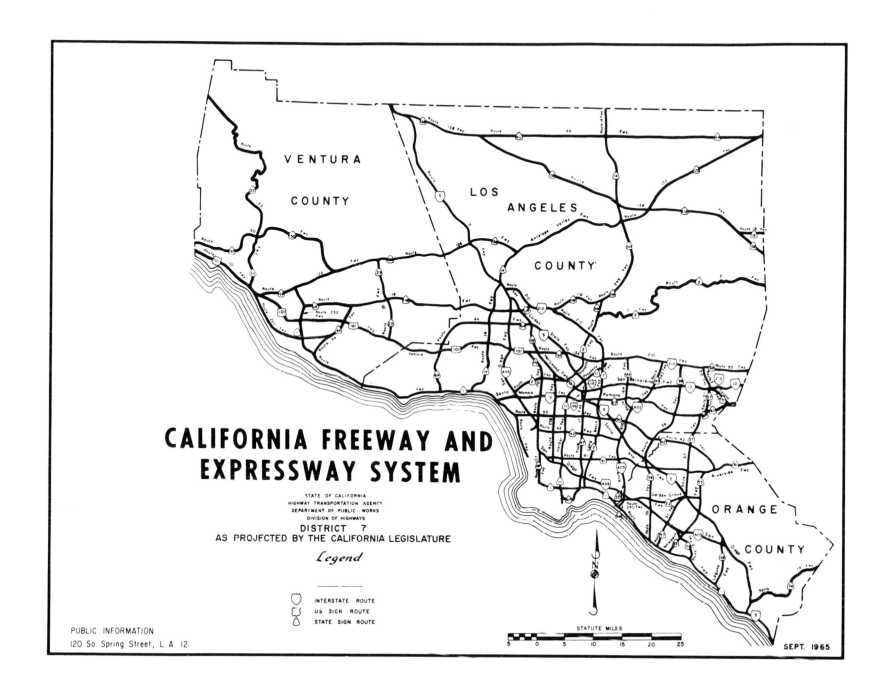

CALIFORNIA FREEWAY AND EXPRESSWAY SYSTEM

STATE OF CALIFORNIA
HIGHWAY TRANSPORTATION AGENCY
DEPARTMENT OF PUBLIC WORKS
DIVISION OF HIGHWAYS

DISTRICT 7
AS PROJECTED BY THE CALIFORNIA LEGISLATURE

Legend

INTERSTATE ROUTE
US SIGN ROUTE
STATE SIGN ROUTE

VENTURA COUNTY

LOS ANGELES COUNTY

ORANGE COUNTY

STATUTE MILES
5 0 5 10 15 20 25

SEPT. 1965

PUBLIC INFORMATION
120 So. Spring Street, L.A. 12

121

Disposable Freeway (left.)

The construction of freeway interchanges was complicated by the need to maintain a normal flow of traffic on existing freeways. This photo, taken in 1959, is a northward view of the Harbor freeway detour around the site of the Santa Monica freeway separation. The first detour required a second detour, this time on heavily traveled Venice Boulevard. A temporary bridge was therefore built over the temporary freeway. (Courtesy of CAL-TRANS.)

Stockpiled Embankment (right.)

About 226,000 cubic yards of excess excavation from the Harbor freeway were transported to this site at Arlington Avenue in Torrance for eventual use in the embankment of the San Diego freeway. To ensure an adequate supply of inexpensive fill to carry elevated freeways, the state set up numerous dumping sites on freeway rights-of-way, and collected earth of acceptable quality from a wide variety of public agencies and private contractors. This photo was taken in 1960; two years later this portion of the freeway was opened. (Courtesy of CALTRANS.)

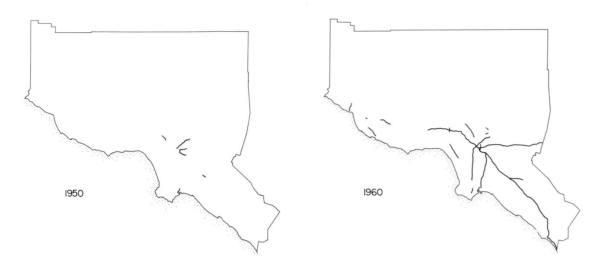

1950　　　　1960　　　　1965

1970

Growth of a System

The freeway system began as a few short segments that upgraded
existing highways: the Arroyo Seco Parkway replaced a portion
of North Figueroa (to the extent of usurping its tunnels); a new
Aliso Street bridge built to freeway standards crossed the Los Angeles River; a mile of parkway straightened Cahuenga Pass.
When large-scale construction began in the 1950s, priority was
assigned to the radial routes feeding downtown. During the
1960s, as these main arterials were completed, construction was
refocused on the circumvential routes lacing the suburban periphery. The 1970s were a time for closing the gaps in the system,
and few new freeways were begun, although nearly as much
freeway mileage was opened in that decade as was in existence
in 1960.

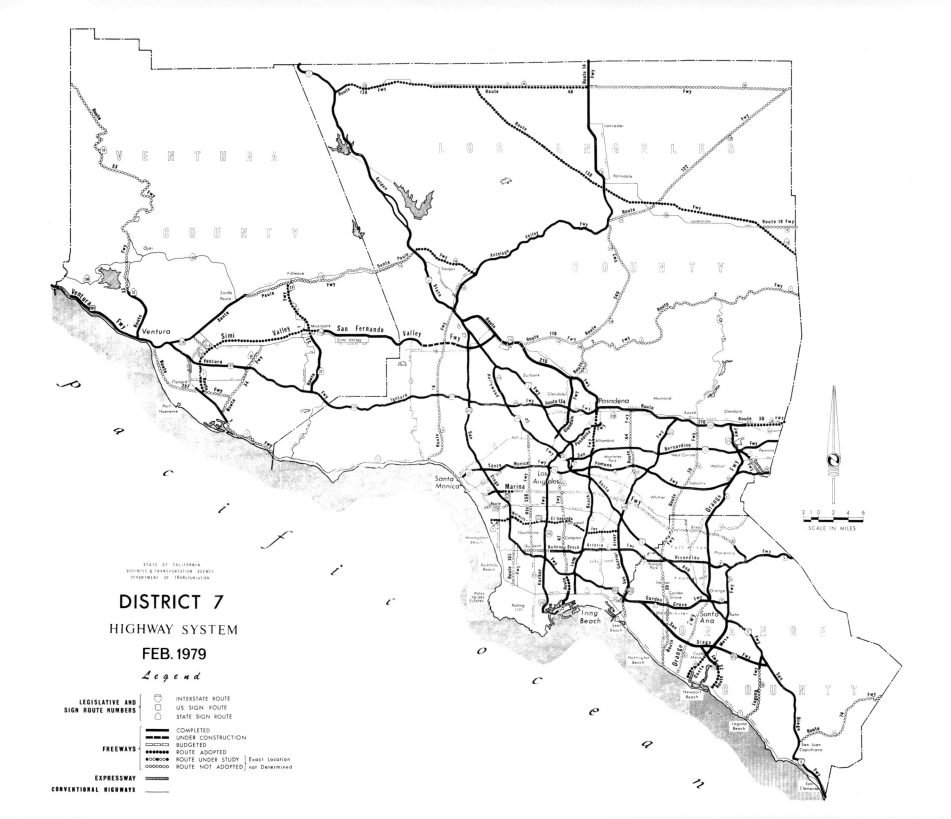

DISTRICT 7

HIGHWAY SYSTEM

FEB. 1979

Legend

LEGISLATIVE AND
SIGN ROUTE NUMBERS

INTERSTATE ROUTE
U.S. SIGN ROUTE
STATE SIGN ROUTE

FREEWAYS

COMPLETED
UNDER CONSTRUCTION
BUDGETED
ROUTE ADOPTED
ROUTE UNDER STUDY   Exact Location
ROUTE NOT ADOPTED   not Determined

EXPRESSWAY

CONVENTIONAL HIGHWAYS

STATE OF CALIFORNIA
BUSINESS & TRANSPORTATION AGENCY
DEPARTMENT OF TRANSPORTATION

cial priorities now stress maintenance, rehabilitation, and reconstruction; operational improvements to increase traffic flow and safety and to encourage higher vehicle occupancy rates; and making the freeways more environmentally compatible through landscaping and walls to cut down noise. Little new construction is even planned. The legislature, in response to specific public pressures, began to delete routes from the master plan of freeways in the late 1960s. Now even that is unnecessary; of the nearly 200 miles of unconstructed routes officially adopted for District VII by the Highway Commission, probably less than 30 miles stand any chance of being built. They are, in descending order of probability, completion of the Artesia freeway to the Harbor freeway, the Norwalk–El Segundo (formerly the Century) freeway, the Long Beach freeway connection to the Foothill freeway, completion of the San Fernando–Simi Valley freeway to the Moorpark freeway, and some extension of the Newport freeway toward the ocean. The only reason the 15.5 mile Century freeway may be constructed is that it was declared an interstate route and therefore will receive about 92 percent federal funding. (Furthermore, much of the right-of-way has already been cleared, and something must be done with what has become a wasteland. Even so, it took seven years of litigation, and agreements to build replacement housing for 4,400 removed units, to get the freeway through.) State funds are so tight that federal programs overwhelmingly dominate revenues directed toward capital outlays; after paying all the expenses of running the system and making minor improvements, the state can barely cover its 8 percent share of matching funds.[139]

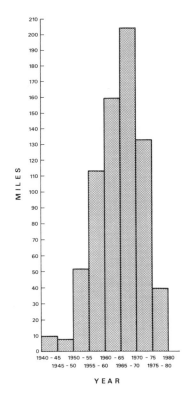

New Freeway Mileage per Five-Year Period,
1940-1980

The Rise and Fall of the Construction Program

These tables summarize the opening of the freeway system in Los Angeles, Orange, and Ventura counties. The sudden leap beginning around 1950 represents the passage of the Collier-Burns Highway Act, which legislated a steady influx of money for construction. The flattening out of the curve in the late 1970s represents the decline of the construction program, partly a result of changing transportation priorities, but even more a result of rising construction costs eroding the value of highway tax monies.

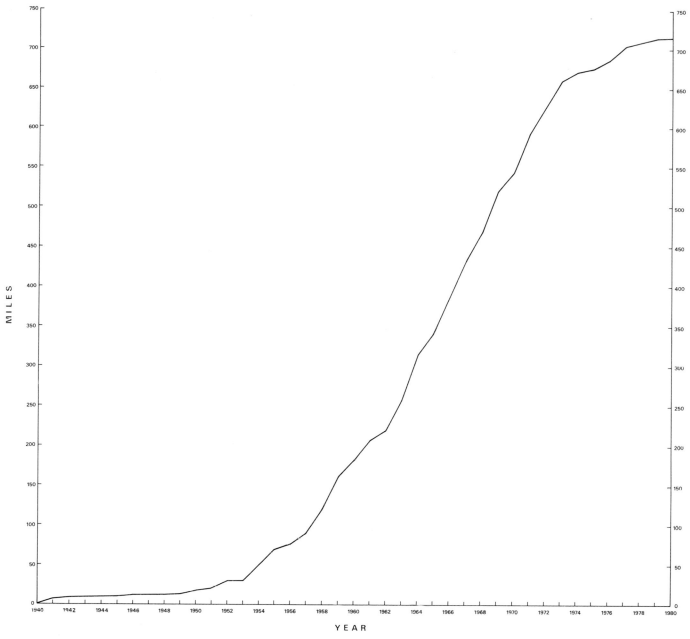

Cumulative Freeway Mileage, 1940-1980

Freeway name[1]	State highway route number(s) ("I" signifies Interstate rte.)	Miles open[2]	First segment open	Last segment open	Average daily traffic (at highest volume breakpoint, 1979)
Antelope Valley	14	52.0	1963	1974	37,500: west of jct. with fwy. 5, Los Angeles
Artesia[3]	91 (west of fwy. 5)	17.6	1968	1975	195,000: east of Paramount Avenue, Long Beach
Corona	71	1.4	1971	1972	23,200: south of jct. with fwy. 210, Pomona
Corona Del Mar	73	2.0	1977	1979	40,500: south of Bear Street, Costa Mesa
Foothill	I 210 (from fwy. 5 to fwy. 30) 30 (from fwy. 210 to Foothill Blvd.)	41.2[4]	1955	1977	153,000: east of jct. with fwy. 134, Pasadena
Garden Grove	22	12.6	1964	1967	138,000: west of jct. with fwy. 5, Santa Ana
Glendale[5]	2	8.8	1958	1978	81,000: east of jct. with fwy. 5, Los Angeles
Golden State	I 5 (north of fwy. 101)	71.5	1956	1975	182,000: south of jct. with fwy. 134, Los Angeles
Harbor	11 (south of fwy. 101)	22.8	1952	1970	206,000: south of 8th and 9th Street connections, Los Angeles
Hollywood	101 (from fwy. 11 to fwy. 134) 170 (from fwy. 134 to fwy. 5)	16.1	1940	1948	220,000: west of jct. with fwy. 11, Los Angeles
Laguna	133	1.1	1970		18,000: south of jct. with fwy. 405.
Long Beach	7 (north of rte. 1) no number[6] (south of rte. 1)	20.4 1.6	1952	1965	158,000: south of jct. with fwy. 5, Commerce
Marina[7]	90	1.9	1968	1972	51,000: west of jct. with fwy. 405, Los Angeles
Metropolitan Bypass[8]	138	1.5	1967		2,300: east of jct. with fwy. 5
Moorpark	23	8.0	1970	1971	34,000: north of jct. with fwy.101, Thousand Oaks
Newport[9]	55	13.3	1962	1973	163,000: south of Edinger Avenue, Tustin
Orange	57 (from fwy. 5 to fwy. 10) I 210 (from fwy. 10 to fwy. 30)	23.4	1969	1976	160,000: north of jct. with fwy. 91, Placentia
Ojai	33	5.5	1956	1970	23,300: north of jct. with fwy. 101, Ventura
Pacific Coast	1	6.4	1957		16,100: north of Hueneme Road
Pasadena	11 (north of fwy. 101)	8.0	1940	1953	133,000: north of Hill Street, Los Angeles
Pomona	60	30.4	1965	1971	165,000: east of jct. with fwy. 7
Riverside	91 (east of fwy. 5)	18.7	1958	1971	162,000: west of Harbor Boulevard, Fullerton
San Bernardino	I 10 (east of fwy. 101)	30.5	1943	1957	168,000: east of Soto Street, Los Angeles
San Diego	I 405 (from fwy. 5 south to fwy. 5) I 5 (south of southern jct. with fwy. 405)	93.7	1957	1969	233,000: north of jct. with fwy. 10, West Los Angeles

Freeway name[1]	State highway route number(s) ("I" signifies Interstate rte.)	Miles open[2]	First segment open	Last segment open	Average daily traffic (at highest volume breakpoint, 1979)
San Gabriel River	I 605	27.7	1964	1971	168,000: north of jct. with fwy. 91, Dairy Valley
Santa Ana	I 5 (from fwy. 405 to fwy. 101) 101 (from fwy. 5 to fwy. 11)	43.0	1944	1958	200,000: east of jct. with fwy. 10, Los Angeles
Santa Monica	I 10 (west of fwy. 5)	16.2	1961	1966	236,000: west of Normandie Avenue, Los Angeles
Santa Paula	126	13.1	1963	1965	27,000: west of Victoria Avenue, Ventura
Simi Valley—San Fernando Valley[10]	118	20.9[11]	1968	1977	51,000: west of L.A./Ventura County line
Terminal Island	47 (from Seaside Blvd. to Sepulveda Blvd.)	2.6	1948		18,500: north of Anaheim Street, Long Beach
Ventura	101 (west of fwy. 170) 134[12] (from fwy. 170 to fwy. 210)	80.4	1955	1974	228,000: west of jct. with fwy. 405, Sherman Oaks
Vincent Thomas Bridge	47 (from fwy. 11 to Seaside Ave.)	1.9	1970[13]		26,000
Yorba Linda[14]	90	2.3	1970		29,000: south of Orangethorpe Avenue, Yorba Linda

[1]Gives name commonly used, whether officially authorized or used by default. A few freeways are known by other than their official names; such instances are explicitly noted.

[2]Gives mileage located in the California Department of Transportation's District VII, composed of Los Angeles, Orange, and Ventura counties. Many of these freeways continue beyond county limits.

[3]The 4.7 miles of freeway west of the Long Beach freeway officially comprise the Redondo Beach freeway.

[4]The final 5.3-mile segment of the Foothill freeway is scheduled for completion in 1981.

[5]The 4.4-mile segment north of freeway 134 is officially named the Frank Lanterman freeway.

[6]South of state highway 1, the Long Beach freeway is not part of the state system; rather, it is under the jurisdiction of the city of Long Beach.

[7]Previously the Richard M. Nixon freeway, the name was officially changed in 1976.

[8]This freeway is merely a long exit ramp off the Golden State freeway at the north end of Los Angeles County. It was originally planned to extend 72 miles to the San Bernardino County line.

[9]Officially named the Costa Mesa freeway.

[10]Officially, the San Fernando Valley freeway is that portion of route 118 which is east of the Los Angeles/Ventura County line, and the Simi Valley freeway is the portion west of the county line.

[11]The completion of the 5.5-mile gap is scheduled for 1983.

[12]The Ventura freeway officially ends at the Golden State freeway. The stretch continuing east has not been officially named; it is often called "freeway 134."

[13]Although the Vincent Thomas Bridge was opened in 1964, it did not become a "freeway" until 1970, when a California Highway Commission resolution simply declared it so despite the lack of the median divider usually required for such a classification.

[14]Officially an expressway, as it does not contain at least four lanes for any mile-long segment.

Building before and after the Urban Deluge

Constructing freeways through built-up areas was extremely costly, in both a financial and a social sense. By preceding de-velopment and building through rural and uncultivated land, the price of the freeway was kept down and the disruption of peo-ple's lives was minimized. A further benefit of early construction was that future development would conform to the structural order defined by the freeway, resulting in a better-integrated

urban landscape. Unfortunately, the anticipation of future freeway need became self-fulfilling. As freeways induced further
growth, the points connected by rural routes merged into a single, indistinguishable mass of suburbia. The accompanying
photos, both taken in 1956, show the Golden State freeway
under construction in Burbank (looking southeast, with the
Alameda interchange in the foregound) and the Santa Ana freeway through Tustin (also looking southeast, at the Tustin Avenue
interchange). (Courtesy of CALTRANS.)

Who Built the Freeways?

Los Angeles' history has been one continuous real estate enterprise, with land speculation a driving force for its never-ending growth. The first great boom was a railroad boom, fed by unprecedented railroad-sponsored promotional campaigns. The early electric railways not only served the land and promoted it, they were also subdividers of the first order; it was real estate, not transit fares, which supported railway construction. Real estate supported a large share of the population as well, either directly or indirectly, bearing the fruit of cash profits. Large land corporations were joined by independent speculators, and huge sums were earned (and lost) in the repackaging of property for homeowners and businesses. The cities grew, new suburban communities were opened, and the metropolis began to take shape, not according to any plan but rather at the subdivider's discretion.

With the establishment of city and regional planning commissions in the early 1920s, the voice of public authority became louder. The documents produced by these two commissions, as well as by assorted ad hoc planning committees, provide us a twofold look at the area's history: they are both blueprints for self-conscious change and contemporary sources of perceived trends and themes. In the effort to curb uncontrolled development of the city by private interests, planning in Los Angeles was clearly creating models for future urban expansion. Traffic congestion, flooding, and irresponsible subdivision spoke to the inadequacy of private enterprise and fragmented municipal authority to solve mounting developmental problems and ensure the desired quality of life. But it is easy to take the notion of planning too literally. In many ways it was simply an attempt to regulate, rationalize, and expedite trends that were perceived to be spontaneous, and so it was more a product than a creator of historical developments.

A major reason that Los Angeles planners have often played a subservient role in the course of events is the area's consistently high rate of growth. The rate was phenomenal during the two planning commissions' first decade, a period when crucial precedents were set in managing the area's decentralization. In its first nine months of operation, for instance, the Regional Planning Commission was called upon to review more than 800 plans for new tracts in unincorporated territory. Los Angeles was being most actively shaped by private real estate developers and, with limited resources and staff, the commission found it difficult simply to keep pace with the onrush of private development.[140] The early drafting of decentralized street plans was perceived as a necessary step toward ensuring that the inevitable development would be orderly. The emphasis on highway construction in the region's periphery was explained by Gordon Whitnall, president of the regional commission:

When we faced the matter of subdivision in the County of Los Angeles . . . subdivisions which were coming like a sea wave rolling over us . . . we reached the conclusion that it would be absolutely necessary to go out into the country and try to beat the subdivider to it by laying out adequate systems of major and secondary highways at least.[141]

Similar problems attended freeway planning some twenty years later. As noted above, the combination of a depression and a world war, while accelerating some state and national planning activities, had re-

Queuing Up for More Freeways

Heavy traffic (shown in lower middle of photo) is backed up for a detour around the construction site of the Alameda Street grade separation over the Santa Ana–Hollywood freeway in 1953. Scenes of congestion were cited as implicit testimony to the popular desire for more freeways: traffic jams were read as public opinion polls by freeway planners. The four-level stack is visible in the background. (Courtesy of CALTRANS.)

133

tarded progress in highway construction. Postwar programs were initiated in an atmosphere of urgency. For example, a major reason for not giving more consideration to putting electric railway tracks down much of the Hollywood freeway—a somewhat popular notion at the time—was that it would delay construction at least five years. In the words of a highway commissioner, "the need for this Hollywood Parkway facility was so great, not only for the San Fernando Valley but the whole metropolitan area, that this delay wasn't justified."[142]

As in the 1920s, new waves of subdivisions encouraged highway construction in areas still awaiting development. The rapid increase in population and its widespread distribution required, as a local head of the Division of Highways pointed out, "consideration of the growth trend rather than present-day traffic pattern as being the proper consideration for long-range planning."[143] Furthermore, acting on long-range planning by building highways in advance of immediate need allowed for less expensive right-of-way and construction costs and offered, as in past highway improvements, an opportunity to control the inevitable growth. "If the freeway can be constructed before there is any appreciable development," wrote another highway official, "it can be established as the guide for the future trend of development in the area."[144]

In a sense, planners on all levels have consistently tried to play down their active role in public policy. Government planning agencies are, after all, bureaucracies, and as such they must walk the often thin line between vested interests and taxpaying citizens. The planning profession has had the added problem of being a relatively new discipline, and even today its functionaries must handle questions of legitimization.

Planners have often had to guard against being considered utopian visionaries.

On the other hand, the principal makers of planning policy for Los Angeles have been far from eccentric. Rather, they have usually been of the same class as and of one mind with both residents and subdividers. For example, Olmsted and Cheney, compilers of *A Major Traffic Street Plan,* were chief consultants on the design of Palos Verdes Estates, whose plans had been released the year before publication of the report.[145] This residential development, located almost 20 miles southwest of downtown, was one of the first major subdivisions to be completely dependent on the automobile. Their coauthor, Harland Bartholomew, wrote elsewhere that "we should decentralize, spread our values over a large area and automatically by this distribution of business and traffic solve the traffic problem."[146]

By the same measure, highway officials were proud of the role they played in opening up rural and undeveloped land for the burgeoning population of Los Angeles. New homes, schools, businesses, and industrial plants all testified to the success of the freeway.[147] With the same sense of pride, the freeway's contribution to the modern capitalist economy was also praised: "Freeways are a means of helping free enterprise cope with the fantastic expansion that is being required of it. Our competitive economy is founded on lessening the economic costs of production and distribution of goods and services."[148] The freeway as a social expenditure joined private capital in facilitating the suburban life-style and serving the prevailing middle-class ethos.

If highway and freeway development has fallen short of its potential in encouraging a just and intelli-

Structural Continuity

Most of the routes of Los Angeles freeways evolved from previous modes of transportation. Four generations of landscape features are shown here: the Los Angeles River, the Southern Pacific railroad (and freight yard), Riverside Drive, and the Golden State freeway (under construction in 1962). With the superimposition of each new transportation improvement the pattern becomes even more permanent. (Courtesy of CALTRANS.)

gently planned community structure, it is not for lack of a "general agreement as to what form of community structure we would wish should we be able to determine it," as one early critic suggested.[149] As has been seen, transportation planning in Los Angeles displayed a clear and consistent vision of the preferred community. Variant reports, such as a comprehensive rapid transit plan presented by Kelker and De Leuw in 1925, were often shelved precisely because they were not consistent with the favored view. Highway and freeway planning, as it proceeded confidently, regularly assumed a popular consensus.

Presumably this collective vision was fairly representative of Los Angeles residents, if their unquestioned taste for dispersal and their deep infatuation with the automobile may be taken as indications of popular sentiment. The planners simply substituted an engineering technique—the traffic survey—for conventional political processes in assessing the general will. Traffic congestion became a political statement, and a highway official could reasonably argue that

continuous traffic studies of the Harbor Freeway as its construction has progressed show the wisdom of the local planning agencies in anticipating a complete network of freeways to adequately serve the tremendous desire for motor vehicle travel in the Los Angeles Metropolitan area.[150]

As a consequence, plans were often presented as being dictated by "reality" and therefore as embodying the only rational option. Such planning, characterized more as a technique or a "science" than as an art, emphasized the priority of the data and, sidestepping all political implications, obscured the possibility of choice.

For what is most apparent in so many of the planning reports is the perceived lack of real alternatives. Transportation programs for the Los Angeles area have all followed the precedent of that early report in 1924. Within that street plan was found a faint recognition that traffic congestion can in itself be self-limiting and force people toward alternatives to traditional streets and highways. At the end of the discussion, however, was the assertion, made manifest by the "trend of things," that "it is the part of wisdom and of conservatism to aim for greater thoroughfare capacity rather than for less."[151] This same "manifest wisdom," prevailing throughout all later planning, provided a leading rationale for the freeway system.

It would indeed be difficult to dispute the manifest nature of such wisdom, given the type of community Los Angeles has evidently chosen to be. It is naive to expect that some Philosopher-Planner would have steered us clear of the incessant accommodation of incessantly growing vehicular traffic. Attempts to restrict use of the automobile, from the 1920 downtown parking ban to restricted car-pool lanes on the Santa Monica freeway in 1976, have all fallen victim to popular resistance. Freeway construction was the logical progression in facilitating automotive mobility. Indeed, there seems to be something inevitable about both the urban form pioneered by Los Angeles and the construction of a freeway system to serve it, once a large enough population has been given the technological means to pursue a vision that is basically anti-technological.

Los Angeles' urban form has been, perhaps to an unprecedented extent, a reflection of choice. To understand why the region became the prototypical dispersed metropolis one must keep in mind the ideal that informed that choice. For fully a century Los Angeles has faithfully adhered to an American bourgeois ideal, an ideal forged primarily from Protestant midwestern and New England small-town and rural sensibilities. Los Angeles was pioneered by the well-to-do, those most capable of actualizing their cultural ideals, and they set the tone for its future development. With its subsequent growth in the early decades of the twentieth century, Los Angeles emerged as America's first essentially middle-class metropolis. Southern California was the right place at the right time, a relatively virgin landscape waiting to be exploited by advancing technology and rising incomes. It was one of America's great experiments, an attempt to build a modern city free from the traumas of overcrowding and the gray ugliness of high-density urbanization. As such, it blazed the trail for much of the nation's future development.

The fact that so many of the city's early converts were midwesterners is not surprising. The Midwest was particularly restless during the late nineteenth and early twentieth centuries. Much of southern California's original mystique was custom-made by midwesterners for midwesterners, and it made Los Angeles a likely stopping point for those who could afford to forsake economic opportunities near home and strike out for a homeowner's paradise of sunny skies and orange trees. But this white American-born base was soon transcended; present-day Los Angeles shows blacks, Mexicans, Japanese, Koreans, and Europeans all buying into a similar vision of the good life. Los Angeles is far from alone in providing a testament to this American ideal. If Los Angeles has begun to lose favor with many Americans, it is not because their values have changed; it is simply that sheer accessibility has soiled an essential element in the vision, the pastoral retreat. Thus, new and improved replicas of Los Angeles have sprung up throughout California, across the Southwest, on the borders of older cities, and indeed throughout the United States. They are monuments to the restlessness of the American spirit and to its contradictory loyalty to a homely, hometown ideal.

138

Now I used to think that I was cool
Running around on fossil fuel
Until I saw what I was doing
Was driving down the road to ruin.
— James Taylor[1]

It was not difficult, during the height of the 1979 gas crisis, to forecast the end of the automobile's prodigal reign and to imagine the freeways standing vacant like some modern Versailles attesting to the sins of excess. Anyone listening to the car radio while awaiting a turn at the gas pumps heard the announcers joke about converting the freeways into bike paths, or skate paths, or tennis courts. It seemed as if obituaries were being written everywhere for the southern California way of life.

Needless to say, the reports of the automobile's demise were exaggerated. It certainly takes more than a panicky month to change an ingrained habit: witness what followed the 1973 crisis. But it is hard to imagine our energy problems vanishing, no matter how hard we might try to ignore them. Fuel supplies can only become less secure, pump prices can only continue to rise, and we can expect only more governmental policies directed toward curbing fossil fuel consumption. It would seem all but certain that we are facing the end of an era.

Just what the transportation future will actually be is less clear. It seems that the only certainty about predictions is that they will be wrong. But if I were to hazard a guess I would say that things will continue essentially the same as they have in the past. We will still be driving automobiles, relating to them as a private means of transporting ourselves wherever we choose to go. Transit patronage will rise to some extent, as more people who work downtown and in other urban centers start taking the bus to work—driving, of course, to the bus stop. It is even very likely that Los Angeles will get a subway, but that additional carrier will make very little difference, probably so little that no more rail systems will be attempted. Finally, the freeways will retain their central place in Los Angeles; in fact, as energy supplies diminish, the freeway's dominance in both the economic and the psychological geography can only increase.

A fuel crisis says little about the relative merit of the automobile vis-à-vis other forms of transportation. What it does say is that we need to use less gasoline. When faced with a shortage we rely on a limited repertoire of immediate responses. Our major response is to drive fewer miles and refrain from speeding. Some of us take the bus more often or try to get into a car pool. And we queue up, for hours if necessary, to purchase a commodity we cannot do without. These immediate responses require that we endure a fair amount of discomfort, but they do get us by. When the pressure eases, conditions veer back toward "normal": we drive more, speed more, ride the bus less, and decide to leave the car pool. Not all of us, of course, and so a fuel crisis does have a long-term effect in changing enough habits so as to make a difference.[2] That is one benefit of having a fuel crisis. An-

other is that it reminds us that we need to take more active steps toward long-term conservation.

The most significant action apropos of curbing gasoline consumption which has been foisted upon us is the rise in prices at the pump. It is foolish to expect, or even to desire, that a scarce but essential commodity will be sold at a price that encourages its waste. Yet gasoline prices, when compared with the costs of other commodities, remained fairly constant for years.[3] Recent price increases by OPEC have changed that relationship, and the decontrol of gasoline prices will change it even more. As an incentive to conserve (or, more accurately, as a disincentive to waste), skyrocketing fuel costs are undoubtedly effective. Such increases may not be the best of all possible ways—they disrupt the economy and add one more hardship for the poor—but they are the only measure that seems to have worked. That gasoline now costs more than a dollar a gallon may be, in consideration of long-range transportation prospects, the best thing that has happened in years.

It seems fairly evident that the latest series of price increases has done more to affect the way we think about gasoline than anything since World War II. A wise government would give conservation a further boost by levying new domestic taxes on gasoline, anticipating the inevitable price rises that will drain our economy through foreign "taxation." But that may be too much to ask of politicians. A wise government would have imposed such a tax years ago. A levy of 35 cents a gallon was indeed part of President Carter's 1977 energy package before it was disemboweled by Congress. Another proposal worthy of consideration is coupon rationing which, unlike "price" rationing, is less favorable to the wealthy. Such a measure, however, became a feasible option only after fuel prices had soared to a previously unimaginable level; and not only would rationing be unwieldy, but the politics involved would probably guarantee that no truly effective program could ever get out of Congress.

What the federal government has done is to regulate automobile efficiency, which is the second important step toward dealing with the energy problem. The Energy Policy and Conservation Act of 1975 mandated fuel economy standards for new automobiles marketed or imported after 1977, and by 1985 each manufacturer's new car fleet must average 27.5 miles per gallon. That is almost double the current average for American cars now on the road; it will be, when effected, the first significant increase in automobile efficiency since the times of the Model A.[4] Substantially higher prices at the pump make gas-efficient cars extremely marketable, as anyone who has been on the waiting list for a Honda Civic will tell you. In addition, a "gas-guzzler tax," passed in 1978 and going into effect with the 1980 model line, will further discourage the purchase of the most inefficient vehicles.[5]

One prediction for Los Angeles is therefore certain: southern Californians, like all Americans, will be driving smaller cars that use less gas. The potential effect of this change is mind boggling. Transportation economist Charles Lave has reported that simply increasing fuel efficiency by raising the average rate from 15.0 to 15.2 miles per gallon would save more energy than doubling public transit patronage.[6] There is no single conceivable strategy, short of banning half our cars

from the streets, which will provide the savings in store for us in a few years through improved automobile technology. It may still be advisable, of course, to encourage transit patronage and car-pooling, measures that do a lot to ease highway congestion. But apropos of energy, attacking the problem at the source and reducing gasoline consumption by private automobiles is overwhelmingly the simplest and the most effective response.

Because I have every reason to expect that gas prices will continue to rise and that the average automobile will become much more efficient, I see no reason to think that the other aspects of our transportation future will be significantly different. Every advantage that recommended the automobile to most Americans during the past fifty years will continue to do so; and Los Angeles will remain an "Autopia." Future gas crises may require short-term readjustments, but their long-term effect will be a return to an equilibrium supported by ever more efficient automobile technology. The psychology of car ownership will surely change, with "sleek" and "sporty" replacing "powerful" and "luxurious" as preferred adjectives, and auto makers will boast their latest estimates on control of pollution and increased mileage rates. What we are witnessing in many respects is more the end of a fashion than of an era.

But what of mass rapid transit, of fixed-rail systems, of subways and elevated lines? No doubt many would hope that Los Angeles would now come to its collective senses and build a more reasonable alternative to the chaos of private cars. Long-term supporters of rail transit must now feel vindicated: L.A. sealed its own fate and is now paying the wages of having thrice voted down rail systems in recent years (1968, 1974, 1976). Probably most people would be as surprised as I was to learn that fixed-rail transit would not help at all. The automobile remains a far superior form of transportation. When augmented by a good bus system, it can actually beat rail transit at its own game.

Many of us—myself included—have long cherished a set of transportation myths. We assume mass transit is the obvious response to an energy crisis. After all, it is self-evident that higher occupancy vehicles are more efficient. But rapid transit is more complicated than that, and only recently has there been extensive research to investigate the assumed superiority of fixed-rail and other public transit systems. Not only have older systems received further scrutiny, but for fifteen years there have been experiments financed by the Urban Mass Transit Administration (over $6.5 billion worth),[7] as well as the BART project in San Francisco, to test transit-related questions.

The Bay Area Rapid Transit system, constructed as it was in a perfect setting, provides a particularly useful test of a modern rail system. San Francisco has a concentrated downtown business district, staffed by suburbanites making long commutes (nearly twice as long as the L.A. average) from narrow strips of low-density residential development.[8] Hardly any other city could have so favorable a public climate for mass transit, where cable cars and streetcars still survive and are as central a part of the civic image as the freeway is in Los Angeles. (In 1959 new freeway building was actually banned in San Francisco.) Yet BART, like all modern transit projects, has failed to keep its promise.

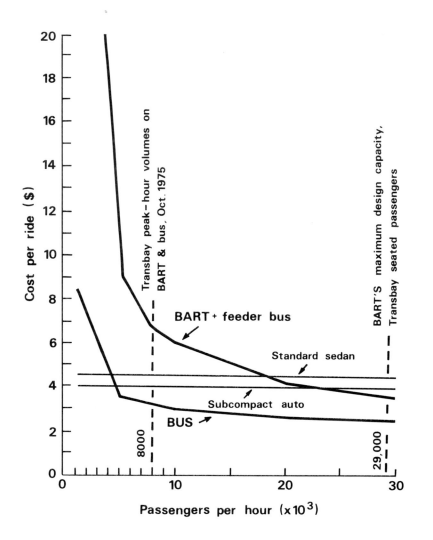

TIME REQUIRED TO REPAY BART ENERGY INVESTMENT

Situation	Years to repay	
	14 miles/gal. automobile efficiency	27.5 miles/gal. automobile efficiency
Current BART (130,000 trips/day, 30 percent load factor, 46.5 percent of passengers from automobiles)	535	Never; more energy wasted each year
Current but with 75 percent of passengers from automobiles	163	Never; more energy wasted each year
Current but with 50 percent load factor	139	502
Current but with 260,000 trips/day	266	Never; more energy wasted each year
Ideal (260,000 trips/day, 50 percent load factor, 75 percent of passengers from automobiles)	44	168

NOTE: Load factor is a measure of used capacity, that is, the percentage of seats actually used. BART's current load factor is about average for the United States. No system has ever achieved a 50 percent load factor or is likely to do so, given the need to run trains both with and against traffic and during both peak and off-peak hours.

Evaluating Rail Rapid Transit

There may be good reasons to build subways and other heavy rail transit systems, but neither economy nor energy efficiency are among them. The accompanying tables show how San Francisco's Bay Area Rapid Transit system (BART) fares on both accounts. Studies of the full costs of carrying one passenger on a transbay ride shows that even if BART were to achieve its full design efficiency, it would cost more per passenger trip than would the use of buses; and it may continue to cost more than a private automobile. A separate study of BART's energy costs, which include the energy used in construction, shows that it will take many years of energy savings to repay that investment—if BART is lucky. More realistic scenarios show an energy loss. (Sources: first table from Melvin M. Webber, The BART Experience—What Have We Learned? *Institute of Urban and Regional Development, University of California, Berkeley, 1976, p. 24; second table from Charles A. Lave, "Rail Rapid Transit and Energy: The Adverse Effects,"* Transportation Research Record *648 [1977], 17.)*

The best assets of fixed-rail transit systems these days are public ignorance and a strong desire to believe. Professor Lave has summarized what must be the first four commandments for rapid-transit advocates: good transit systems can attract people out of their cars, decrease private automobile ownership, save scarce energy resources, and be more economical than cars.[9] Lave proves that the above assumptions are myth, and BART belies that myth as well as any system.

The BART system has attracted relatively few people from their cars. Only about 35 percent of its passengers had previously made the trip by driving their own cars. About half of them, on the other hand, had previously ridden buses or been riders in car pools, with the former category predominating. Buses, by the way, are substantially more energy efficient than subways, and car pools require virtually no extra energy. In addition, BART had the same effect as all transportation improvements in the past—from the first streetcars to the freeways— of generating trips that were not made before. Not only were roughly 15 percent of BART trips induced, but by removing some 14,000 vehicles from the streets and highways, new automobile trips were encouraged as well. The net result has been increased accessibility, meaning an increase in the number of trips but little overall reduction in highway use.[10]

BART has had no effect on decreasing car ownership even among its patrons. The average number of cars per BART household is no less than the average car ownership among its users before they switched to rapid transit. (The weighted average is actually a little higher.) BART does not replace the second car, it merely supplements it. As Lave observes, "one should not be surprised if a family that switches its commuting trips to transit still retains second cars for its non-work trips."[11] BART will not take you to the market, drive the kids to school, or transport you to all the other places that account for 60 percent of your car's mileage.

The situation is really depressing when one evaluates BART in terms of energy, which is probably the most salient criterion in contemporary discussions. BART comes close to wasting energy. Its operating efficiency lies somewhere between that of a bus and that of a car, but because it draws heavily from former bus riders its actual savings are small. According to Lave, who used ridership figures that are somewhat biased in favor of BART and credited the system with saving the energy that would have been needed to construct highways to accommodate its present patrons, it will take BART 535 years of energy savings merely to pay back the initial energy investment used to build the system in the first place! That is less than 0.2 percent annual return on energy investment. And the calculation ignores the fact that if the average auto fuel efficiency should ever reach the 27.5 miles per gallon that Congress has mandated, BART will operate 15 percent less efficiently than a private automobile. Even if BART should do the seemingly impossible and double its patronage, divert 75 percent of its passengers from cars, and operate at a 50 percent load factor, it would take 168 years of operation before it would break even. Any conditions that could affect so radical and unprecedented a change in transit patterns would also surely turn many people toward maximum-efficiency cars. Realistically speaking, no matter what happens, BART will have been a waste of energy.[12]

If that conclusion is not depressing enough, rapid transit's worst liability is its cost. It is about two-thirds more expensive than even a private auto–based system of transportation, but it must charge less to attract riders. It therefore requires a public subsidy larger than any highway lobbyist would ever have dared to ask for. Lave reports the 1975 national transit deficit at $1.7 billion to serve 2.5 percent of urban travel, and that deficit has been rising at an average rate of 59 percent a year.[13] BART researchers have compared the cost of a transbay trip by subway with the cost of the same trip by bus, standard sedan, and subcompact auto. They weighted their figures in favor of transit by calculating all conceivable auto-related expenses, including air-pollution and nonmonetary impacts such as the noise endured by neighbors, and by hypothesizing an optimally effective transit system. The most transit-favored estimate showed BART costing $6.67 per transbay trip, as compared with $4.49 for a standard sedan, $4.05 for a subcompact, and $3.21 for a bus. Estimates that were less favorable to BART, but still based on reasonable assumptions, rated a subway trip at $11.96 and a standard sedan at only $7.79. In all cases, bus transit was the least costly and rail rapid transit the most expensive.[14]

Finally, the huge subsidy required by BART cheapens commutes for a generally well-to-do clientele. By attracting long-distance suburban commuters traveling to the central business district, BART draws most heavily from the upper levels of income distribution. Yet BART is heavily financed by local sales taxes and property taxes. The result is that "the percentage of income paid to provide tax support for each ride

taken is 40 times greater for an individual in the lowest income group than for one in the highest group. Clearly, the poor are paying and the rich are riding."[15]

It would be gratifying if we could say that BART's wastefulness is unique. We cannot reach that conclusion, however; Lave contends that it is "clear that to the extent that BART is atypical, it is atypically efficient."[16] It is true that the system has been unduly plagued by operational and labor problems, but there is no guarantee that its problems are exceptional. In any event, BART's showing in regard to energy and cost is so bad that significant improvement cannot possibly be expected, no matter what its future. Such transit systems simply do not work, at least not well enough to justify the tremendous investment. Certainly they offer no solution to the problems of energy and mobility facing the country today.

Given so poor a showing, why has mass transit, so long suffering from falling patronage and public neglect, suddenly become the darling of proponents of urban transportation? Why do so many people automatically assume that, as energy gets tight, subways and other rapid transit facilities will rise inevitably from the ashes of the decrepit, archaic freeway?

One reason is that we are caught up in a set of antiquated notions that equate "real cities" with the "real rapid transit" of elevateds and subways (mostly built when electric railways were the mainstay of urban transport). We base our notions on the exceptions, on the few cities that, because they developed when average incomes were low and technology was primitive, maintain a unique pattern of settlement in which rail rapid transit could survive, largely because local government was willing to subsidize its operation.[17]

We employ a nostalgic symbol of "the good old days" and refurbish it with the space-age technology of a science-fiction fantasy, creating a mythological cure for real social problems.

If a myth is good, if it serves its function of quelling our anxieties when we are faced with the complexities of modern social life, then we will battle the obstacles of reason in its defense. A particularly blatant example is a report prepared by consultants for the Southern California Rapid Transit district in 1974, consultants who have been researching transportation policy in Los Angeles for nearly two decades. After hundreds of thousands of dollars were spent to reevaluate previous estimates for a proposed fixed-rail system, it was discovered that earlier studies contained inflated patronage projections. The new figures showed that the large heavy-rail system long under study was simply not justified. But it takes more than mathematics to kill a deity. The researchers simply dismissed the earlier findings, arguing that "all the results noted . . . are contrary to common sense and seem to ignore the re-alistics [sic] of everyday life in the Los Angeles area."[13] They then projected an "expectable system capture potential" based primarily on the inclusion of every commuter driving more than half an hour to work.[18]

I must confess that I was deeply disheartened to discover that a modern fixed-rail system was not the solution to Los Angeles' transportation problems. I enjoy subways and find them much more exciting than freeways. I like the pedestrian environments they support; I enjoy visiting subway cities much more than nonsubway cities (though I have never lived in any city that had subways). Although I own a car, I regu-larly ride buses in Los Angeles, recognizing the advantages of public transit. But talking about subways and downtown people movers at so critical a time only diverts attention from real solutions to transportation and energy problems. Politicians who focus on rail and other "fixed-guideway" systems are modern Marie Antoinettes who, upon learning that their constituents cannot buy gas to run their cars, suggest that they ride transit.

There are other factors that may justify high-technology mass-transit systems besides cost and energy. They are compact, and they often have a less adverse impact than automobiles (unless, of course, they in turn encourage even more automobile trips to the areas they serve). Perhaps downtown Los Angeles would be improved by a people-mover system; I have no immediate arguments against the notion that Disneyland provides a workable model for a society. Perhaps we should build a subway beneath Wilshire Boulevard, thereby giving the popular 83 bus a chance to operate underground. But such measures will waste energy, do little to end congestion, and cost a lot of money. The $2 billion estimated for the subway would buy nearly half a million Volkswagen Rabbits. Everybody driving on Wilshire could simply be given a new car and we would save money, save energy, and reduce congestion; none of these purposes will probably be served by the subway itself.

Fortunately, there is another way of providing mass rapid transit in Los Angeles: use the freeways for buses. Operating buses on freeways is not a new idea, but there are some relatively new strategies for making such a transit program more attractive (see the Appendix for further discussion). The most important proposal is to build more fixed guideways designed for the exclusive use of high-occupancy vehicles. Such guideways, like the 11-mile El Monte busway on the San Bernardino freeway, free buses and car pools from the need to do battle in rush-hour congestion, making them a more truly rapid form of public transit.

The California Department of Transportation (Caltrans) already has several proposed busway systems on the boards.[19] The most comprehensive suggestion calls for exclusive guideways on 100 miles of freeway, served by 100 stations (which include on-line bus stops) and 30,000 commuter parking spaces. The estimated capital cost to construct this system is about 1.5 billion 1978 dollars (which does not include the cost of building 24 miles of guideway included in the original designs for the proposed Century freeway and Long Beach freeway extension, or the expenses involved in the existing 11 miles on the San Bernardino). An additional $715 million or so would be allocated to purchase 1,000 new buses which would run on the guideways as well as on an additional 328 miles of mixed-flow freeway. Although the combined price of over $2.3 billion is a lot of money, it is a bargain compared with the $2 billion needed for only 18 miles of subway. Whether the entire system will ever actually be built is open to doubt, but Caltrans is prepared to begin advance planning on exclusive guideways for parts of the Harbor and Santa Ana freeways, and both projects are eligible for 92 percent federal funding. (As of this writing, progress has been delayed on these projects for up to two years. Owing to local political pressures for fixed-rail transit, an executive-level order was issued to restudy the proposals, now for the third time, so as to compare them with the alternative of running rapid transit trains along the freeways.)

The addition of exclusive bus and car-pool lanes to already existing major freeways would provide virtually all the features of a subway. Busways, like subways, are fixed-guideway systems with an exclusive right-of-way to serve major corridors of urban movement. They can offer frequent service between on-line stations, much as any fixed-rail system does, but they have the added advantage of flexibility, as conventional buses do. Buses need not stop at every station, permitting a variety of express services. Some buses, like park-and-ride ones, can pick up all their passengers at a particular point. Others can pick up passengers on traditional surface routes and then head toward the busway, reducing the need for transfers. Exclusive busways have been shown to attract the same clientele as subways—usually middle-class suburbanites who would rather not fight freeway traffic in driving to the office. Contrary to what one might expect, most such commuters really do not care if the vehicle they are riding is a sleek, space-age electric train or a comfortable bus; they care about how quickly and reliably they get from their homes to their places of work.[20]

The use of buses for such commuters has another advantages: once the rush hour is over, lots of vehicles are available to serve the local needs of central city residents. The discount price tags of such systems also mean, at least theoretically, that more money could be spent in such areas. Thus a commitment to buses instead of subways means that we can really help those who most need public transit: working-class commuters who need crosstown service to industrial

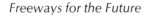
Freeways for the Future

The construction of exclusive bus and carpool lanes may offer the most rational response to future transportation needs by encouraging more intensive use of existing facilities. The 135-mile busway system presently proposed would provide fixed-guideway rapid transit at a fraction of the cost of a comparable rail system. Design standards stipulate, however, that these exclusive lanes be built to rail specifications for possible future conversion. Such a busway system, if built, would exert a strong and continuing influence on the metropolis no matter what the future transportation scenario should be. Shown here is the San Bernardino busway to the right of the San Bernardino freeway, looking west toward downtown. (Photo by Mason Dooley.)

148

jobs; the elderly who need buses to go shopping, see their doctors, or visit friends; and all others who do not commute downtown everyday to jobs, who do not have the money to buy cars, or who, for some reason or other, do not drive. Whereas fixed-rail transit is a regressive burden on those who are dependent on public transportation, better bus service gives them precisely what they need.

Freeway bus lanes have one other advantage over fixed-rail transit: they can actually save energy. The cost of constructing two lanes of freeway on an existing right-of-way is a fraction of the amount needed to dig a subway, and buses are the most energy-efficient form of transportation.[21] Whether busways will save very much energy is open to debate. Much depends on to what extent external factors encourage people to switch to buses or car pools for getting to work. There is also that omnipresent devil of all transportation improvements: induced speed and induced travel. A Caltrans study revealed that its present ramp-metering program actually raised energy consumption slightly, because it permitted travel at higher speeds.[22] Should the busways have the intended impact of reducing freeway congestion, we can expect similar results as well, somewhat undermining the initial energy gains. In any event, if we want to build a mass rapid transit system in Los Angeles, fixed-guideway bus and car-pool lanes are by far the most practical program at hand, offering the least expensive and the most effective service conceivable.

I have one final observation apropos the future of transportation in Los Angeles. No matter what the scenario, we can expect the freeways to become more important in the spatial organization of urban life. They will continue to encourage the aggregation of certain types of economic activity, as they have been doing for the past thirty years. This influence can only be accelerated by the proposed busway systems, for it further entrenches the freeway's dominance of public movement. The freeways are in fact a much more effective concentrator of activity than any fixed-rail system could be, because virtually everybody uses them at least some of the time and they accommodate all kinds of trips. Take BART again as a point of comparison. With the probable exception of the downtown San Francisco financial district, BART has had little effect on urban form, especially in the suburban periphery of the Bay Area. There have been none of the high-rise offices or apartments, none of the compact shopping malls or industrial parks, which the freeway system has inspired in greater Los Angeles (and I would assume in greater San Francisco as well).[23] Ironically, if the time should ever come when we really want a fixed-rail transit system in Los Angeles, we will have not only the exclusive rights-of-way of freeways and busways to build them on, but we will also be much closer to an urban pattern appropriate to such a system.

But I will leave that subject to the daydreams of futurists. A far more realistic expectation is for more of the same, interrupted by an occasional attack of collective anxiety during a fuel shortage, disciplining any tendency to lapse back into gross excess. One thing is certain: the extreme value granted mobility in our society, a value incarnate in cars and freeways, will be one of the last to go.

Transportation planning in Los Angeles has been consistently marked by two features: systematic adaptation to the automobile and continuing inability to execute significant public transit improvements. The neglect of public transportation was not for lack of vision. From 1906 on, a series of proposals for mass rapid transit have been put forward, most of them based on an electrified rail system. Attempts to act on these plans, however, were plagued by numerous obstacles, many of which highway and freeway development could circumvent. The following is a brief look at two particularly critical periods, both marked by rail rapid transit proposals that had a good chance of being realized, and at the reasons for the failure to implement them.

The 1920s

Although Los Angeles' first real city plan—the *Major Traffic Street Plan,* presented in 1924—was restricted explicitly to improvements in streets, it acknowledged the importance of coordinating the traffic system with street railways, rapid transit, and railroads (not to mention flood protection and drainage systems, schools, playgrounds, and parks). Since the streetcar was assumed to be necessary and desirable, "its freedom of movement must be provided for."[1] But the plan gave few details as to how the electric railway would fit into a comprehensive plan for improving regional transportation. This information was provided the following year, in a work prepared for the city and regional planning commissions by Kelker, De Leuw, and Company of Chicago. Their *Report and Recommendations on a Comprehensive Rapid Transit Plan for the City and County of Los Angeles* addressed itself to the same basic problems as had the *Street*

Plan: traffic congestion and the role of transportation in the development of the metropolis. In the concern expressed in the letter of transmittal, the 1925 plan harmonizes with its automotive-oriented predecessor in stressing that "a clear cut recognition of the fundamental relationship of transportation to the growth of a city is essential to the determination of a sound developmental policy." This study, however, turned toward improvement of the electric railway system as the key to the city's future. It opens with the following argument:

Los Angeles has become a large metropolitan center and it is of vital importance, at this time, that transportation facilities be planned upon a scale commensurate with the present and prospective development of the City and County. The phenomenal growth in population and industrial activity, together with the tremendous increase in street traffic, makes the construction of rapid transit lines not only necessary, but imperative if an adequate, quick, and convenient means of public transportation is to be provided and traffic conditions are to be improved.[2]

The report, in effect, recognized the transformation of Los Angeles from a rural to a metropolitan region. As Nelson and Clark have more recently observed, "there was something not quite urban about a city that had no subways or elevated trains, but instead depended on the street car or interurban for mass transit."[3] The Kelker, De Leuw plan was an attempt to rectify the contradiction by constructing those very subways and elevateds which would have allowed interurban lines to efficiently accommodate intraurban patterns of movement.

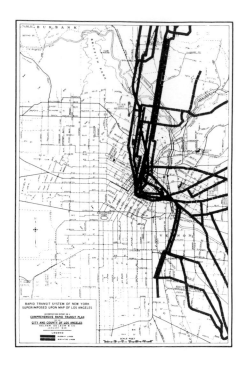

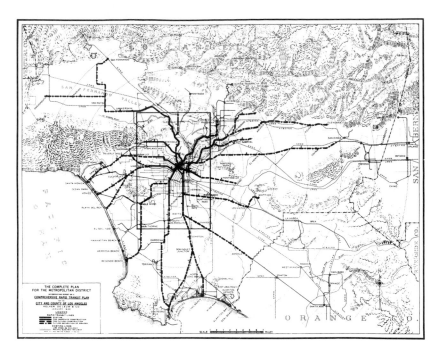

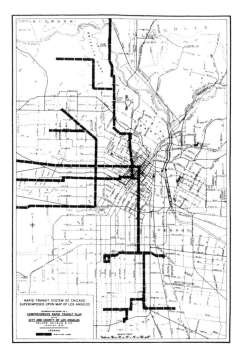

Rapid Transit Plan, 1925

These three plates appear in the Kelker, De Leuw and Co. report submitted to the City and Regional Planning commissions. The complete plan was the most ambitious public transit proposal ever suggested in southern California. The existing rapid transit visible on the Los Angeles map was the 0.8-mile Hollywood subway and a few grade separations, all in the downtown area. Comparison with eastern cities reveals some of the problems facing such a system in Los Angeles. New York, which began constructing elevateds in the 1880s, had in 1925 an overall population density of 31 persons per acre; Chicago, which began its elevateds in the 1890s, had 22 persons per acre. Los Angeles had an overall population density of 4.2 persons per acre, with 10.2 per acre in urbanized areas. In 1925 the average Angeleno rode transit half as often as the average Chicagoan and less than a third as often as a New Yorker.

What the report offered was a remarkably extensive rapid transit plan. If the proposals had been completely carried out, the system would serve virtually every developed corner of the county. Comparison of the plan with the systems in four other United States cities showed that it would have provided the most extensive rapid transit system then, or now, in existence.

The heart of the plan was a two-stage construction of subways and elevateds. Four basic radial passenger lines were scheduled for completion within ten years. Eventually this core system would be elaborated by extensions connecting with communities on the county's perimeter. The total system would have included about 26 miles of subways and 85 miles of elevated lines, as well as extensive private surface rights-of-way.[4] The proposal embodied three supportive elements: improvement of Pacific Electric freight facilities, an increase in crosstown streetcar service, and development of crosstown bus service. The latter two improvements showed a recognition of the fact that people were focusing less on the downtown area than on outlying districts, a movement that had already become significant owing to the motor car. But the map outlining the system clearly illustrates an emphasis on the central district, and so only a few bypass routes were detailed.

The Kelker, De Leuw proposals were predicated on increased public interest in rapid transit. The authors explicitly recognized that even expanded patronage would not form a self-sustaining basis for construction and operation. The improvements were to be funded primarily through city and county bonds and assessments, except for freight improvements, which were to be the responsibility of the Pacific Electric Railway alone. The plan would have required administrative as well as financial assistance from public authority so as to implement a suggested coordination of transit operations. It is not unlikely that the authors would have preferred complete municipalization of all public transportation, yet the nature of the necessary agreements or consolidation was left undecided in recognition of the complex political maneuvering required.

The report also briefly summarized the street traffic problem per se, at the same time commending the *Major Traffic Street Plan*. The rapid-transit plan was obviously conceived as a complement to the street plan, and it did, in fact, provide the missing element suggested by the earlier report. But even massive street improvements could do only so much, or so Kelker and De Leuw argued. Increasingly, people would have to resort to public transportation to cope with the inevitable saturation of the central business district.[5]

Like every proposal for publicly sponsored rail rapid transit in Los Angeles history, the Kelker, De Leuw report never got beyond the planning stage. Though the transit proposals may very well have been a step toward a better Los Angeles, they were not so for the reasons advanced. Kelker and De Leuw were working with a set of assumptions that were no longer quite accurate for describing the sort of city Los Angeles was becoming. Public rapid transit, though perhaps desirable, would no longer be a necessity for a major metropolitan center. And more unprecedented, neither would a vital downtown district.

Inherent in the report was a contradiction with the earlier street plan and with the trend of events in general which would prevent its actualization: any fixed-rail rapid transit system, especially the radially aligned plan presented, would work to preserve, if not to intensify, patterns of concentration. Kelker and De Leuw were not unaware of Los Angeles' uniqueness. They cited the low-density population and the large number of single-family homes as among the region's more alluring charms. Nevertheless, their argument that efficient and reasonably priced rapid transit would only aid in continuing the orderly spread of population[6] was apparently unconvincing. It was on this issue—the preferred vision for future development of the metropolis—that debate centered.

The most important challenge to the proposal came from the City Club of Los Angeles, an influential organization of professionals which concerned itself with civic issues.[7] A seven-member committee was formed to consider the Kelker, De Leuw report. Several particulars of the plan, such as "circumstantial lines" and even limited subway or elevated lines, were endorsed. Yet all but one committee member agreed that implementation of a comprehensive fixed-rail rapid transit system would prove contrary to the area's best interests.

The committee members' argument was simple. The most important issue in transportation planning, they said, was relief of congestion. Subways and elevated railways would work toward the contrary; they would concentrate, and therefore congest, population. With the automobile and the telephone, such solutions were no longer necessary; nor, according to the majority report, were they desirable. Los Angeles was pioneering a new urban form, for "the great city of the future will be a harmoniously developed community of local centers and garden cities, a district in which the need for transportation over long distances at a rapid rate will be reduced to the minimum."[8] Swayed by arguments such as these, both city and county governments shelved the Kelker, De Leuw proposal.

The City Club report, issued late in January 1926, cast a dark shadow over prospects for implementation of the rapid transit plan. A second major blow came three months later.

Early in the same month the Pacific Electric had joined the Southern Pacific, Santa Fe, and Union Pacific railroads in putting forward a plan that suggested a partial sharing of facilities. A major proposal in the plan was to build four miles of elevated trolley lines in the downtown area which would eliminate 18,000 individual street crossings each day. Two new passenger terminals were also suggested: one at Fourth and Central streets, to be shared by Southern Pacific, Union Pacific, and Pacific Electric, and the second to be a separate Santa Fe terminal farther east. This package was opposed by the *Los Angeles Times,* which preferred a single union station located near the traditional Plaza. The *Times*-sponsored plan would have eliminated the Pacific Electric from participation, including the elevated railways. Debate over the two proposals focused on the elevated lines, and a referendum was set to decide the issue.[9]

Proponents of the plan sponsored by the rail companies included the Los Angeles and other regional chambers of commerce, the traffic commission, numerous civic groups, and all the major local papers except the *Times.* They argued that a union terminal was unnecessary (as Los Angeles was not a midway stop on rail trips, a single transfer site was useless) and that it was essential to aid the Pacific Electric, which carried three times as many passengers as all the railroads combined. "The fatal weakness of the Plaza Terminal Plan," said the *Los Angeles Examiner,* "is that it leaves the Pacific Electric entirely out of the picture."[10]

But Harry Chandler and the *Times* mounted a formidable opposition. Launching a journalistic barrage against the proposal for elevated lines, the newspaper urged voters to "Keep the L out of Los Angeles." It argued the merits of a palatial union station, held up the specter of railroad monopolies trampling on "the people's" will, and mounted sharp attacks against elevated railways. The paper ran up to five "articles" a day ("editorials" would be a more precise description), blasting elevated lines and frequently running photographs of disasters on such lines in the East. The *Times* used the occasion to attack not only the modest

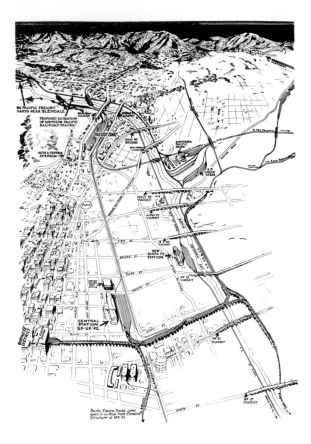

Defeated Elevated Railway Proposal

This sketch shows the railroad companies' plan for two new rail stations, which was defeated by the voters in 1926. Four miles of elevated railway were to be built in the mostly industrial eastern section of downtown, carrying passengers heading for points north, east, and south. Although the plan was supported by downtown business interests and most of the daily newspapers, it was bitterly opposed by the Los Angeles Times. A single union station excluding Pacific Electric was selected instead for the Plaza area. (Source: Union Pacific System, et al., The Solution of Los Angeles Station Problem, *1925.)*

railroad plan but the entire concept of the elevated railway, specifically including the Kelker, De Leuw proposal. Often ignoring the fact that at issue were only four miles of overhead construction on private rights-of-way, the newspaper tied the station issue to the eventual construction of 61 miles of elevateds in the central area, many along public streets. The choice, as the *Times* saw it, was to have "a union depot or elevateds," to have a beautiful new terminal the city could be proud of, or "hideous, cluttering, dusty, dangerous, street darkening trestles in our downtown area."[11] (Interestingly, the paper occasionally championed the subway as a wonderful alternative, though it never offered specific proposals. And though it condemned elevateds as "expensive," it never mentioned that even the most elaborate ones would cost a fourth as much as the simplest subways.)[12] Despite the inconsistency of its campaign, however, the *Times* did in all likelihood reflect the prevailing popular sentiment. In any event, the straw vote saw the Plaza site narrowly approved and the "El" soundly defeated.

The inability of local rapid transit proponents to get their proposals off the planning boards and out of political chambers reflects more than a simple rejection of "eastern" devices. A 1906 subway proposal was killed by a business recession. Expenses chopped the Hollywood subway, opened in 1925, down to a tunnel less than a mile long from its envisioned four-mile course.[13] Finances were, as always, the insurmountable obstacle. The privately held Pacific Electric corporation could finance only the most modest capital improvements. (The four miles of elevated tracks included in the PE-backed terminal plan would have been affordable, at $2 million, only because construction costs would have been shared by the more capital-rich railroads.) A comprehensive system of any sort would have required public backing. Kelker and De Leuw were asking for $120 million for the first stage of their plan alone.[14] Yet it was a difficult time to secure such backing, as rapid transit had to compete with all other municipal improvements, such as schools, water supply, flood control, and an expanding array of public services, including highway improvements. The Kelker, De Leuw proposal was submitted after the *Major Traffic Street Plan* had already been approved and partly funded.[15] Since the proposal followed almost immediately upon the ideological and financial commitment to automotive transportation, it is questionable whether area voters would have approved the bonds necessary for the sys-

tem's construction, had they been given the choice. One can only imagine the strength of the *Times* opposition to a bond issue for elevated lines. And it certainly did not help that the most articulate municipal policymakers were members of the professional middle classes, and in Los Angeles that meant they were automobile commuters. If elevateds would help to ease traffic congestion, the proposal was certainly worthy of consideration, but the prime concern was to make life easier for the automobile.

The situation was further complicated by the inclusion in the public debate of indirectly related issues, such as the argument over the merits of a union station. Three years earlier, in 1923, a subway station proposal was defeated in large part because of a furor over trees. Hoping to fit the Hollywood subway into a more comprehensive system, transit supporters had won substantial political backing for a connecting station under centrally located Pershing Square. Opponents objected that the high ceiling required for the construction would destroy most of the trees in the square. A city council ordinance requiring a ceiling below the ten-foot-deep root system of the trees terminated the project.[16] (A city, of course, can change its collective mind. In 1951 Pershing Square was excavated and 200,000 cubic yards of soil were removed to make way for a three-level, 2,000-car underground garage. New trees were planted in the square. The garage was completed the same year as the downtown freeway interchange, and its supporters associated the two projects as a combined attack on traffic congestion.)[17]

The improbability of private financing of rapid transit proposals becomes obvious when one discovers that the railways could hardly earn their own operating expenses. The compact and heavily traveled downtown streetcar system operated by the Los Angeles Railway stayed in the black through most of the predepression years, but as a paying investment the Pacific Electric was a disaster. From its incorporation in 1911 until 1941 (the beginning of an anomalous good period, owing to World War II) it turned a profit only three times, in 1912, 1913, and 1923.[18] It could survive only as part of the huge Southern Pacific conglomerate. It is obvious with hindsight that the only way a vital system of rail public transit could survive would have been with municipal support.

Such an observation was made as early as 1911, though it was suggested more as a forecast than as an immediate proposal.[19] Fourteen years later the city attempted to purchase the Los Angeles Railway from its owner, Henry Huntington, but the negotiations were halted when Huntington died.[20]

For the Pacific Electric interurban lines, full municipalization was never seriously considered. The closest approximation to that ideal was recommendations of municipal support for rapid transit improvements. A major block to further public participation was the management of Pacific Electric. Mark Foster describes the official attitude toward municipal ownership as one of contempt. In 1928, in its official journal, the company proclaimed that "when the facts are known, then there will be no fear that the radical and half-baked notion [of public ownership] will triumph."[21] This statement, together with analogous statements by private citizens, planners, and utility commission members, underscores a naive apprehension of the future course of the area's history. No one really recognized the severe threat the automobile was presenting to all electric railways. The already difficult financial situation was perceived, even in the 1930s, as a temporary setback.[22] As electric railways were an assumed necessity for any city, their survival was simply assumed. One can only speculate that, had public and corporate officials known better, they would have responded differently.

At the time, each separate defeat for a transit proposal was perceived more as a delay than as a rejection of the whole idea of rapid transit. The cumulative effect of such defeats, however, was disastrous. Even many of the planners originally behind the Kelker, De Leuw proposal became wary. For example, by 1927 Gordon Whitnall, the Regional Planning Commission head who originally backed the proposal, had begun to change his mind, becoming increasingly convinced that the automobile provided the more reasonable alternative. The area was undergoing rapid transformation, and planners feared the inflexibility of fixed-rail transportation facilities. In 1928 the commission cited a New York study which found that subways were proving unable to keep pace with demand and that new construction was creating new centers of congestion. With every passing year of debate the Kelker, De Leuw proposal was becoming more and more untenable.[23]

In Los Angeles, a tendency to decentralization had long been at work, and one might seriously question whether any fixed-rail system could have successfully competed with the area's growing obsession with the car. Rail rapid transit would have required the compromise of a walking city while automotive transit ide-

ally served the preferred pattern. Both Los Angeles planners and voters were ultimately unwilling to make such a compromise.

By failing to replace streetcars with a rapid transit system, Los Angeles effectively cast its lot. The Kelker, De Leuw proposal, offered at a time when passenger revenues (if not profits) of electric rail companies were growing, was a crossroads in the course of the city's self-definition. The rejection of rapid transit improvements stemmed largely from a rejection of the image of the industrial city in favor of the image of a pastoral garden city. With its failure to construct a transportation system appropriate to "a Great American City," Los Angeles firmly committed itself to a redefinition of the nature of an urban metropolis.

The Freeway Era

Later critics of the freeway system would indict it as the archnemesis of public transit, and, to be sure, the freeway is a haven for individual mobility. But freeways were intended to serve an entire community, and throughout the years of their development they were envisioned as a vital supplement to public transportation.

Since *A Transit Program for the Los Angeles Metropolitan Area* appeared in 1939, the freeway has been considered in relationship to public transit. This first report, true to its title, examined the total transportation situation in the metropolis. At the time there were both a million automobiles and a million daily revenue passengers on public transportation in the area,[24] and a large portion of the study was devoted to the issue of mass transit. Based on expected figures for future growth, there is a repeated acceptance of rail rapid transit as the "ultimate solution" for the area's transportation problems. The report offers several possible improvements, including electric railways operating on certain freeways, and perhaps the first suggestion of a Wilshire Boulevard subway and its eventual connection with the San Fernando Valley.

Any attempts to revitalize that mode of transit within the immediate future, however, were dismissed as impractical during the "intermediate stage," owing to prohibitive costs. Transit needs for this period of rapid growth combined with continuing low densities would be best served by running express buses on the rapid transit facilities provided through freeway construction. The operation of this system should remain private, the report argued, though there should be increased public coordination.

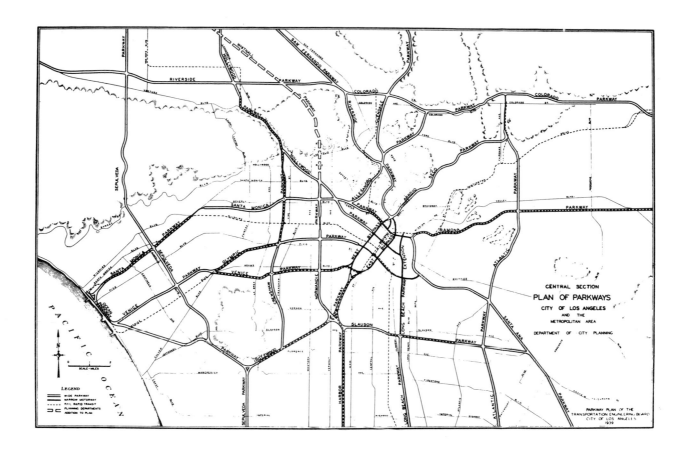

Freeway Transit, 1939

The most influential report in the early planning of the freeway system, prepared by the Transportation Engineering Board of the City of Los Angeles, recommended wide center strips in key portions of the freeway system to be used later for a heavy rail system. Drafters of the plan argued that "the broken lines in the centers of certain double lined parkway routes represent a most intensive and effective use of the investment by providing simultaneously in the same right-of-way for automobile traffic of relatively light passenger capacity and for rail rapid transit trains of radically greater passenger capacity."

Most emphatically, the city was urged not to get into the business of bailing out failing transit operations. In addition, any extra costs accruing from alterations designed to fit highways for bus use would be met from transportation company revenues.[25] Accordingly, the 1939 report lay the groundwork for future action in both freeway and public transit developments.

The freeway system in Los Angeles fulfilled all the basic requirements for providing mass rapid transit: smooth surface, reasonable grades, freedom from interference by other traffic, easy accessibility to business centers, and the capacity to handle large passenger vehicles.[26] Adjusting freeway design to further accommodate buses was repeatedly endorsed throughout the forties and the fifties,[27] but the issue of financing consistently hindered action. Because of restrictions on the use of the Highway Trust Fund (along with Highway Commission and legislative obstinacy), the state refused to contribute directly to the construction of such facilities. Local government was ultimately responsible for bus turnouts and other bus-related improvements, an expense passed on to the bus companies—and thereby to bus patrons—through increased franchise taxes. Only the city of Los Angeles was able to afford such expenditures. Six bus turnouts were constructed between 1949 and 1955, three each on the Hollywood and Harbor freeways, and a few improvements were made on surface level.[28] Needless to say, plans for building even more elaborate facilities for express buses on freeways were never implemented.[29] Thus the opportunity to adjust freeway design to immediate public transportation use was usually passed up.

Express buses have long used the freeways, but their service during peak hours was always a problem. Caught in heavy automobile traffic, they produced all the inconveniences of public transit without affording any of its benefits. Not until the 1970s was any major innovation introduced to fit the freeway system to public transportation. In 1974 an 11-mile express busway was opened along the San Bernardino freeway from downtown to El Monte, complete with on-line stations. This single experiment suggests the importance of dramatically visible changes in affecting the popular notion of a freeway's function.[30]

Another persistent proposal was to use the center divider of the freeway to carry fixed-rail systems. This option was argued frequently during the late forties and early fifties. Its most vocal proponent was the Rapid Transit Action Group, an organization that included top officials of the State Division of Highways, the Public Utilities Commission, the County Regional Planning Com-

Freeway Trolleys

Pacific Electric trolley cars used the center divider of the original 1.8-mile Cahuenga Pass segment of the Hollywood freeway. The Division of Highways joined the city of Los Angeles in financing the improvements in order to make use of the rail company's right-of-way. An additional 1.1 miles of track were placed in the freeway's right-of-way with the 1949 extension to Lankersheim. Operation was halted in 1952 when the entire Van Nuys – Cahuenga Pass line was discontinued. The abandoned 48-foot median strip was purchased by the Division of Highways to be used for additional freeway lanes to reduce mounting congestion. These photos were taken from the Pilgrimage Bridge. (Top photo courtesy of Henry E. Huntington Library; bottom photo courtesy of CALTRANS.)

mission, and all concerned city departments (such as City Engineer Lloyd Aldrich, Board of Public Utilities head Charles Bean, and Mayor Fletcher Bowron), as well as the executives of both local rail companies and prominent private citizens.

The essential argument in the group's report, *Rail Rapid Transit* (1948),[31] was that the time had come for construction of a rapid rail system, and its combination with the freeway system offered an unprecedented economic opportunity. The report recommended rail operation for all or part of seven freeways, as well as several routes on private rights-of-way. Financing was to be secured through bonds offered by a metropolitan rapid transit district. No highway money would—or could—be used.

Other voices spoke for similar programs. The Assembly Fact Finding Committee on Highways, Streets, and Bridges, after passage of the Collier-Burns Highway Act, began to deliberate on such proposals. Particular attention was paid to running rails down the Hollywood freeway extension toward downtown.[32] Plans were also offered for overhead suspended systems, such as monorails, down the center divider. At any given time some plan or other, suggesting the use of freeways for fixed-guideway rights-of-way, was being considered.

One of the most thorough investigations of the whole rapid transit question during this period was conducted by the Assembly Interim Committee on Public Utilities and Corporations. Its *Preliminary Report on Rapid Transit for the Los Angeles Area* (1950) resulted from a series of hearings, as well as a public survey, aimed at determining the best public transportation policy for the area. The committee considered all four of the basic measures then being debated: a monorail system running on freeways, on private rights-of-way, on surface streets, and through downtown subways; an electric train system with the same basic qualities; an extensive electric subway serving downtown only, with surface rail or bus connections; and express buses on freeways.[33] The last proposal was the one endorsed by the committee.

The committee's conclusions offer an important reminder as to why no action was taken on a fixed-rail measure at a time when extensive freeway construction would have made it as economical as it could ever be. The same problems surfaced then as had faced the Kelker, De Leuw proposal twenty-five years earlier and would face those dealing with similar proposals twenty-five years later.

Although some form of public transportation was widely regarded as a necessity, there was sharp disagreement as to which form was best, and this division hampered particularly the rail proponents. The study accompanying the 1950 report showed that while 40 percent of the population preferred some form of fixed-rail transit, this support was divided among the three alternatives. Freeways with buses, receiving a 47 percent favorable response, were far and away the most popular choice. When respondents were asked whether they would favor buses on freeways, if they could be convinced that this alternative would cost less to construct and operate, be more flexible, give more extensive and quicker overall service, be available sooner, and require no additional taxes, the support jumped to almost 80 percent.[34] Except for the issue of travel time, all the above propositions were conceded to be fairly accurate.

The issue of financing has always been a major barrier to rapid rail systems. The genius of the Collier-Burns Highway Act was to allocate highway user taxes for freeway construction, making freeways, in a real sense, self-supporting. Rail operations, on the other hand, had been unprofitable for years, in other major cities as well as in Los Angeles. Though many argued that an improved system would pay for itself, many others disagreed, feeling that buses alone could be operated at a profit. And in either case, construction would probably have required some additional tax burden. Only 18 percent of those polled, however, would support a bond issue secured simply by property taxes, which was the most likely measure to be employed and one that would require approval by two-thirds of the voters.[35] Obviously the times were not ripe for the notion of publicly subsidized transit. (It is important to remember that as late as 1976 Los Angeles County residents rejected a locally financed transit system, one quite similar to those under discussion in the late 1940s. It has taken 80 percent federal funding to keep the notion of fixed-rail transit alive in Los Angeles, and even the process of obtaining necessary matching funds from the state will require tricky legislative maneuvering.)

The ultimate impasse in the question of mass transit was that most people simply did not want to use it. It was conceived as the choice of necessity. The pilot study accompanying the interim committee's 1950 report showed that 74 percent of those using public transit did so because they had to, not because they wanted to. Only 23 percent of those polled used it even for the regular daily trips to work. Those using automobiles cited a number of reasons to avoid public transit and, with the exception of speed, those reasons could not be eliminated. Uncomfortably crowded vehicles, the bother of using transfers, the difficulty of carrying tools or packages, and other inconveniences would plague even the most modern system. And apropos of speed, new freeway construction would continue to make the private automobile a superior choice. The report concluded that

At least insofar as public transportation is concerned the big majority of people use it as little as possible. The indications are that the trend is away from the use of public transportation instead of toward it. The hope that the *percentage* of the people will increase who will use a new and improved system of public transportation appears to be rather dim. This significant situation is one that must be given serious consideration in planning a new public transportation program.[36]

By the 1950s public transit had become less a viable transportation alternative and more a form of transportation welfare. Transit was a bad investment; in 1958 both of Los Angeles' private operators gladly sold their holdings to the Metropolitan Transit Authority. Public transportation, however, was a social necessity, serving those unfortunates who could not afford to own automobiles: the poor, the old, the young, and frequently the housewife.[37] Nevertheless, the overwhelming majority preferred the private car; it was eccentric to choose transit freely. Supporters of public transportation lacked the strong political base, the political clout, available to freeway proponents, for a majority of southern Californians used the private automobile.

All these factors contributed to the overwhelming support for private transportation and the pitifully small support for mass transportation. But even if the most extensive plans for public transit had been developed, there is disagreement among experts as to whether they would have been successful. Critics of such systems were probably correct in claiming that the urban form of Los Angeles was not particularly conducive to successful fixed-rail transit. Transportation economist George Hilton notes the lack of geographical barriers to sprawl, an economy based on nonclustering industries such as petroleum, aerospace, motion pictures, and agriculture, as opposed, for example, to Manhattan's finance, garment, and entertainment districts, and the cultural ingredients encouraging homeownership and private transportation—all have worked against a fixed-rail system and will continue to do so.[38] At issue in contemporary debates is whether these patterns have changed, or whether such transit systems could accelerate changes in what was once the preferred pattern, and, perhaps most important, whether such changes would be desirable.

NOTES

I. Prologue

[1]Quoted from "Atlantis," Part VIII of *The Bridge,* in *The Complete Poems and Selected Letters and Prose of Hart Crane,* ed. Brom Weber (Garden City: Anchor Books, 1966), p. 116.

II. Intuitions of Meaning

[1]Quoted in Wolf Von Eckardt, *A Place to Live: The Crisis of the Cities* (New York: Delacort Press, 1967), p. 27.

[2]Claiborne Pell, *Megalopolis Unbound* (New York: Praeger, 1966), p. 72.

[3]See Paul T. McElhiney, "Evaluating Freeway Performance in Los Angeles," *Traffic Quarterly* 54 (July 1960), 301-302; W. A. McDaniel, "Re-evaluating Freeway Performance in Los Angeles," (M.A. thesis, UCLA, 1971), pp. 18-23.

[4]California, Division of Highways, *The California Freeway and Expressway System: 1968 Progress and Problems* (Sacramento, 1969), p. 2.

[5]Los Angeles Regional Transportation Study (LARTS), 1976 base-year calculations.

[6]Richard E. Preston, "The Changing Form and Structure of the Southern California Metropolis, Part I," *California Geographer* 12 (1971), 17.

[7]Francine F. Rabinowitz and James Lamare, "After Suburbia What? The New Communities Movement in Los Angeles," in Werner Z. Hirsch, ed., *Los Angeles: Viability and Prospects for Metropolitan Leadership* (New York: Praeger, 1971), pp. 169-206.

[8]Daniel J. Boorstin, *The Americans: The Democratic Experience* (New York: Vintage Books, 1974), p. 269.

[9]Richard Austin Smith, "Los Angeles: Prototype of a Supercity," *Fortune* 71 (March 1965), p. 202.

[10]See *The Automobile: Its Province and Its Problems,* vol. 116 of *Annals of the American Academy of Political and Social Science* (Nov. 1924), pp. 199-246. This section of volume 116 of the *Annals,* entitled

"City Plans for Motor Traffic," outlines recently established plans in New York City, Chicago, Philadelphia, Detroit, St. Louis, and Los Angeles.

[11]Los Angeles County Regional Planning Commission, *Master Plan of Highways* (Los Angeles, 1941), p. 51.

[12]E. Gordon Ericksen, "The Superhighway and City Planning: Some Ecological Considerations with Reference to Los Angeles," *Social Forces* 28 (May 1950), 433.

[13]Milton Stark, "L.A. Renaissance: Freeway Service Key Factor in Downtown Growth, Renewal," *California Highways and Public Works* 40 (Sept.-Oct. 1961), 29-45.

[14]Albert C. Martin (architect responsible for the Arco and Bank of America towers, the Security Pacific building, and the Wells Fargo building, now under construction) in Henry Sutherland, "New 'Main Street' Changing L.A.," *Los Angeles Times,* 19 Feb. 1967, J. p. 1.

[15]Howard J. Nelson and William A. V. Clark, *The Los Angeles Metropolitan Experience: Uniqueness, Generality, and the Goal of the Good Life* (Cambridge, Mass.: Ballinger, 1976), p. 27.

[16]Ibid., p. 27.

[17]Richard E. Preston, "Freeway Impact on the Central Business District: The Case of Long Beach," *California Geographer* 4 (1963), 9-19.

[18]Richard E. Preston and Donald W. Griffin, "The Pattern of Major Retail Centers in the Los Angeles Area," *California Geographer* 9 (1968), 1-26.

[19]W. L. Fahey, "Santa Ana Freeway Has Induced Industrial and Recreational Development," *California Highways and Public Works* 34 (Sept.-Oct. 1955), 1-4.

[20]Dudley F. Pegrum, *Urban Transport and the Location of Industry in Metropolitan Los Angeles,* Occasional Paper no. 2, Bureau of Business and Economic Research, UCLA, 1963.

[21]United States Department of Commerce, Area Redevelopment Administration, *Hard Core Unemployment and Poverty in Los Angeles* (Washington, 1965), pp. 76-78 and Appendix, "Major Factors in Industrial Location," by Joel Leigner; Edward T. Telford, "L.A. Freeways," *California Highways and Public Works* 41 (March-April 1962), 42-57.

[22]See Los Angeles County Regional Planning Commission, *Master Plan of Land Use* (Los Angeles, 1941), p. 43; Los Angeles County Regional Planning Commission, "1975 Land Use" (map).

[23]*Los Angeles Times,* 28 Nov. 1963.

[24]Stuart L. Hill, "Glendale Report: Reconstruction Study Shows Freeway Benefits," *California Highways and Public Works* 43 (March-April 1964), 42-47.

[25]Reyner Banham, *Los Angeles: The Architecture of Four Ecologies* (New York: Penguin Books, 1971), p. 175.

[26]Nelson and Clark, *Los Angeles Metropolitan Experience,* p. 25; Los Angeles County Regional Planning Commission, "1975 Land Use."

[27]Anthony Downs, "Land-Value Impacts of Transportation Arteries and How They Affect New City Development," in *Urban Problems and Prospects* (Chicago: Markham, 1970), pp. 228-250.

[28]Stuart L. Hill, *The Effect of Freeways on Neighborhoods: An Analysis of the Relationship of Mobility to Community Values* (Sacramento: California Division of Highways, 1967); California Division of Highways, *Beverly Hills Freeway: Community Benefit Analysis of Alternative Route Location* (Los Angeles, 1964).

[29]"Los Angeles in a New Image," *Life,* 20 June 1960, p. 75.

[30]Benjamin Stein, *Dreemz* (New York: Harper & Row, 1978), p. 48.

[31]Kevin Lynch, *Images of the City* (Cambridge: MIT Press, 1960), pp. 51-67.

[32]Ibid., p. 57.

[33]Mark M. Jones, "Finding a Freeway: Environmental Clues in a Path-Choosing Task" (MA thesis, UCLA, 1971).

[34]See Martin Heidegger, "Building Dwelling Thinking," in *Basic Works,* ed. David Farrell Krell (New York: Harper & Row, 1977), pp. 323-339.

[35]John C. Everitt, "Community and Propinquity in the City," *Annals of the Association of American Geographers* 66 (March 1976), 104-116.

[36]Los Angeles Department of City Planning, *The Visual Environment of Los Angeles* (Los Angeles, 1971), pp. 8-11.

[37]Los Angeles Regional Transportation Study (LARTS), *Base Year Report: 1967 Origin-Destination Survey* (Los Angeles, 1971), pp. 47-48.

[38]Suzanne Keller, *The Urban Neighborhood: A Sociological Perspective* (New York: Random House, 1968), p. 53.

[39]Woodrow Wilson Nichols, Jr., "Spatio-Perceptive Analysis of the Effect of the Santa Monica and Simi Valley Freeways on Two Selected Black Residential Areas in Los Angeles County" (Ph.D. diss., UCLA 1973), p. 56.

[40]Nelson and Clark, *Los Angeles Metropolitan Experience,* p. 31.

[41]William Irwin Thompson, "Los Angeles: Reflections at the Edge of History," *Antioch Review* 28 (Fall 1968), 265.

[42]H. Marshall Goodwin, "California's Growing Freeway System" (Ph.D. diss., UCLA, 1969), p. 374.

[43]California Assembly Interim Committee on Natural Resources, Planning, and Public Works, *Highway and Freeway Planning* (Sacramento, 1965), p. 22.

[44]Christopher Tunnard and Boris Pushkarev, *Man Made America: Chaos or Control?* (New Haven: Yale University Press, 1963), p. 218.

[45]Nelson and Clark, *Los Angeles Metropolitan Experience,* p. 52.

[46]Bessie A. McClenahan, *The Changing Urban Neighborhood: From Neighbor to Nigh-Dweller* (Los Angeles: University of Southern California, 1929), p. 79.

[47]Sam Bass Warner, Jr., *The Urban Wilderness* (New York: Harper & Row, 1972), p. 48.

[48]United States Bureau of the Census, *Current Population Reports,* Series P-26, no. 76-5 (Washington, Sept. 1977).

[49]Warner, *Urban Wilderness,* p. 142.

[50]Robert M. Fogelson, *The Los Angeles Riots* (New York: Arno Press—New York Times, 1969), pp. 131-132; see also ibid., p. 73 (from the McCone Commission Report).

[51]Timothy Tyler, "Where the Auto Reigns Supreme," *Time,* 3 April 1973, p. 48.

[52]Steven V. Roberts, "Ode to a Freeway," *New York Times Magazine,* 15 April 1973, p. 42.

[53]LARTS, *1967 Origin-Destination Survey,* pp. 54, 59.

[54]Joan Didion, "The Diamond Lane Slowdown," *Esquire* 86 (Aug. 1977), 36.

[55]William Bronson, "Home is a Freeway," *Cry California* (Summer 1966), repr. in John and La Ree Caughey, *Los Angeles: Biography of a City* (Berkeley, Los Angeles, London: University of California Press, 1976), pp. 433-438.

[56]E.g., Nelson and Clark, *Los Angeles Metropolitan Experience,* p. 52, who feel that Banham has "overstated the case."

[57]Banham, *Los Angeles,* p. 213.

[58]"Freeway Blues: The Dread L.A. Breakdown," *Los Angeles Times,* 4 Sept. 1974, I, p. 1.

[59]Thomas Pynchon, "A Journey into the Mind of Watts," *New York Times Magazine,* 12 June 1966, repr. in *The California Dream,* ed. Dennis Hale and Jonathan Eisen (New York: Collier Books, 1968), p. 253.

[60]Richard M. Michaels, "The Effect of Expressway Design on Driver Tension Responses," *Public Roads* 32 (Dec. 1962), 107-112.

[61]Didion, "Diamond Lane," p. 35.

[62]See McElhiney, "Evaluation Freeway Performance"; McDaniel, "Re-evaluating Freeway Performance."

[63]Joan Didion, *Play It As It Lays* (New York: Bantam Books, 1970), p. 14.

[64]Christopher Rand, *Los Angeles, the Ultimate City* (New York: Oxford University press, 1967), p. 57.

[65]Charles T. Powers, "The Accident, or Why Timothy S. Kinderton Sort of Wishes He Hadn't Taken the Freeway Thursday Morning," *Los Angeles Times West Magazine,* 24 Sept. 1972, p. 10.

[66]Banham, *Los Angeles,* p. 215.

[67]Melvin M. Webber, *The BART Experience—What Have We Learned?,* Institute of Urban and Regional Development, University of California, Berkeley, 1976, pp. 31-32.

[68]Downs, "The Law of Peak-Hour Congestion," in *Urban Problems,* pp. 176-191.

[69]Hunter S. Thompson, *Fear and Loathing: On the Campaign Trail '72* (New York: Popular Library, 1973), p. 24.

[70]California Department of Transportation, District VII Freeway Operations Branch, unpublished vehicle occupancy studies.

[71]Alan M. Voorhees & Associates, *Final Report: A Study of Tech-niques to Increase Commuter Vehicle Occupancy on the Hollywood Freeway* (Berkeley, 1975), pp. 3, 86-93.

[72]See esp. Roberts, "Ode to a Freeway"; Eleanor Hoover, "Freeway Mystique: More Than 'Getting There,'" *Los Angeles Times,* 11 May 1975, II, p. 1.

[73]Hoover, "Freeway Mystique."

[74]William Warren Bartly, III, *Werner Erhard: The Transformation of a Man, The Founding of est* (New York: Clarkson N. Polter, 1978), p. 166.

[75]Thomas Pynchon, *The Crying of Lot 49* (New York: Bantam Books, 1966), pp. 79-80.

[76]Powers, "The Accident," p. 10.

[77]See David Barry, "Thunder Road," *New West,* 31 July 1968, pp. 35-38; Tom Wolfe, *The Kandy-Kolored Tangerine-Flake Streamline Baby* (New York: Pocket Books, 1965), pp. 62-93.

[78]Stein, *Dreemz,* p. 22.

[79]James Q. Wilson, "The Political Culture of Southern California," *Commentary* 43 (May 1967), p. 40.

[80]Deanne Barkley, *Freeway* (New York: Macmillan, 1978), p. 214.

[81]Richard Lillard, *Eden in Jeopardy: The Southern California Experience* (New York: Knopf, 1966), p. 194.

[82]Tom S. Reck, "Raymond Chandler's Los Angeles," *Nation,* 20 Dec. 1975, p. 661.

[83]Banham, *Los Angeles,* pp. 174-175.

[84]Lawrence Halprin, *Freeways* (New York: Reinhold, 1966), p. 5.

[85]Ibid., p. 16.

[86]Anselm L. Strauss, "Strategies for Discovering Urban Theory," in *The American City,* ed. Anselm L. Strauss (Chicago: Aldine, 1968), p. 517.

[87]Robert de Roos, "Los Angeles," *National Geographic* 122 (Oct. 1962), 451-501.

[88]Roberts, "Ode to a Freeway," p. 30.

[89]*Highway and Freeway Planning,* p. 23.

[90]Owen B. Shoemaker, letter to the editor, *Los Angeles Times,* 21 March 1972.

[91]See Leo Marx, *The Machine in the Garden* (New York: Oxford University Press, 1964).

[92]Lillard, *Eden in Jeopardy,* p. 204.

[93]From "The Cement Octopus," words and music by Malvina Reynolds, copyright 1964, Schroeder Music Co. (ASCAP).

[94]"Freeways Called Good Neighbors," *Los Angeles Times,* 27 Jan. 1974; Goodwin, "Growing Freeway System," p. 576.

[95]Ted Thackery, Jr., "Californians Still Like Freeways with Restraints," *Los Angeles Times,* 11 April 1973, I, p. 15.

[96]California Department of Transportation and Southern California Association of Governments, *1976 Urban and Rural Travel Survey,* Vol. II: *Summary of Findings: Attitudinal Data* (Los Angeles, 1978), p. 50.

[97]Didion, *Play It As It Lays,* p. 13.

98Ibid., p. 14.
99Ibid., p. 161.
100Barkley, *Freeway*, p. 49.
101Ibid., p. 231.
102Ibid., p. 229.
103Pynchon, *Lot 49*, p. 14.
104Ibid., p. 72.
105Ibid., p. 132.
106Ibid., p. 84.
107Lawrence P. Spingarn, "Freeway Problems," in *Freeway Problems and Other Poems* (Van Nuys, Calif.: Perivale Press, 1970), p. 17.
108Hart Crane, "Modern Poetry," in *The Complete Poems and Selected Letters and Prose of Hart Crane*, ed. Brom Weber (Garden City: Anchor Books, 1966), p. 262.

III. History

1Larry McMurtry, *Moving On* (New York: Simon and Schuster, 1970), pp. 647-648.
2See Robert M. Fogelson, *The Fragmented Metropolis: Los Angeles, 1850-1930* (Cambridge: Harvard University Press, 1967), pp. 43-62.
3Carey McWilliams, *Southern California: An Island on the Land* (Santa Barbara and Salt Lake City: Peregrine Smith, 1973), p. 118.
4Glenn S. Dumke, *The Boom of the Eighties in Southern California* (San Marino: Huntington Library, 1944), p. 48.
5United States Census Office, *Eleventh Census of the United States: 1890*, Vol. I: *Population* (Washington, 1895), pp. 70–71, 370.
6James E. Vance, Sr., "California and the Search for the Ideal," *Annals of the Association of American Geographers* 66 (1972), 185-210.
7Dumke, *Boom of the Eighties*, p. 32.
8Ibid., p. 223.
9Charles Lummis, "The Lion's Den," *Out West* 19 (1 Oct. 1903), as quoted in Laurence R. Veysey, "Southern California Society, 1867-1910: A Study in the Forms of Regional Self-Awareness" (M.A. thesis, University of Chicago, 1957), p. 19.
10"The Kirkman-Harriman Pictorial and Historical Map of Los Angeles County, 1860 AD" (Los Angeles, 1937).
11Dumke, *Boom of the Eighties*, pp. 7-24; Southern California Writers' Project, *Los Angeles* (New York: Hastings House, 1951), pp. 406-407; Rockwell D. Hunt and William S. Amert, *Oxcart to Airplane* (Los Angeles: Powell Publishing Co., 1929), p. 161.
12Howard J. Nelson, "The Spread of an Artificial Landscape over Southern California," in *Man, Time, and Space in Southern California*, ed. William L. Thomas, Jr., special supplement to *Annals of the Association of American Geographers* 49 (Sept. 1959), 84.
13Ibid., p. 85.
14Ibid.
15Hunt and Amert, *Oxcart to Airplane*, p. 190.
16Spencer Crump, *Ride the Big Red Cars: How Trolleys Helped Build Southern California* (Corona del Mar: Trans-Anglo Books, 1970), pp. 35-37.
17George W. Hilton and John F. Due, *The Electric Interurbans in America* (Stanford: Stanford University Press, 1960), pp. 406-407.
18Ibid., p. 406; Kelker, De Leuw, and Co., *Report and Recommendations on a Comprehensive Rapid Transit Plan for the City and County of Los Angeles* (Chicago, 1925), p. 58.
19Crump, *Big Red Cars*, p. 55.
20Pat Adler, "Watts: A Legacy of Lines," *Westways* 58 (Aug. 1966), 22-24.
21Crump, *Big Red Cars*, p. 119.
22Automobile Club of Southern California, *Traffic Survey* (Los Angeles, 1937), p. 11.
23Dudley Pegrum, *Residential Population and Urban Transport*, Occasional Paper no. 3, Bureau of Business and Economic Research, UCLA, 1964, p. 10.
24Fogelson, *Fragmented Metropolis*, p. 203.
25Mark Foster, "The Model-T, the Hard Sell, and Los Angeles' Urban Growth: The Decentralization of Los Angeles during the 1920's," *Pacific Historical Review* 44 (Nov. 1975), 461.
26Leon Moses and Harold Williamson, "The Location of Economic Activity in Cities," *Economic Review* 57 (May 1967), 211-222.
27Fogelson, *Fragmented Metropolis*, p. 151.
28See ibid., pp. 85-92; Crump, *Big Red Cars*, pp. 27-127 passim.
29Crump, *Big Red Cars*, p. 60.
30Charles N. Glaab and A. Theodore Brown, *The History of Urban America* (London: Macmillan, 1967), p. 282.
31Crump, *Big Red Cars*, p. 37.
32Fogelson, *Fragmented Metropolis*, pp. 78-79.
33Glaab and Brown, *Urban America*, pp. 135-136.
34Arthur M. Schlesinger, *The Rise of the City, 1878–1898* (New York: Macmillan, 1933), pp. 58-61.
35Ibid., pp. 24-28, 55-57, 62-67.
36Fogelson, *Fragmented Metropolis*, pp. 79-82.
37McWilliams, *Southern California*, p. 102.
38Lewis Atherton, *Main Street on the Middle Border* (Bloomington: Indiana University Press, 1954), pp. 4, 11, 336.
39Fogelson, *Fragmented Metropolis*, pp. 144-145.
40McWilliams, *Southern California*, p. 169.
41Robert Gregory Brown, "The California Bungalow in Los Angeles: A Study in Origins and Classifications" (M.A. thesis, UCLA, 1964).
42Joseph Lilly, "Metropolis of the West," *North American Review* 232 (Sept. 1931), 242. See also Sarah Comstock, "The Great American Mirror: Reflections from Los Angeles," *Harper's* 156 (May 1928), 715-723; McWilliams, *Southern California*, pp. 156-175.
43From Raymond Chandler, *The Little Sister*, as quoted by Philip

Durham, "Raymond Chandler's Los Angeles," in John and LaRee Caughey, *Los Angeles: Biography of a City* (Berkeley, Los Angeles, London: University of California Press, 1976), pp. 333-334.

[44]Glaab and Brown, *Urban America*, pp. 154-159; Sam Bass Warner, Jr., *Streetcar Suburbs: The Process of Growth in Boston, 1870–1900* (Cambridge: Harvard University Press, 1962), p. 160; Sam Bass Warner, Jr., *The Urban Wilderness: A History of the American City* (New York: Harper & Row, 1972), p. 201.

[45]Mark Foster, "The Decentralization of Los Angeles during the 1920's" (Ph.D. diss., University of Southern California, Los Angeles, 1971), p. 40.

[46]See Fogelson, *Fragmented Metropolis*, pp. 79-80.

[47]Stephan Thernstrom, "The Growth of Los Angeles in Historical Perspective: Myth and Reality," in Werner Z. Hirsch, ed., *Los Angeles: Viability and Prospects for Metropolitan Leadership* (New York: Praeger, 1971), pp. 8-11.

[48]Margaret L. Bright and Dorothy S. Thomas, "Interstate Migration and Intervening Opportunities," *American Sociological Review* 6 (Dec. 1941), 780-781.

[49]Fogelson, *Fragmented Metropolis*, pp. 68-75.

[50]McWilliams, *Southern California*, p. 175.

[51]See ibid., p. 150; Fogelson, *Fragmented Metropolis*, pp. 75-77.

[52]Fogelson, *Fragmented Metropolis*, pp. 72-74.

[53]Atherton, *Main Street*, p. 22.

[54]Fogelson, *Fragmented Metropolis*, pp. 70-72; Richard Weiss, *The American Myth of Success: From Horatio Alger to Norman Vincent Peale* (New York: Basic Books, 1969), pp. 145-169. See also Peter J. Schmitt, *Back to Nature: The Arcadian Myth in Urban America* (New York: Oxford University Press, 1969).

[55]See McWilliams, *Southern California*, pp. 249-272.

[56]Page Smith, *As a City upon a Hill* (Cambridge: MIT Press, 1966), p. 26.

[57]McWilliams, *Southern California*, p. 129.

[58]Glenn Cunningham, "Comments on Howard J. Nelson's 'The Spread of an Artificial Landscape over Southern California,'" *Annals of the Association of American Geographers* 49 (Sept. 1959), p. 99.

[59]Fogelson, *Fragmented Metropolis*, p. 151.

[60]Ibid., p. 169.

[61]Kelker, De Leuw, *Comprehensive Rapid Transit Plan*, p. 35.

[62]Howard J. Nelson and William A. V. Clark, *The Los Angeles Metropolitan Experience: Uniqueness, Generality, and the Goal of the Good Life* (Cambridge, Mass.: Ballinger, 1976), p. 51; Los Angeles Traffic Commission, *A Major Traffic Street Plan for Los Angeles*, prepared by Frederick Law Olmsted, Jr., Harland Bartholomew, and Charles Henry Cheney (Los Angeles, 1924), p. 11.

[63]Attributed to Edwin Bates in McWilliams, *Southern California*, p.135.

[64]Foster, "Model-T," p. 463.

[65]Ibid., p. 476.

[66]Ibid., p. 477.

[67]Fogel, *Fragmented Metropolis*, p. 92.

[68]Ibid., p. 94; Foster, "Decentralization," pp. 141-142.

[69]*Major Traffic Street Plan*, p. 12.

[70]Ibid., p. 37.

[71]Ibid., p. 12.

[72]Foster, "Decentralization," p. 140.

[73]Ashleigh Brilliant, "Some Aspects of Mass Motorization in Southern California, 1919-1929," *Southern California Quarterly* 47 (June 1965), 191-196.

[74]Fogelson, *Fragmented Metropolis*, p. 250.

[75]*Major Traffic Street Plan*, pp. 12, 9.

[76]Ibid., pp. 12, 16.

[77]Ibid., p. 29.

[78]Ibid., p. 18.

[79]Foster, "Decentralization," p. 52.

[80]*Major Traffic Street Plan*, p. 51.

[81]Bion J. Arnold, "The Transportation Problem of Los Angeles," *California Outlook*, 4 Nov. 1911.

[82]Foster, "Decentralization," p. 165.

[83]*Major Traffic Sheet Plan*, p. 7.

[84]Fogelson, *Fragmented Metropolis*, p. 132.

[85]Nathanael West, *The Day of the Locust*, in *Miss Lonelyhearts and The Day of the Locust* (New York: New Directions, 1962), p. 156.

[86]Automobile Club of Southern California, *Traffic Survey*, pp. 20-21.

[87]Pegrum, *Residential Population*, p. 10.

[88]Foster, "Model-T," p. 473.

[89]Reyner Banham, *Los Angeles: The Architecture of Four Ecologies* (New York: Penguin Books, 1971), p. 84.

[90]Dudley Pegrum, *Urban Transport and the Location of Industry in Metropolitan Los Angeles*, Occasional Paper no. 2, Bureau of Business and Economic Research, UCLA, 1963.

[91]Los Angeles County Regional Planning Commission, *Master Plan of Highways* (Los Angeles, 1941), p. 29.

[92]Los Angeles Department of City Planning, *A Parkway Plan for the City of Los Angeles and the Metropolitan Area* (Los Angeles, 1941), p. 22.

[93]Fogelson, *Fragmented Metropolis*, p. 179.

[94]Foster, "Decentralization," p. 89.

[95]Fogelson, *Fragmented Metropolis*, p. 183.

[96]Crump, *Big Red Cars*, p. 203.

[97]*Master Plan of Highways*, p. 29.

[98]Donald M. Baker, *A Rapid Transit System for Los Angeles, California*, report to the Central Business District Association (Los Angeles, 1933).

99Los Angeles County, Office of Chief Administrative Officer, *Summary of Transit Surveys* (Los Angeles, 1951?), pp. 9-10 (summarizing two Pacific Electric engineering surveys from 1949).

100*Poor's Directory of Directors and Executives* (New York: Standard and Poor's Corporation, 1946, 1955).

101Crump, *Big Red Cars,* p. 209.

102Bernard C. Snell, "American Ground Transport," in U.Ş. Senate, Committee on the Judiciary, *The Industrial Reorganization Act: Hearing on S. 1167,* 93d Cong., 2d sess. Part 4: *Ground Transportation Industries,* 1974, pp. A30-A33; "Material Relating to the Testimony of George Hilton," in ibid., pp. 2228-2267. For a more recent discussion of the conspiracy theory see Jonathan Kwitny," The Great Transportation Conspiracy," *Harpers* 262 (Feb. 1981), 14.

103Los Angeles County Regional Planning Commission, *A Comprehensive Report on the Regional Plan of Highways: Section 2-E, San Gabriel Valley* (Los Angeles, 1929), pp. 17, 47-52.

104Ibid., p. 42; *Comprehensive Report: Section 4, Long Beach—Redondo Area* (Los Angeles, 1931), p. 144.

105*Master Plan of Highways,* p. 75; *Comprehensive Report: San Gabriel,* p. 48.

106*Master Plan of Highways,* p. 33.

107Most of the information in the next four paragraphs was taken from Christopher Tunnard and Boris Pushkarev, *Man Made America: Chaos or Control?* (New Haven: Yale University Press, 1963), pp. 160-169.

108Ibid., p. 164.

109Ibid., p. 165.

110Los Angeles Citizens' Committee on Parks, Playgrounds, and Beaches, *Parks, Playgrounds, and Beaches for the Los Angeles Region,* submitted by Olmsted Brothers and Bartholomew and Associates (Los Angeles, 1930), pp. 13, 96.

111See H. Marshall Goodwin, Jr., "From Dry Gulch to Freeway," *Southern California Quarterly* 47 (Summer 1965), pp. 73-102. (An excerpt appears in Caughey, *Los Angeles.*)

112Automobile Club of Southern California, *Traffic Survey,* pp. 12, 31.

113Ibid., letter of transmittal.

114John B. Rae, *The Road and the Car in American Life* (Cambridge: MIT Press, 1971), p. 82.

115Los Angeles Transportation Engineering Board, *A Transit Program for the Los Angeles Metropolitan Area* (Los Angeles, 1939), letter of transmittal; Samuel W. Taylor, "Freeways Shape the Modern City," in *Freedom of the American Road,* ed. William Laas (Dearborn: Ford Motor Co., 1956), pp. 67-70.

116*Transit Program,* p. vii.

117*Parkway Plan,* p. 37.

118Ibid., p. 14.

119Ibid., pp. 7, 9, 10, 49.

120Los Angeles County Regional Planning Commission, *Freeways for the Region* (Los Angeles, 1943), pp. 3, 12, 27.

121Ibid., pp. 13-15, 26-27.

122Nelson, "Artificial Landscape," pp. 80-81, 87-96.

123David Gebhard and Harriette Von Breton, *L.A. in the Thirties, 1931-1941* (Santa Barbara and Salt Lake City: Peregrine Smith, 1975), p. 9.

124Nelson, "Artificial Landscape," p. 80.

125California Division of Highways, *Eighth Biennial Report* (Sacramento, 1932), p. 143, and "Map Showing State Highway System."

126California Division of Highways, *Ninth Biennial Report* (Sacramento, 1934), p. 15; Los Angeles County Regional Planning Commission, *State Highways in Los Angeles County* (Los Angeles, 1935).

127California, Assembly Fact Finding Committee on Highways, Streets, and Bridges, *Digest of Testimony* (Sacramento, 1949), p. 74.

128Goodwin, "Dry Gulch," pp. 78-79, 93-94.

129Robert J. Hatfield, "Arroyo Seco Freeway Extension Becomes a $4,000,000 Defense Highway Project," *California Highways and Public Works* 19 (Sept. 1941), 6-8; A. N. George, "Easterly Gateway to L.A. Involves Structure for Freeways," *California Highways and Public Works* 19 (Feb. 1941), 13-16.

130H. Marshall Goodwin, Jr., "California's Growing Freeway System" (Ph.D. diss., UCLA, 1969), p. 151.

131Ibid., pp. 314-320.

132Ibid., p. 312.

133*Los Angeles Times,* 14, 18 June 1947.

134Richard O. Davis, *The Age of Asphalt: The Automobile, The Freeway, and the Condition of Metropolitan America* (Philadelphia: Lippincott, 1975), pp. 3-27.

135Goodwin, "Freeway System," p. 85.

136Ibid., pp. 324-346.

137California Transportation Commission, "Financing Transportation in California, Vol. II: Background," in *1978 Biennial Report* (Sacramento, 1979) pp. ii, 17, 20.

138See Kathleen Armstrong, "Litigating the Freeway Revolt: Keith v. Volpe," *Ecology Law Review* 2 (Winter 1972), 761-799.

139Heinz Heckeroth, "The Changing California Highway Program," *Transportation Research Record* 654 (1977), 23-77; Richard M. Zettel, *California's Highway Program in the Seventies: A System in Jeopardy,* Institute of Transportation Studies, University of California, Berkeley, 1976.

140Mel Scott, *American City Planning Since 1870* (Berkeley, Los Angeles, London: University of California Press, 1971), p. 202.

141Foster, "Model-T," p. 472.

142Harrison Baker in California, Assembly Fact Finding Committee on Highways, Streets and Bridges, *Final Report* (Sacramento, 1949), p. 90; see also pp. 123-136, 165-178.

143Edward T. Telford, "District VII Freeway Report," *California Highways and Public Works* 36 (Jan.-Feb. 1957), 8-9.

144P. O. Harding, "Big Job: Role of Division of Highways in Development of the Freeway System for the Los Angeles Metropolitan Area," *California Highways and Public Works* 31 (March-April 1955), 6.

[145]Fogelson, *Fragmented Metropolis*, p. 157.

[146]Harland Bartholomew, "The Urban Auto Problem," *Proceedings of the Twelfth National Conference of City Planners*, 51 (19-20 April 1920), 99.

[147]See W. L. Fahey, "Santa Ana Freeway Has Induced Industrial and Recreational Development," *California Highways and Public Works* 34 (Sept.-Oct. 1955), 1-13; P. O. Harding, "Revealing Direct Benefits from Freeway Development," *California Highways and Public Works* 34 (July-Aug. 1955), 6-10.

[148]Stuart L. Hill, "Freeway Impact: Santa Ana Project Saves Users $7,000,000 in Five Years," *California Highways and Public Works* 42 (July-Aug. 1963), 23.

[149]Paul Shuldiner, "The Rationale behind the Los Angeles Freeway System," paper prepared for CHP 226, University of California, Berkeley, 1957, p. 13.

[150]C. G. Beer, "Traffic Studies: Need for Network of Freeways in Los Angeles Clearly Evident," *California Highways and Public Works* 32 (Sept.-Oct. 1953), 31; see also Harding, "Big Job," p. 14.

[151]*Major Traffic Street Plan*, pp. 18-19.

IV. Epilogue: The End of an Era?

[1]James Taylor, "Traffic Jam," on *JT* (CBS, Columbia Records, 1977).

[2]See California Department of Transportation, *Effect of the Current Fuel Shortage in California: Travel and Related Factors*, Report 3 (Sacramento, Sept. 1979).

[3]Bureau of the Census, *United States Historical Abstract (1979)*, pp. 490-491.

[4]Bureau of the Census, *Historical Statistics of the United States, Colonial Times to 1970*, Series Q (Washington, 1976), pp. 156-162.

[5]See Mark Leepson, "Auto Research and Regulation," *Editorial Research Report* 8 (23 Feb. 1979), 146-164.

[6]Charles A. Lave, "The Mass Transit Panacea and Other Fallacies about Energy," *Atlantic Monthly* 244 (Oct. 1979), 40. The increase in average mileage by 0.2 mpg and the doubling of transit patronage would each result in approximately a 1.3 percent energy savings.

[7]Charles A. Lave, "Transportation and Energy: Some Current Myths," *Policy Analysis* 4 (Summer 1978), 299-301.

[8]Melvin M. Weber, *The BART Experience—What Have We Learned?*, Institute of Urban and Regional Development, University of California, Berkeley, 1967, pp. 1-5.

[9]Lave, "Transportation and Energy," p. 297.

[10]Weber, *BART*, pp. 7-12; Charles A. Lave, "Rail Rapid Transit and Energy: The Adverse Effects," *Transportation Research Record* 648 (1977), 15.

[11]Lave, "Transportation and Energy," p. 305.

[12]Lave, "Transportation and Energy," pp. 301-305; Lave, "Rail Rapid Transit," pp. 14-30.

[13]Lave, "Transportation and Energy," pp. 306-307.

[14]Weber, *BART*, pp. 23-29.

[15]Ibid., pp. 19-23.

[16]Lave, "Transportation and Energy," p. 303.

[17]Andrew Marshall Hamer, *The Selling of Rail Rapid Transit* (Lexington, Mass.: Lexington Books, 1976), pp. 9-12.

[18]Kaiser Engineers and Daniel, Mann, Johnson, and Mendenhall, *Subarea and Total System Analysis (Task 8.5.1)* (Los Angeles, 1974), pp. III, 10-14, as quoted in Peter Marcuse, "Mass Transit for the Few: Lessons from Los Angeles," School of Architecture and Urban Planning, University of California, Los Angeles, 1975, pp. 12-14.

[19]California Department of Transportation, District VII, *Freeway Transit Element of the Regional Transit Development Plan for Los Angeles County* (Los Angeles, 1978).

[20]Martin Wachs, "The Case for Bus Rapid Transit in Los Angeles," unpublished position paper, School of Architecture and Urban Planning, University of California, Los Angeles, 1975, passim.

[21]Caltrans estimates that the high-level guideway alternative would save 8 percent of the energy that would be used if no new guideways were built. See "Technical Analysis," in *Freeway Transit Element*, pp. 133-135.

[22]California Department of Transportation, District VII, *Progress Report for the Upgrade and Control for the Los Angeles Area Freeway Network* (Los Angeles, 1978), pp. 38-39.

[23]See Weber, *BART*, pp. 12-19.

V. Appendix

[1]Los Angeles Traffic Commission, *A Major Traffic Street Plan for Los Angeles*, prepared by Frederick Law Olmsted, Jr., Harland Bartholomew, and Charles Henry Cheney (Los Angeles, 1924), pp. 9, 18, 14.

[2]Kelker, De Leuw, and Co., *Report and Recommendations on a Comprehensive Rapid Transit Plan for the City and County of Los Angeles* (Chicago, 1925), p. 1.

[3]Howard J. Nelson and William A. V. Clark, *The Los Angeles Metropolitan Experience: Uniqueness, Generality, and the Goal of the Good Life* (Cambridge, Mass.: Ballinger, 1976), p. 60.

[4]Mark Foster, "The Decentralization of Los Angeles during the 1920's" (Ph.D. diss., University of Southern California, Los Angeles, 1971), p. 119.

[5]Kelker, De Leuw, *Comprehensive Rapid Transit Plan*, p. 36.

[6]Ibid., p. 6.

[7]City Club of Los Angeles, *Report on Rapid Transit*, supplement to *City Club Bulletin*, 30 (Jan. 1926).

[8]Ibid., p. 4.

[9]Union Pacific System, Atchison, Topeka, and Santa Fe Railway, and Southern Pacific Company, *The Solution of the Los Angeles Station Problem* (Los Angeles, 1925); *Los Angeles Examiner,* April 1926, passim; *Los Angeles Times,* April 1926, passim.

[10]*Los Angeles Examiner,* 27 April 1926.

[11]*Los Angeles Times,* 1 Feb. 1926.

[12]Kelker, De Leuw, *Comprehensive Rapid Transit Plan,* p. 7.

[13]Foster, "Decentralization," pp. 114-117.

[14]Kelker, De Leuw, *Comprehensive Rapid Transit Plan,* p. 118. This figure does not include the $13 million investment expected of the Pacific Electric Railway Corporation for expansion of freight-connected facilities.

[15]Mark Foster, "The Model-T, the Hard Sell, and Los Angeles' Urban Growth: The Decentralization of Los Angeles during the 1920's," *Pacific Historical Review* 44 (Nov. 1975), 472.

[16]Foster, "Decentralization," pp. 114-116.

[17]"Underground Garage Nears Completion," *Western City* 25 (April 1952).

[18]Spencer Crump, *Ride the Big Red Cars: How Trolleys Helped Build Southern California* (Corona del Mar, Calif.: Trans-Anglo Books, 1970), App. E, p. 251.

[19]Bion J. Arnold, "The Transportation Problem of Los Angeles," *California Outlook,* 4 Nov. 1911.

[20]Foster, "Decentralization," pp. 95-96.

[21]Ibid., p. 99.

[22]Mark Foster, "City Planners and the Evolution of Urban Transportation in the United States, 1900-1940," paper read at Social Science History Association Meeting, Ann Arbor, 23 Oct. 1972.

[23]Foster, "Decentralization," pp. 126-129.

[24]Los Angeles Transportation Engineering Board, *A Transit Program for the Los Angeles Metropolitan Area* (Los Angeles, 1939), p. 85.

[25]Ibid., pp. 7, 14, 38, 86.

[26]Los Angeles Board of Public Utilities, *Mass Transportation Facilities in Various Large Cities* (Los Angeles, 1952), p. 5.

[27]For example, see Los Angeles City Planning Commission, *Mass Transit Facilities and the Master Plan of Parkways* (Los Angeles, 1942); California Legislature Joint Fact Finding Committee on Highways, Streets, and Bridges, *Final Report* (Sacramento, 1947), pp. 132-133; California Assembly Interim Committee on Transportation and Commerce, *Transcript of Proceedings, Hearings by the Subcommittee on Rapid Transit Problems* (Sacramento, 1954).

[28]California Assembly Interim Committee on Public Utilities and Corporations, *Final Report* (Sacramento, 1962), p. 51.

[29]De Leuw, Cather, and Co., et al., *Recommended Program for Improvement of Transportation and Traffic Facilities in the Metropolitan Area* (Los Angeles, 1945); Los Angeles Metropolitan Traffic Association, *Express Busses on Freeways* (Los Angeles, 1953).

[30]John F. Maloney, "Eleven Mile Busway Will Serve Los Angeles Region," *Public Works* 105 (Aug. 1974); Southern California Association of Governments, *San Bernardino Freeway Express Busway: Evaluation of Mixed-Mode Operations* (Los Angeles, 1978).

[31]Rapid Transit Action Group, *Rail Rapid Transit* (Los Angeles, 1948).

[32]California Assembly Fact Finding Committee on Highways, Streets, and Bridges, *Final Report* (Sacramento, 1949), pp. 67-203.

[33]California Assembly Interim Committee on Public Utilities and Corporations, *Preliminary Report on Rapid Transit for the Los Angeles Area* (Sacramento, 1950), pp. 10-14.

[34]Ibid., pp. 36-37.

[35]Ibid., pp. 15-17.

[36]Ibid., pp. 14-15, 31-35.

[37]Ibid., p. 34. Housewives, who made up most of the category of "non-employed persons," used public transit at a much higher rate than employed persons. Although 25 percent of the latter used public facilities on a daily basis (4-7 times weekly) as compared with 14 percent for the unemployed, fully 60 percent of the employed used transit less than once a month or never, whereas only 32 percent of the unemployed fell into that category.

[38]George W. Hilton, "Rail Transit and the Pattern of Modern Cities: The California Case," *Traffic Quarterly* 12 (July 1967).

BIBLIOGRAPHY

Books

Adams, Henry. *The Education of Henry Adams*. Ed. Ernest Samuels. Boston: Houghton Mifflin, 1973.

Atherton, Lewis. *Main Street on the Middle Border*. Bloomington: Indiana University Press, 1954.

The Automobile: Its Province and Its Problems. Vol. 116 of *Annals of the American Academy of Political and Social Science*. Nov. 1924.

Banham, Reyner. *Los Angeles: The Architecture of Four Ecologies*. New York: Penguin Books, 1971.

Barkley, Deanne. *Freeway*. New York: Macmillan, 1978.

Bartly, William Warren, III. *Werner Erhard: The Transformation of a Man, The Founding of est*. New York: Clarkson N. Polter, 1978.

Boorstin, Daniel J. *The Americans: The Democratic Experience*. New York: Vintage Books, 1974.

Caughey, John and LaRee. *Los Angeles: Biography of a City*. Berkeley, Los Angeles, London: University of California Press, 1977.

Crane, Hart. *The Complete Poems and Selected Letters and Prose of Hart Crane*. Ed. Brom Weber. Garden City: Anchor Books, 1966.

Crump, Spencer. *Ride the Big Red Cars: How Trolleys Helped Build Southern California*. Corona del Mar, Calif.: Trans-Anglo Books, 1970.

Davis, Richard O. *The Age of Asphalt: The Automobile, The Freeway, and the Condition of Metropolitan America*. Philadelphia: Lippincott, 1975.

Didion, Joan. *Play It As It Lays*. New York: Bantam Books, 1970.

Downs, Anthony. *Urban Problems and Prospects*. Chicago: Markham Publishing Co., 1970.

Dumke, Glenn S. *The Boom of the Eighties in Southern California*. San Marino, Calif.: Huntington Library, 1944.

Fogelson, Robert M. *The Fragmented Metropolis: Los Angeles, 1850-1930*. Cambridge: Harvard University Press, 1967.
————. *The Los Angeles Riots*. New York: Arno Press—New York Times, 1969.
Gebhard, David, and Harriette Von Breton. *L.A. in the Thirties, 1931-1941*. Santa Barbara and Salt Lake City: Peregrine Smith, 1975.
Glaab, Charles N., and A. Theodore Brown. *The History of Urban America*. London: Macmillan, 1967.
Hale, Dennis, and Jonathan Eisen. *The California Dream*. New York: Macmillan, 1968.
Halprin, Lawrence. *Freeways*. New York: Reinhold, 1966.
Hamer, Andrew Marshall. *The Selling of Rail Rapid Transit*. Lexington, Mass.: Lexington Books, 1976.
Heidegger, Martin. *Basic Works*. Ed. David Farrell Krell. New York: Harper & Row, 1977.
Hilton, George W., and John F. Due. *The Electric Interurbans in America*. Stanford: Stanford University Press, 1960.
Hirsch, Werner Z., ed. *Los Angeles: Viability and Prospects for Metropolitan Leadership*. New York: Frederick A. Praeger, 1971.
Hunt, Rockwell D., and William S. Amert. *Oxcart to Airplane*. Los Angeles: Powell Publishing Co., 1929.
Keller, Suzanne. *The Urban Neighborhood: A Sociological Perspective*. New York: Random House, 1968.
Lass, William, ed. *Freedom of the American Road*. Dearborn: Ford Motor Co., 1956.
Lillard, Richard. *Eden in Jeopardy: The Southern California Experience*. New York: Alfred A. Knopf, 1966.
Lynch, Kevin. *Images of the City*. Cambridge: MIT Press, 1960.
McClenahan, Bessie A. *The Changing Urban Neighborhood: From Neighbor to Nigh-Dweller*. Los Angeles: University of Southern California, 1929.
McMurtry, Larry. *Moving On*. New York: Simon and Shuster, 1970.
McWilliams, Carey: *Southern California: An Island on the Land*. Santa Barbara and Salt Lake City: Peregrine Smith, 1973.
Marx, Leo. *The Machine in the Garden*. New York: Oxford University Press, 1964.
Nelson, Howard J., and William A. V. Clark. *The Los Angeles Metropolitan Experience: Uniqueness, Generality, and the Goal of the Good Life*. Cambridge, Mass.: Ballinger Publishing Co., 1976.
Pegrum, Dudley. *Residential Population and Urban Transport*. Occasional Paper no. 3. Bureau of Business and Economic Research. University of California, Los Angeles, 1964.
————. *Urban Transport and the Location of Industry in Metropolitan Los Angeles*. Occasional Paper no. 2. Bureau of Business and Economic Research. University of California, Los Angeles, 1963.
Pell, Claiborn. *Megalopolis Unbound*. New York: Frederick A. Praeger, 1966.
Pynchon, Thomas. *The Crying of Lot 49*. New York: Bantam Books, 1966.
Rae, John B. *The Road and the Car in American Life*. Cambridge: MIT Press, 1971.
Rand, Christopher. *Los Angeles, the Ultimate City*. New York: Oxford University Press, 1967.
Schlesinger, Arthur M. *The Rise of the City, 1878-1898*. New York: Macmillan, 1933.
Schmitt, Peter J. *Back to Nature: The Arcadian Myth in Urban America*. New York: Oxford University Press, 1969.
Scott, Mel. *American City Planning since 1870*. Berkeley, Los Angeles, London: University of California Press, 1971.
Smith, Page. *As a City upon a Hill*. Cambridge: MIT Press, 1966.
Southern California Writers' Project. *Los Angeles*. New York: Hastings House, 1951.
Spingarn, Lawrence P. *Freeway Problems and Other Poems*. Van Nuys, Calif.: Perivale Press, 1970.
Stein, Benjamin. *Dreemz*. New York: Harper & Row, 1978.
Strauss, Anselm L., ed. *The American City*. Chicago: Aldine Publishing Co., 1968.
Thompson, Hunter S. *Fear and Loathing: On the Campaign Trail '72*. New York: Popular Library, 1973.
Tunnard, Christopher, and Boris Pushkarev. *Man Made America: Chaos or Control?* New Haven: Yale University Press, 1963.
Von Eckardt, Wolf. *A Place to Live: The Crisis of the Cities*. New York: Delacort Press, 1967.
Warner, Sam Bass, Jr. *Streetcar Suburbs: The Process of Growth in Boston, 1870-1900*. Cambridge: Harvard University Press, 1962.
————. *The Urban Wilderness: A History of the American City*. New York: Harper & Row, 1972.
Webber, Melvin M. *The BART Experience—What Have We Learned?* Institute of Urban and Regional Development. University of California, Berkeley, 1976.
Weiss, Richard. *The American Myth of Success: From Horatio Alger to Norman Vincent Peale*. New York: Basic Books, 1969.
West, Nathanael. *Miss Lonelyhearts and The Day of the Locust*. New York: New Directions, 1962.
Wolfe, Tom. *The Kandy-Kolored Tangerine-Flake Streamline Baby*. New York: Pocket Books, 1965.
Zettel, Richard M. *California's Highway Program in the Seventies: A System in Jeopardy*. Institute of Transportation Studies. University of California, Berkeley, 1976.

Articles

Adler, Pat. "Watts: A Legacy of Lines." *Westways* 58 (Aug. 1966): 22-24.

Armstrong, Kathleen. "Litigating the Freeway Revolt: Keith v. Volpe." *Ecology Law Review* 2 (Winter 1972): 761-799.

Arnold, Bion J. "The Transportation Problem of Los Angeles." *California Outlook,* 4 Nov. 1911.

Barry, David. "Thunder Road." *New West,* 31 July 1978, pp. 35-38.

Bartholomew, Harland. "The Urban Auto Problem." *Proceedings of the Twelfth National Conference of City Planners* 51 (19-22 April 1920).

Beer, C. G. "Traffic Studies: Need for Network of Freeways in Los Angeles Clearly Evident." *California Highway and Public Works* 32 (Sept.-Oct. 1953):31-36.

Bright, Margaret L., and Dorothy S. Thomas. "Interstate Migration and Intervening Opportunities." *American Sociological Review* 6 (Dec. 1941):773-783.

Brilliant, Ashleigh. "Some Aspects of Mass Motorization in Southern California, 1919-1929." *Southern California Quarterly* 47 (June 1965):191-208.

Comstock, Sarah. "The Great American Mirror: Reflections from Los Angeles." *Harper's* 156 (May 1928):715-723.

Didion, Joan. "The Diamond Lane Slowdown." *Esquire* 86 (Aug. 1977):35-37.

Ericksen, E. Gordon. "The Superhighway and City Planning: Some Ecological Considerations with Reference to Los Angeles." *Social Forces* 28 (May 1950):429-434.

Everitt, John C. "Community and Propinquity in the City." *Annals of the Association of American Geographers* 66 (March 1976):104-116.

Fahey. W. L. "Santa Ana Freeway Has Induced Industrial and Recreational Development." *California Highways and Public Works* 34 (Sept.-Oct. 1955):1-13.

Foster, Mark. "The Model-T, the Hard Sell, and Los Angeles' Urban Growth: The Decentralization of Los Angeles during the 1920's." *Pacific Historical Review* 44 (Nov. 1975):459-484.

"Freeway Blues: The Dread L.A. Breakdown." *Los Angeles Times,* 4 Sept. 1974, I, p. 1.

"Freeways Called Good Neighbors." *Los Angeles Times,* 27 Jan. 1974.

George, A. N. "Easterly Gateway to L.A. Involves Structure for Freeways." *California Highways and Public Works* 19 (Feb. 1941):13-16.

Goodwin, H. Marshall, Jr. "From Dry Gulch to Freeway." *Southern California Quarterly* 47 (Summer 1965):73-102.

_____. "Right-of-Way Controversies in Recent California Highway-Freeway Construction." *Southern California Quarterly* 56 (Spring 1974):61-103.

Harding, P. O. "Big Job: Role of Division of Highways in Development of the Freeway System for the Los Angeles Metropolitan Area." *California Highway and Public Works* 34 (March-April 1955):6.

_____. "Revealing Direct Benefits from Freeway Development." *California Highways and Public Works* 31 (July-Aug. 1955):6-10.

Hatfield, Robert J. "Arroyo Seco Freeway Extension Becomes a $4,000,000 Defense Highway Project." *California Highways and Public Works* 19 (Sept. 1941):6-8.

Herbert, Ray. "L.A. Area Freeways Displace 3,000 a Year." *Los Angeles Times,* 28 June 1973, II, p. 1.

Heckeroth, Heinz. "The Changing California Highway Program." *Transportation Research Record* 654 (1977):23-27.

Hill, Stuart L. "Freeway Impact: Santa Ana Project Saves Users $7,000,000 in Five Years." *California Highways and Public Works* 42 (July-Aug. 1963):21-24.

_____. "Glendale Report: Reconstruction Study Shows Freeway Benefits." *California Highways and Public Works* 43 (March-April 1964):42-47.

Hilton, George W. "Rail Transit and the Pattern of Modern Cities: The California Case." *Traffic Quarterly* 12 (July 1967):379-392.

Hoover, Eleanor. "Freeway Mystique: More Than 'Getting There.'" *Los Angeles Times,* 11 May 1975, II, p. 1.

Lave, Charles A. "The Mass Transit Panacea and Other Fallacies about Energy." *Atlantic Monthly* 244 (Oct. 1979):39-43.

_____. "Rail Rapid Transit and Energy: The Adverse Effects." *Transportation Research Record* 648 (1977):14-30.

_____. "Transportation and Energy: Some Current Myths." *Policy Analysis* 4 (Summer 1978):297-315.

Leepson, Mark. "Auto Research and Regulation." *Editorial Research Report* 8 (23 Feb. 1979):146-164.

Lilly, Joseph. "Metropolis of the West." *North American Review* 232 (Sept. 1931):239-245.

"Los Angeles in a New Image." *Life,* 20 June 1960, pp. 74-87.

McElhiney, Paul T. "Evaluating Freeway Performance in Los Angeles." *Traffic Quarterly* 54 (July 1960):296-312.

Maloney, John F. "Eleven Mile Busway Will Serve Los Angeles Region." *Public Works* 105 (Aug. 1974):54-57.

Michaels, Richard M. "The Effect of Expressway Design on Driver Tension Responses." *Public Roads* 32 (Dec. 1962):107-112.

Moses, Leon, and Harold Williamson. "The Location of Economic Activity in Cities." *Economic Review* 57 (May 1967):211-222.

Nelson, Howard J. "The Spread of an Artificial Landscape over Southern California." In *Man, Time, and Space in Southern California.* Ed. William L. Thomas, Jr. Special supplement to *Annals of the Association of American Geographers* 49 (Sept. 1959):80-100.

Powers, Charles T. "The Accident, or Why Timothy S. Kinderton Sort of Wishes He Hadn't Taken the Freeway Thursday Morning." *Los Angeles Times, West Magazine,* 24 Sept. 1972, pp. 7-13.

Preston, Richard E. "The Changing Form and Structure of the Southern California Metropolis, Part I." *California Geographer* 12 (1971):5-21.

_____. "The Changing Form and Structure of the Southern California Metropolis, Part II." *California Geographer* 13 (1972):32-48.

_____. "Freeway Impact on the Central Business District: The Case of Long Beach." *California Geographer* 4 (1963):9-19.

Preston, Richard E., and Donald W. Griffin. "The Pattern of Major Retail Centers in the Los Angeles Area." *California Geographer* 9 (1968):1-26.

Pynchon, Thomas. "A Journey into the Mind of Watts." *New York Times Magazine,* 12 June 1966. Repr. in *The California Dream.* Ed. Dennis Hale and Jonathan Eisen. New York: Collier Books, 1968.

Reck, Tom S. "Raymond Chandler's Los Angeles." *Nation,* 20 Dec. 1975, pp. 661-663.

Roberts, Steven V. "Ode to a Freeway." *New York Times Magazine,* 15 April 1973, pp. 20-42.

Roos, Robert de. "Los Angeles." *National Geographic* 122 (Oct. 1962):451-501.

Smith, Richard Austin. "Los Angeles: Prototype of a Supercity." *Fortune* 71 (March 1965): 98-106, 200-212.

Stark, Milton. "L.A. Renaissance: Freeway Service Key Factor in Downtown Growth, Renewal." *California Highways and Public Works* 40 (Sept.-Oct. 1961): 29-45.

Sutherland, Henry. "New 'Main Street' Changing L.A." *Los Angeles Times,* 19 Feb. 1967, J. p. 1.

Telford, Edward T. "District VII Freeway Report: Accomplishments during 1956 and Outlook for Future." *California Highways and Public Works* 36 (Jan.-Feb. 1957):1-18.

————. "L.A. Freeways." *California Highways and Public Works* 41 (March-April 1962):42-57.

Thackery, Ted, Jr. "Californians Still Like Freeways—with Restraints." *Los Angeles Times,* 11 April 1973, I, p. 15.

Thompson, William Irwin. "Los Angeles: Reflections at the Edge of History." *Antioch Review* 28 (Fall 1968):261-275.

Tyler, Timothy. "Where the Auto Reigns Supreme." *Time,* 3 April 1973, pp. 48-49.

"Underground Garage Nears Completion." *Western City,* 25 (April 1952).

Vance, James E., Sr. "California and the Search for the Ideal." *Annals of the Association of American Geographers* 66 (1972):185-210.

Wilson, James Q. "The Political Culture of Southern California." *Commentary* 43 (May 1967):37-45.

Woehlke, Walter V. "The Corn Belt in California: How Climate Is Moving the Middle West." *Sunset* (Aug. 1921): pp. 29-32.

Government Documents and Transportation Studies

American Society of Civil Engineers. Los Angeles Section. *The Los Angeles Freeway System: Past, Present, and Future.* Los Angeles, 1970.

Automobile Club of Southern California. *Traffic Survey.* Los Angeles, 1937.

Baker, Donald M. *A Rapid Transit System for Los Angeles, California.* Report to the Central Business District Association. Los Angeles, 1933.

California Legislature. Assembly. Fact Finding Committee on Highways, Streets, and Bridges. *Digest of Testimony.* Sacramento, 1947.

————. *Final Report.* Sacramento, 1949.

————. Interim Committee on Natural Resources, Planning, and Public Works. *Highway and Freeway Planning.* Sacramento, 1965.

————. Interim Committee on Public Utilities and Corporations. *Final Report.* Sacramento, 1962.

————. *Preliminary Report on Rapid Transit for the Los Angeles Area.* Sacramento, 1950.

————. Interim Committee on Transportation and Commerce. *Transcript of Proceedings, Hearings by the Subcommittee on Rapid Transit Problems.* Sacramento, 1954.

————. Joint Fact Finding Committee on Highways, Streets, and Bridges. *Final Report.* Sacramento, 1947.

California Department of Public Works. Division of Highways. *Beverly Hills Freeway: Community Benefit Analysis of Alternative Route Location.* Sacramento, 1964.

————. *Eighth Biennial Report.* Sacramento, 1932.

————. *Ninth Biennial Report.* Sacramento, 1934.

————. *Tenth Biennial Report.* Sacramento, 1936.

————. *The California Freeway and Expressway System: 1968 Progress and Problem.* Sacramento, 1969.

————. *The Effect of Freeways on Neighborhoods: An Analysis of the Relationship of Mobility to Community Values.* Prepared by Stuart Hill. Sacramento, 1967.

California Department of Transportation. *Effect of the Current Fuel Shortage in California: Travel and Related Factors.* Report 3. Sacramento, Sept. 1979.

————. *1979 Traffic Volumes on the California State Highway System.* Sacramento, 1979.

————. District VII. *Freeway Transit Element of the Regional Transit Development Plan for Los Angeles County.* Los Angeles, 1978.

————. "Mileage Summary." Computer printout. Los Angeles, 1979.

————. *Progress Report for the Upgrade and Control Program for the Los Angeles Area Freeway Network.* Los Angeles, 1978.

California Department of Transportation and Southern California Association of Governments. *1976 Urban and Rural Survey.* Vol. II: *Summary of Findings: Attitudinal Data.* Los Angeles, 1978.

California. Transportation Commission. *1978 Biennial Report.* Sacramento, 1979.

City Club of Los Angeles. *Report on Rapid Transit.* Supplement to *City Club Bulletin,* 30 (Jan. 1926).

De Leuw, Cather, & Co., Harold M. Lewis, and Joe R. Ong. *Recommended Program for Improvement of Transportation and Traffic Facilities in the Metropolitan Area*. Los Angeles, 1945.

Kelker, De Leuw, and Company. *Report and Recommendations on a Comprehensive Rapid Transit Plan for the City and County of Los Angeles*. Chicago, 1925.

Los Angeles. Board of Public Utilities. *Mass Transportation Facilities in Various Large Cities*. Los Angeles, 1952.

————. City Planning Commission. *Mass Transit Facilities and the Master Plan of Parkways*. Los Angeles, 1942.

————. Community Analysis Bureau. *The State of the City, 1975*. Vol. X, Part II: *Accessibility*. Los Angeles, 1976.

————. Department of City Planning. *A Parkway Plan for the City of Los Angeles and the Metropolitan Area*. Los Angeles, 1941.

————. *The Visual Environment of Los Angeles*. Los Angeles, 1971.

Los Angeles Citizens' Committee on Parks, Playgrounds, and Beaches. *Parks, Playgrounds, and Beaches for the Los Angeles Region*. Submitted by Olmsted Brothers and Bartholomew and Associates. Los Angeles, 1930.

Los Angeles County. Office of Chief Administrative Officer. *Summary of Transit Surveys*. Los Angeles, 1951(?).

————. Regional Planning Commission. *A Comprehensive Report on the Regional Plan of Highways: Section 2-E, San Gabriel Valley*. Los Angeles, 1929.

————. *A Comprehensive Report on the Regional Plan of Highways: Section 4, Long Beach—Redondo Area*. Los Angeles, 1931.

————. *Freeways for the Region*. Los Angeles, 1943.

————. *Master Plan of Highways*. Los Angeles, 1941.

————. *Master Plan of Land Use*. Los Angeles, 1941.

————. *State Highways in Los Angeles County*. Los Angeles, 1935.

Los Angeles Metropolitan Parkway Engineering Committee. *Interregional, Regional, and Metropolitan Parkways*. Los Angeles, 1946.

Los Angeles Metropolitan Traffic Association. *Express Busses on Freeways*. Los Angeles, 1953.

Los Angeles Metropolitan Transportation Association. *Review of Pacific Electric Railway Company's Right-of-Way as Potential Routes for Metropolitan Rapid Transit Lines in Los Angeles Metropolitan Area*. Prepared by Leslie Appel. Los Angeles, 1955. Typed copy in UCLA Public Affairs Library.

Los Angeles Regional Transportation Study. *Base Year Report: 1967 Origin-Destination Survey*. Los Angeles, 1971. Los Angeles Traffic Commission. *A Major Traffic Street Plan for Los Angeles*. Prepared by Frederick Law Olmsted, Jr., Harland Bartholomew, and Charles Henry Cheney. Los Angeles, 1924.

Los Angeles Transportation Engineering Board. *A Transit Program for the Los Angeles Metropolitan Area*. Los Angeles, 1939.

Rapid Transit Action Group. *Rail Rapid Transit*. Los Angeles, 1948.

Southern California Association of Governments. *San Bernardino Freeway Express Busway: Evaluation of Mixed-Mode Operations*. Los Angeles, 1978.

Union Pacific System, Atchison, Topeka, and Santa Fe Railway, and Southern Pacific Company. *The Solution of the Los Angeles Station Problem*. Los Angeles, 1925.

United States. Census Office. *Eleventh Census of the United States: 1890*. Vol. I: *Population*. Washington, 1895.

United States. Congress. Senate. Committee on the Judiciary. *The Industrial Reorganization Act: Hearing on S. 1167*. 93d Cong., 2d sess., 1974.

————. Department of Commerce. Area Redevelopment Administration. *Hard Core Unemployment and Poverty in Los Angeles*. Washington, 1965.

————. Bureau of the Census. *Current Population Reports*. Series P-26, no. 76-5. Washington, Sept. 1977.

————. *Fifteenth Census of the United States: Population*. Washington, 1933.

————. *Historical Statistics of the United States, Colonial Times to 1970*. Washington, 1976.

————. *United States Statistical Abstract*. Washington, 1979.

Voorhees, Alan M., & Associates. *Final Report: A Study of Techniques to Increase Commuter Vehicle Occupancy on the Hollywood Freeway*. Berkeley, Calif., 1975.

Unpublished Materials

Brown, Robert Gregory. "The California Bungalow in Los Angeles: A Study in Origins and Classifications." M.A. thesis, University of California, Los Angeles, 1964.

Foster, Mark. "City Planners and the Evolution of Urban Transportation in the United States, 1900-1940." Paper read at Social Science History Association meeting, Ann Arbor, 23 Oct. 1972.

————. "The Decentralization of Los Angeles during the 1920's." Ph.D. dissertation, University of Southern California, Los Angeles, 1971.

Goodwin, H. Marshall, Jr. "California's Growing Freeway System." Ph.D. dissertation, University of California, Los Angeles, 1969.

Jones, Mark M. "Finding a Freeway: Environmental Clues in a Path-Choosing Task." M.A. thesis, University of California, Los Angeles, 1971.

McDaniel, W. A. "Re-evaluating Freeway Performance in Los Angeles. M.A. thesis, University of California, Los Angeles, 1971.

Marcuse, Peter. "Mass Transit for the Few: Lessons from Los Angeles." Mimeographed. School of Architecture and Urban Planning, University of California, Los Angeles, 1975.

Nichols, Woodrow Wilson, Jr. "Spatio-Perceptive Analysis of the Effect of the Santa Monica and Simi Valley Freeways on Two Selected Black Residential Areas in Los Angeles County." Ph.D. dissertation, University of California, Los Angeles, 1973.

Shuldiner, Paul. "The Rationale behind the Los Angeles Freeway System." Paper prepared for CHP 226, University of California, Berkeley, 1957.

Veysey, Laurence R. "Southern California Society, 1867–1910: A Study in the Forms of Regional Self-Awareness." Ph.D. dissertation, University of Chicago, 1957.

Wachs, Martin. "The Case for Bus Rapid Transit in Los Angeles." Position paper, School of Architecture and Urban Planning. University of California, Los Angeles, 1975.

Maps

Automobile Club of Southern California. "Automobile Road Map of Los Angeles County, California." Los Angeles, 1934(?)

_____. "Metropolitan Los Angeles." Los Angeles, 1941.

California. Department of Transportation. "District 7 Highway System, February 1977."

Daum, W. H., & Staff. "Industrial Area Map for Los Angeles and Orange Counties." Los Angeles, 1976.

"Kirkman-Harriman Pictorial and Historical Map of Los Angeles County, 1860 A.D." Los Angeles, 1937.

Los Angeles County. Regional Planning Commission. "1975 Land Use."

Los Angeles Times. Marketing Research. "Regional Shopping Centers and Department Stores: Los Angeles, Orange, Riverside, San Bernardino, and Ventura Counties." Los Angeles, 1979.

Securities First National Bank of Los Angeles. "Motor Map of Southern California." Los Angeles, 1930.

Van Doren, William. "L.A.'s Rail Transit System: 'The One That Got Away.'" Los Angeles, 1979.

Western Economic Research Co. "Cities, Communities, and Freeway Map." Sherman Oaks, 1972.

_____. "Family Income." Sherman Oaks, 1972.

_____. "Negro Population." Sherman Oaks, 1972.

_____. "New High Rise Office Buildings." Sherman Oaks, 1978.

_____. "New Hi-Rise Apartment Buildings." Sherman Oaks, 1974.

_____. "Population Distribution." Sherman Oaks, 1972.

_____. "Spanish Population." Sherman Oaks, 1972.

INDEX

Compositor: Scientific Composition
   Printer: Halliday Lithograph
   Binder: Halliday Lithograph
     Text: Optima
  Display: Optima